The D...

SAINTS

A Concise Guide to Patron Saints

✤

This authoritative guide to patron saints is invaluable to anyone who wishes to find a compassionate and powerful mediator for prayers of thanks, petition, or intercession. It is the only directory of saints arranged according to need or situation. For everything from abandoned children to zoos, a saint has been designated as a special intercessor.

The entries in this unique sourcebook detail the saints' lives, dates of canonization, and the reason for each saint's relevance in a particular area. It is simple to locate the patron saints for hundreds of areas by consulting the directory's easy-to-use listing of concerns and subjects, which includes: specific professions, such as nurses, teachers, or military personnel; acts of nature or weather; and other topics as varied as illnesses, family problems, and love and marriage. This lexicon of saints and their patronages provides a quick reference guide for anyone seeking inspiration, hope, and comfort.

The Directory of
SAINTS

A Concise Guide
to Patron Saints

Annette Sandoval

A SIGNET BOOK

SIGNET
Published by the Penguin Group
Penguin Books USA Inc., 375 Hudson Street,
New York, New York 10014,U.S.A.
Penguin Books Ltd, 27 Wrights Lane, London W8 5TZ, England
Penguin Books Australia Ltd, Ringwood, Victoria, Australia
Penguin Books Canada Ltd, 10 Alcorn Avenue,
Toronto, Ontario, Canada M4V 3B2
Penguin Books (N.Z.) Ltd, 182–190 Wairau Road,
Auckland 10, New Zealand

Penguin Books Ltd, Registered Offices: Harmondsworth, Middlesex, England

Published by Signet an imprint of Dutton Signet,
a division of Penguin Books USA Inc.
Previously published in a Dutton edition.

First Signet Printing, May, 1997
10 9 8 7 6 5 4 3 2 1

COVER PHOTOGRAPHS, CLOCKWISE FROM UPPER LEFT-HAND SIDE:

1. Francesco del Cossa. Santa Lucia. c1470. The Granger Collection, New
York. 2. Master Theoderich. St. Hieronymous. Before 1365. Tempera on
panel, 103 x 112.8 cm. National Museum, Prague, Czech Republic. Erich
Lessing / Art Resource, N.Y. 3. Crespi, Giovanni Battista. Saint Michael.
Castello Sforzesco, Milan, Italy. Scala / Art Resource, N.Y. 4. Anonymous,
15th century. Lombard School. Ex-voto of Saint Catherine of Siena. Musée
des Beaux-Arts, Nîmes, France. Giraudon / Art Resource, N.Y. 5. Perugino,
Pietro. Saint Sebastian. Oil on wood. 15th century. The Granger Collection,
New York. 6. Lieferinxe, Josse. Saint Catherine of Alexandria. Panel from an
altarpiece. Musée du Petit Palais, Avignon, France. Giraudon / Art Resource,
N.Y. 7. Garofalo. Saint Catherine of Alexandria. Wood. The Granger
Collection, New York. 8. Orazio Gentileschi. Saint Cecila and an Angel.
Canvas, c1610. The Granger Collection, New York. 9. Anonymous, 13th
century. Saint Clare and Eight Stories from Her Life. S. Chiara, Assisi, Italy.
Scala / Art Resource, N.Y.

 REGISTERED TRADEMARK—MARCA REGISTRADA

Printed in the United States of America

To Maria and Manuel Sandoval
for my life's first breath.
To Patrick Phalen
for reminding me to exhale.

[Handwritten inscription:]

Julie

"Saints Will aid
ymun will aid"

Best

[signature]

3/12/90

Acknowledgments

My thanks to the University of San Francisco, for allowing me the use of their library. Thank you, Father Cameron Ayres, S.J., for your useful leads.

A special thanks to the good people at the San Francisco Public Library.

Contents

✤

Introduction

⁜

Getting the Most Out of Prayer

Prayer is an expression of faith and trust, meant to enrich our lives. It is integral to all religious practices, often acting as a prism, allowing glimpses into a culture's structure, values, and history. Whether in a congregation or alone, each one of us could be summed up by how we choose to pray.

When we are in need, our prayers often sound more like commands than appeals. Requesting anything from heaven is like dealing with an employer. To storm into the office and demand a day off just might get you too much time on your hands. Think of God as the big boss and the saints as management. Flatter them, point out some nice things. Be grateful for today, or, when praying to a saint, include something up their alley. If you have children, you may want to thank God for those little miracles. After all, God is a family man himself.

There is nothing wrong with flattering heaven, so long as you are sincere. Remember, heaven is one hundred percent on your side and really does want what is best for you. In short, show some appreciation first, then ask.

What Is a Saint?

Saints are extraordinary people who have lived their lives based on holy principles. God has bestowed gifts upon these individuals in the form of bilocation, levitation, stigmata, and so on. These pious individuals devoted themselves unconditionally to the service of Christ and their fellow man. In death, they are the compelling link between heaven and earth.

A Brief History of Saints

Saint: *Sanctus* (Latin). Sanctified or consecrated. The word *saint* was first used in the Old Testament and referred to God's chosen people, the Israelites.

During the early days of Christianity, the New Testament described saints as the followers of Jesus Christ and his teachings. After the death and resurrection of Christ, the distinction of saint shifted to those who suffered martyrdom for their Christian beliefs. To die for "the cause" was actually encouraged for the first three centuries. Only by imitating Christ's examples, it was believed, was one assured of eternal life with God.

Feast days are the celebration of the death and rebirth of these heroes, memorialized each year on the anniversary of their admittance into heaven. For the potential martyrs who, through no fault of their own, were deprived of a lingering death, the title of confessor was bestowed. It meant that they had openly expressed their faith in Jesus Christ and were willing to suffer the consequences of imprisonment, or better yet, death.

In the fourth century, Constantine, the first Christian emperor, granted tolerance to Christianity, which in turn became the official Roman religion—thus ending the religious practice of paganism in Rome. Since the veneration of Martin of Tours, in 397, dying of natural causes has since become acceptable for sainthood.

The "white martyrs" of the fourth century were led by Saint Anthony, the father of monasticism. They blazed a trail onto the desert sands, retreating to the caves near Koman and Mount Pispir. Shedding themselves of earthly pleasures, especially sex, the "Anchorites," or hermits, searched for unity with God through self-denial. Some of the hermits were venerated for their virtuous lives.

About this time, the words *latria* or worship of God in Christ, and *doulia* or veneration of saints, were introduced into the church's vocabulary. This dogma reduced any potential rivalries between heavenly bodies by earthly cults.

Between the sixth and the tenth centuries, Roman Catholicism experienced an upsurge in the number of saints. It was the time of great power for the church, which had unsurpassed influence over many of the monarchies of the day. Founders of new monastic orders roamed uncharted lands, in search of the uncivilized in dire need of soul-saving. The requirements for sainthood were pretty minimal: à couple of miracles and/or popularity were all one needed to be placed on the "canon" or "list." Feast days were added to calendars, commemorating the day of rebirth through death. The times were so lenient that saints were molded out of religious fiction, as in the cases of Saints Catherine of Alexandria and Christopher.

The plethora of mythical saints dissipated toward the latter part of the tenth century. In 993, Pope John XV demanded concrete proof of Saint Ulric of of Augsburg's piety and reverence before allowing the canonization process to take place. Pope Sixtus V composed the Sacred Congregation of Rites, allowing the church to assess the beatification and canonization process, while streamlining the calendar of saints. Pope Urban VIII drafted a well-structured decree, in which the papacy acquired total authority over the selection of Roman Catholic saints.

In 1918, the Roman Catholic Church adopted the first Code of Canon Law as the system for the canonization of saints. Pope John XXIII called for global alterations of this code, which took effect on November 27, 1983, under Pope John Paul II.

How Does One Become a Saint?

After close to two millennia, the title of saint is reserved for the few holy men and women who have made it through the gauntlet of bureaucracy in the Vatican. Becoming a saint in the past was a long and expensive process. It took decades, even centuries, and ran into untold millions of dollars.

In 1983, Pope John Paul II released *Divinus perfectonis Magister*, which decentralized the process of canonization away from the pope. Regional bishops are now responsible for selecting potential saints by thoroughly researching the background of the deceased. Then they send all of the collected data for their nominee to the Vatican. A *postio*, or biographical volume, is then written and studied by a jury of eight theologians. To pass, six of the eight must vote in favor of the candidate. The *postio* is then reviewed by a committee of bishops and cardinals. When they give the okay, the *postio* is placed on the pope's desk for his review. One miracle is mandatory for nonmartyrs, though not necessary for martyrs. If he approves, the pope will then declare the individual as *blessed*, and that person may be honored back in his or her hometown. This process is called *beatification*. An additional miracle must be attributed to both martyrs and nonmartyrs before the final step of canonization takes place. The pope then makes a universal declaration, in which all Roman Catholics will acknowledge the individual as a saint, and will venerate him or her from that day forth.

What's the Difference Between a Patron and a Regular Saint?

A patron is a saint who is able to intercede on behalf of mankind in specific circumstances. In order to become a patron saint, the deceased must first meet all of the qualifications of a regular saint. From the over 4,500 saints listed in Roman martyrology, the church decides who will be the intercessors or mediators for specific occupations, situations, or places. Usually, an enduring cult or revered traditions are responsible in the selection of patronages. There is often a link between the early saint and his or her patronage. For example, Saint Lawrence (third century) was griddled to death, making him the patron saint of cooks.

Saint Joseph and the Blessed Virgin Mary have the distinctions of being superior patrons. Joseph was declared the protector of the Universal church in 1870 by Pius IX, while Mary has been listed in the canon as Catholicism's prominent saint. The practice of assigning holy protectors began in the 1630s.

PART ONE

PATRONAGES OF THE SAINTS

No one heals himself by wounding another.

—St. Ambrose

ABANDONED CHILDREN: Jerome Emiliani, founder. Italian (1481–1537). A prisoner of war set free after praying to the Virgin Mary, who then devoted his life to the care of orphans. Founder of several orphanages, a home for reformed prostitutes, and the Order of the Samashi; introduced the catechism system of teaching. Jerome died while tending to the sick. Also patron of orphans. Canonized 1767; feast day, February 8.

ACADEMICS: Thomas Aquinas, theologian. Neapolitan (1225–1274). His aristocratic family was so against his religious pursuits they locked him away for fifteen months. The attempt to change his mind proved futile. The greatest thinker of the Middle Ages; author of volumes of theological works, including *Summa contra Gentiles* and *Summa theologica*. Declared a Doctor of the Church in 1567. Also patron of chastity, colleges, pencil makers and schools. Canonized 1323; feast day, January 28.

ACCOMMODATIONS: Gertrude of Nivelles, abbess. Flemish (626–659). When Gertrude's father died, her mother, Itta, founded a monastery at Neville. The fourteen-year-old Gertrude was appointed as the abbess and proved herself deserving of the title. Gertrude's monastic center was known for its hospitality to pilgrims and monks. At the age of thirty, Gertrude lay on her deathbed, fearing that she was unworthy of heaven. St. Ultan assured her that St. Patrick was awaiting her. She died on St. Patrick's Day. The well at her monastery was said to have repellent properties against rodents. Also patron of cats and the recently dead; she is invoked against rats. Feast day, March 17.

ACCOUNTANTS: Matthew, apostle. Galilean (1st century). His name means "gift of God." Also known as Levi; no records of his early life. Tax collector turned apostle; he wrote the first Gospel between 60 and 90, which contains quotes from the Old Testament. He was martyred either in Ethiopia or Persia. Also patron of bankers, bookkeepers, customs agents, security guards, and tax collectors. Feast day, September 21.

ACTORS: 1) Genesius, martyr. Roman (3rd century). Legend. This comedian converted to Christianity while performing a farce of Christian baptism on stage for the Emperor Diocletian in Rome. For refusing the emperor's order to recant, Genesius was tortured, then beheaded while still on stage. Also patron of lawyers, printers, secretaries, and stenographers. Feast day, August 25.

2) Vitus, martyr. Sicilian (3rd century). Legend. After exorcising Emperor Diocletian's son of evil spirits *(chorea)*, he found himself accused of sorcery by the emperor. Vitus was heaved into a vat of boiling water, from which he miraculously emerged unharmed. He and his two companions escaped Rome with the help of an angel

and he is believed to have been martyred in the Lucanian province. Also patron of comedians and dancers; he is invoked against epilepsy. Feast day, June 15.

ACTRESSES: Pelagia, dancer. Antiochian (date unknown). Pious legend. The Bishop Nonnus of Edessa's sermon one day was of a striptease artist, who ". . . goes to all the trouble to keep herself beautiful and to perfect her dancing, but we are considerably less zealous in the care of our diocese and of our own souls." Coincidentally, Pelagia was in attendance at that particular sermon. Immediately following mass, she confessed her sins and was baptized by the bishop. Moving to a cave in Jerusalem, "Pelagia the beardless monk" lived for many years, until her death. Feast day, October 8.

ADOPTED CHILDREN: 1) Clotilde, Queen. French (6th century). She gave birth to the three sons and daughter of King Clovis, before the king's death in 511. The greedy children were at constant odds with one another over control of the kingdom. The rivalry led to the murder of Clodomir, her eldest son. Clotilde quickly adopted his three children, which angered Clotaire, her youngest son. He proceeded to murder two of the small children. Clotilde managed to sneak young Saint Cloud to safety away from his uncle's wrath. Clotilde then spent the rest of her life tending to the needy. Also patron of children's death, parenthood, queens, and widows. Feast day, June 3.

2) Thomas More, martyr. English (1478–1535). Writer, lawyer. Opposed King Henry VIII's divorce of Catherine of Aragon; he was imprisoned for not signing the Act of Succession, which acknowledged Henry and Anne Boleyn's child as England's heir. He was then accused of treason and eventually beheaded. When Thomas was still a child, his mother died. He and his

three siblings were raised by Mother Maude, the family nurse. Also patron of lawyers. Canonized 1935; feast day, June 22.

ADVERTISING: Bernardine of Siena, preacher. Italian (1380–1444). "The people's preacher." At the age of twenty, he took charge of a hospital in Siena during the plague of 1400. In 1417, he set out on foot preaching and converting thousands throughout Italy; he was the second founder of the Friars of the Strict Observance. In spite of his attributes, he believed that witchcraft was running rampant and appears to have been an anti-Semite. His sermons often denounced gambling. Also patron of communications personnel and public relations; he is invoked against uncontrolled gambling. Canonized 1450; feast day, May 20.

AFRICA: 1) Our Lady Queen of Africa. In 1876, Cardinal Lavigerie declared a bronze statue of the Blessed Virgin Mary as the protector of Africa.

2) Moses the Black, monk. Ethiopian (330–405). Moses worked as a servant to an Egyptian family, where he was discharged for stealing. A miraculous transformation led Moses to God in the Sketis desert, where he became a monk. Dressed in a white robe, Moses once told a bishop "God knows I am still dark within." A gang of Berbers stormed the monastery, killing Moses and the other pacifists. Feast day, August 28.

AFRICAN AMERICANS: 1) Benedict the Black, lay-brother. Sicilian (1526–1589). While still a youth, Benedict's master freed him from slavery. Benedict was harassed one afternoon by a group of adolescents for being the son of slaves, yet he never lost his composure. This was witnessed by the head of the Franciscan hermits, who then persuaded Benedict to join the order.

Eventually, he became the superior before it disbanded. He was then assigned as cook to another order, where once again Benedict became its superior. He then asked to be reduced to cook status at yet another community. Also patron of parish missions. Feast day, April 4.

2) Peter Claver, missionary. Catalonian (1580–1654). As a missionary in New Granada (Colombia), he ministered to the 300,000 African slaves brought to Cartagena to work the mines and plantations. Also patron of Colombia and slavery sufferers. Canonized 1888; feast day, September 9.

AGRICULTURAL WORKERS: Phocas, martyr. Paphlagonian (unknown dates). Legend. As an innkeeper and market gardener near the Black Sea, Phocas would give his excess crops to the poor. According to the story, he lodged the soldiers that were sent to kill him. The next morning Phocas revealed himself as the Christian they were to assassinate. Sensing their apprehension, Phocas insisted that they slay him. Once the uncomfortable moment passed, the soldiers beheaded their gracious host. They then buried him in a grave which Phocas had prepared for himself during the night. Also patron of gardeners. Feast day, September 22.

ALCOHOLISM: 1) John of God, founder. Portuguese (1495–1550). He went from soldier, to shepherd, to drifter, to bookseller. At forty, he heard a sermon by John of Avila and went mad with guilt. John of Avila visited him in his cell, where John of God confessed his sins and converted to Christianity. Building a hospital, he devoted his life to the care of the sick and needy. John died trying to save a man from drowning. He was named founder of the Brothers Hospitallers after his death. Also patron of booksellers, heart patients, hospitals, nurses, printers, and the sick. Canonized 1690; feast day, March 8.

2) Monica, mother. Tagastian (331–387). She was married to Patricius, a pagan alcoholic with a bad temper, and converted him to Christianity. With some persistence she also converted her son Augustine, who later became the most distinguished of the Catholic church's intellectuals. Also patron of housewives, infidelity, married women, and mothers. Feast day, August 27.

ALPINISTS: Bernard of Montijoix, priest. Italian (996–1081). He devoted his forty years as a priest to the residence of the Alps. Builder of schools and churches; best known for Great and Little Bernard, two shelters on mountain passes created for travelers of all religions and origins. Also patron of mountaineers and skiers. Feast day, May 28.

ALSACE: Odilia, abbess. Oberheiman (8th century). Her father, a nobleman, was so embarrassed by his newborn's blindness, he gave her to a commoner to raise. Miraculously, Odilia acquired her sight at age twelve, while being baptized. She founded a convent in Odilienberg. Also patron of the blind. Feast day, December 13.

ALTAR BOYS: John Berchmans. Brabanterian (1599–1621). Somehow this Jesuit novice managed hosts of miracles after his death. Also patron of youths. Canonized 1888; feast day, November 26.

AMERICA, CENTRAL AND SOUTH: Rose of Lima, mystic. Peruvian (1586–1617). The daughter of Spaniards, Isabel de Flores y del Oliva (Rose) has the distinction of being the first saint born in the New World. Instead of marrying into comfort, Rose joined the Dominicans as a tertiary. She applied harsh penance to herself; she experienced visions and stigmata (five wounds concurring with the five wounds of Christ). Since her death, Rose has been attributed with saving Lima from countless local earthquakes. Also patron of embroiderers. Canonized 1671; feast day, August 23.

AMERICA, NORTH: Our Lady of Guadalupe. Tepeyac, Mexico. In the winter of 1531, Juan Diego was walking on a hillside where he was visited by the Virgin Mary. Declaring herself as the "Mother of the true God who gives life," she instructed Juan to build a church in her honor. Juan explained Mary's request to Bishop Juan de Zumarraga, who asked for a sign as proof of her appearance. When Juan Diego returned to the hill, he found it covered with roses in full bloom. Juan filled his *tilma* (shawl) at Mary's request, then took the bundle back to the bishop's residence. Juan opened the tilma, letting the roses spill onto the floor, and there on the cloth emerged the likeness of an olive-complexioned Virgin Mary. Also patron of Mexico.

AMPUTEES: Anthony the Great, hermit. Egyptian (251–356). Founder of monasticism, first of the "white martyrs." As a hermit living in a cave, he refused the flock of naked women sent to tempt him. This caused his further retreat to a cave on Mount Kolzim. His followers wore hair shirts while making baskets and brushes to support their intellectual and spiritual search for God. Emperor Constantine was said to visit the wise hermit for counsel. Anthony was over 100 years old when he died. Also patron of basketweavers, brushmakers, gravediggers, and hermits; is invoked against eczema. Feast day, January 17.

ANESTHETISTS: Rene Goupil, martyr. French (1606–1642). First North American martyr. He was a missionary captured at Ossernenon (Auriesville, New York) by the Huron Indians. They tortured him for two months, then he was tomahawked to death for making the sign of the cross on the head of an Indian child. Canonized 1930; feast day, September 26.

ANGINA SUFFERERS: Swithbert, preacher. Northumbrian (647–713). A monk with a knack for converting Germans, Southern Hollanders, and Brabants. He became bishop in 693, converting the Bortuctuarians along the way. Feast day, March 1.

ANGOLA: Immaculate/Sacred Heart of Mary. In 1942, Pope Pius XII sanctified the holiness of Mary's heart, which has since been revered as the embodiment of purity and mercy. In order to achieve the Sacred Heart one must follow the code of the decent Christian: go to mass, recite the rosary, and receive communion, all of which must be done on a regular basis. Also patron of Ecuador, Lesotho, and the Philippines.

ANIMALS: Francis of Assisi, founder. Italian (1181–1226). Although never a priest, he is one of the dominant figures of the Christian religion. Born to a wealthy cloth merchant, Francis lived a lavish and irresponsible life. At twenty, he went to war against Perugia, where he was captured and imprisoned. After his release, Francis experienced several visions of Christ. He then renounced his inheritance and founded the Friars Minor. The first person ever to receive stigmata (five wounds, concurring with the five wounds of Christ) while praying, which never healed. He created the first Nativity scene in 1223. Also patron of Catholic action, ecologists, Italy, merchants, and zoos. Canonized 1228; feast day, October 4.

APOLOGISTS: Justin, martyr. Palestinian (2nd century). After studying various philosophies, he embraced Christianity. He founded a school of philosophy in Rome. Justin was martyred along with five other men and a woman for refusing to worship pagan gods. Also patron of philosophers. Feast day, June 1.

APOPLEXY: Andrew Avellino, priest. Neapolitan (1521–1608). Sent to reform Sant Arcangelo, Andrew discovered the convent had been turned into a house of ill repute by the fallen nuns. Almost losing his life in his effort at reformation, Andrew joined the Theatines. In the midst of a sermon, he suffered an apoplectic attack and remained unconscious for the rest of his life. Some historians believe that Andrew fell into a catatonic state, was mistaken for dead, then buried. He is invoked against sudden death. Canonized 1712; feast day, November 10.

APPENDICITIS, INVOKED AGAINST: Elmo (Erasmus), martyr. Italian (4th century). Legend. One legend has him surviving unharmed Emperor Diocletian's order of execution by bonfire during the Christian persecutions. Another has him tortured to death by having his intestines pulled from him by a windlass. The electrical discharge on a ship's masthead, which sometimes occurs before or after a storm, is believed to be a sign that St. Elmo is protecting the vessel. Also patron of sailors; he is invoked against intestinal disease and seasickness. Feast day, June 2.

APPLE ORCHARDS: Charles Borromeo, bishop/cardinal. Italian (1538–1584). A speech impediment did nothing to stop him from preaching. His uncle, Pope Pius IV, appointed this twenty-two-year-old as cardinal before he was even a priest. He was one of the predominant figures among Roman Catholic reformers in clerical education, which constantly put him at odds with the clergy and aristocracy of the time. He was the originator of Sunday schools for children. The reason for his patronage to apple orchards is unknown. Also patron of catechists and seminarians. Canonized 1610; feast day, November 4.

APPRENTICES: John Bosco, founder. Italian (1815–1888). He and his mother established a refuge for boys. Their "boys town" offered education and apprenticeships in various trades for homeless and exploited youths. He then opened the Daughters of Mary of Christians for neglected girls. John authored three books to help finance his centers. Also patron of editors and laborers. Canonized 1934; feast day, January 31.

ARCHAEOLOGISTS: Damasus, pope. Roman (4th century). Restored the catacombs, shrines, and tombs of martyrs; encouraged the biblical work of St. Jerome. Feast day, December 11.

ARCHERS: Sebastian, martyr. Gaulish (3rd century). A favorite among Renaissance painters. According to legend, he was an officer of the imperial guard. When Sebastian admitted his Christian faith, he was shot with arrows by his former coworkers. Surviving the execution, Sebastian was nurtured back to health by the widow of St. Castulus. When Emperor Diocletian received word of Sebastian's recovery, he sent his guards to club him to death. Also patron of athletes and soldiers. Feast day, January 20.

ARCHITECTS: 1) Barbara, martyr. (4th century.) Religious fiction. This legend goes back to the seventh century, and can be found in writings from Tuscany, Rome, Antioch, Heliopolis, and Nicomedia. A young woman whose pagan father locked her in a tower before leaving on a long journey. Within the walls, she converted to Christianity and had three windows built to signify the

Trinity. When her father returned, he was so infuriated by his daughter's religious preference, he turned her over to the authorities. Barbara was subjected to heinous torture, yet refused to disavow her faith. The judge ordered the father to kill her himself. Atop a mountain he slew his daughter, then was immediately struck dead by a bolt of lightning. Also patron of builders, dying, fire prevention, founders, miners, prisoners, and stonemasons. Feast day, December 4.

2) Thomas, apostle. Galilean (1st century). Brother of St. James; also known as Didymus or the twin; one of the twelve apostles. He was skeptical about the resurrection of Christ (John 20:24–29), until allowed to touch the wounds in the Lord's side and hands; hence, the origin of the phrase "Doubting Thomas." The legend of Thomas began after Pentecost. Thomas was assigned the conversion of India, a task he not only dreaded but refused to undertake. Christ himself failed in his attempt through a dream to talk the apostle into going to India. So, the Lord appeared to a merchant named Abban, en route to India, and arranged to have Thomas sold into slavery. Once he realized the direction that his new master was headed, Thomas gave in to the will of God. In India, he was advanced a hefty sum to build a palace for the Parthian king. Instead, he donated the money to the needy. When the king was informed of Thomas' actions, he ordered the execution of the apostle. Just then, the king's brother died and was brought back to life. He told of his glimpse of heaven, which was enough to sway the king. Thomas' patronage stems from the many churches he built during his pilgrimages. He is believed to have been martyred in India. Also patron of construction workers, East Indies, and India; he is invoked against doubt. Feast day, July 3.

ARGENTINA: Our Lady of Lujan. Over three hundred years ago, a two-foot-tall statue of the Immaculate Conception disappeared from Buenos Aires, then miraculously turned up in Lujan. In 1904, a church was erected around the fragile figurine. Also patron of Uruguay.

ARMENIA: 1) Gregory the Illuminator, bishop. Armenian (257–332). Also known as "Gregory the Enlightener." His father, Ansk, murdered King Khosrov I. Baby Gregory was smuggled out of Armenia before Khosrov's compatriots avenged their king's death. When Gregory grew into manhood, he separated from his family, then was ordained. Years later, Bishop Gregory returned to his native land. When King Khosrov's son learned of his arrival, he abducted Gregory, then tortured him for thirteen years. Ultimately, the king was swayed to Roman Catholicism by his prisoner. The unlikely pair converted most of Armenia. Feast day, September 30.

2) Bartholomew, apostle. Israelite (1st century). Also known as Nathaniel. The authorship of the extra biblical gospel attributed to Bartholomew is questionable. Little else is known about the son of Tolomai. He is believed to have traveled to Ethiopia, India, and Persia; he was martyred in Armenia. In art, he is often depicted flayed. Also patron of trappers. Feast day, August 24.

ARMORERS: Dunstan, bishop. English (910–988). One of the great reformers of church life in England during the tenth century. He rectified Bath and Westminster Abbey. He was advisor to King Edwy, until his accusation of the king's sexual exploits caused Dunstan's exile. A skillful metalworker and harpist. Also patron of blacksmiths, goldsmiths, locksmiths, musicians, and silversmiths. Feast day, May 19.

ART: Catherine of Bologna, visionary. French (1413–1463). Also known as Catherine de Virgi. She is probably best remembered for her vision on Christmas Day of the infant Jesus cradled in Mary's arms, still a popular subject for artists. Died the prioress of the new Poor Clares' Corpus Christi Convent. Also patron of liberal arts. Canonized 1712; feast day, March 9.

ART DEALERS: John the Divine, apostle. Galilean (1st century). Brother of James. Christ called the siblings "sons of thunder." John was referred to as the "disciple whom Jesus loved" (John 21:20–24). Christ, on the cross, left his mother in John's care (John 19:25–27). He was eventually exiled to the island of Patmos. He was the author of the fourth Gospel, three biblical epistles, and the book of the Revelation. Also patron of Asia Minor, editors, friendship, and publishers. Feast day, December 27.

ARTHRITIS, INVOKED AGAINST: James the Greater, apostle. Galilean (1st century). His name James "the Greater" is to differentiate him from the other apostle, James "the Less." He and his brother John "dropped their fishing nets" at the Sea of Galilee and followed Jesus; they were witnesses to both the transfiguration and the agony of Jesus in the garden. James was beheaded in Jerusalem, the first apostle to be martyred. Also patron of Chile, furriers, Guatemala, Nicaragua, pharmacists, pilgrims, and Spain; he is invoked against rheumatism. Feast day, July 25.

ARTISTS: Luke, evangelist. Greek (1st century). Physician and artist. Little is known of his early life. He was the author of the third Gospel and the Acts of the Apostles, which serve as a record of the progression of early

Christianity. He died in Greece at the age of 84. Also patron of butchers, glassworkers, notaries, painters, physicians, and surgeons. Feast day, October 18.

ASIA MINOR: John the Divine, apostle. Galilean (1st century). Brother of James. Christ called the siblings "sons of thunder." John was referred to as the "disciple whom Jesus loved" (John 21:20–24). Christ, on the cross, left his mother in John's care (John 19:25–27). He was eventually exiled to the island of Patmos. He was the author of the fourth Gospel, three biblical epistles, and the book of the Revelation. Also patron of art dealers, editors, friendship, and publishers. Feast day, December 27.

ASTRONAUTS: Joseph of Cupertino, ecstatic. Italian (1603–1663). Born in a shed to an impoverished family, this mentally challenged child was nicknamed "the gaper" by his peers. After failing twice, Joseph was ordained a Franciscan in 1628. His miracles, raptures, and levitations became legendary. Flying over the altar was commonplace, as were his ecstasies. As his following grew, "the flying friar" was moved from one friary to another, eventually dying in obscure seclusion at Osimo. Also patron of aviators and pilots. Canonized 1767; feast day, September 18.

ASTRONOMERS: Dominic, founder. Spanish (1170–1221). During his baptism, Dominic's mother saw a star shining from her son's chest. Soeur Sourire, better known as "The Singing Nun," paid homage to this saint in 1963 with her pop hit, "Dominique." The invention of the rosary is attributed to him. Canonized 1234; died, August 6; feast day, August 8.

ATHLETES: Sebastian, martyr. Gaulish (3rd century). A favorite among Renaissance painters. According to legend, he was an officer of the imperial guard. When Sebastian admitted his Christian faith, he was shot with arrows by his former coworkers. Surviving the execution, Sebastian was nurtured back to health by the widow of St. Castulus. When Emperor Diocletian received word of Sebastian's recovery, he sent his guards to club him to death. Also patron of archers and soldiers. Feast day, January 20.

ATTORNEYS: Ivo Kermartin (Yves), priest. Breton (1253–1303). He studied law in Paris and Orleans. As an attorney, he represented the poor free of charge. At the age of thirty, Ivo was appointed diocesan judge and proved himself to be incorruptible. He became a priest in 1284, aiding his parishioners in both spiritual and legal matters. Also patron of jurists. Canonized 1347; feast day, May 19.

AUSTRALIA: Our Lady Help of Christians. In 1964, Pope Paul VI venerated the Blessed Virgin Mary as the protector of Australia and New Zealand.

AUSTRIA: 1) Our Lady of Mariazell. In 1157, an Austrian figurine of the Blessed Virgin Mary was dedicated by the Benedictine Monastery in Mariazell.

2) Colman, martyr. Irish (11th century). Roman martyrology has a list of 300 saints named Colman. While on a pilgrimage to Jerusalem, Colman was stopped by the suspicious Viennese, who, fearing he was a Moravian spy, tried and hanged Colman. After his death, his body showed no sign of decay. The miracles which have since occurred at his grave have confirmed his holiness. Also patron of horned cattle; he is invoked against hangings. Feast day, October 13.

AUTHORS: Francis de Sales, bishop, writer. French (1567–1622). He earned a doctorate in law at the age of twenty-four. Within five years, surviving numerous assassination attempts, he managed to convert thousands of Calvinists back to Catholicism. Francis' writings include *Introduction to the Devout Life* (1609) and *Treatise on the Love of God* (1616). He was the first to receive beatification at St. Peter's. Also patron of the Catholic press, the deaf, journalists, and writers. Canonized 1877; feast day, January 24.

AVIATORS: 1) Joseph of Cupertino, ecstatic. Italian (1603–1663). Born in a shed to an impoverished family, this mentally challenged child was nicknamed "the gaper" by his peers. After failing twice, Joseph was ordained a Franciscan in 1628. His miracles, raptures, and levitations became legendary. Flying over the altar was commonplace, as were his ecstasies. As his following grew, "the flying friar" was moved from one friary to another, eventually dying in obscure seclusion at Osimo. Also the patron of astronauts and pilots. Canonized 1767; feast day, September 18.

2) Therese of Lisieux, nun. French (1873–1897). Also known as "The Little Flower." She and her five sisters became Carmelite nuns. Author of *The Story of a Soul*, Therese wrote that she would "let fall a shower of roses" (miracles) when she passed on. Dying of tuberculosis on September 30, she kept her word. Also patron of florists, foreign missions, and France. Canonized 1925; feast day, October 1.

A man who governs his passions is master of his world. We must either command them or be enslaved by them. It is better to be a hammer than an anvil.

—St. Dominic

BABIES: 1) Holy Innocents. According to Matthew (2:16–18), Herod feared the new king had been born in Bethlehem, so he ordered that all male infants be slain. They are considered the first martyrs for Christ. Also patrons of foundlings. Feast day, December 28.

2) Zeno, bishop. African (4th century). Ninety-three of this sportsman's sermons in Latin have been preserved by the church, giving an accurate depiction of the traditions and culture in the fourth century. The majority of his homilies are of the birth of Christ, which probably explains his patronage. Canonized 372; feast day, April 12.

BACHELORS: 1) Theobald, layman. Italian (12th century). After rejecting the hand of his employer's daughter, along with a partnership in the family's business, Theobald gained employment as a janitor at the cathedral of Saint Lawrence. Also patron of church janitors and janitors. Feast day, March 9.

2) Christopher, martyr. Lycian (3rd century). Myth. There are a number of legends about the man martyred in Lycia. One goes like this: He was a hideous giant named Offero, who earned a living carrying travelers across the river. He carried a heavy lad one day, claiming to be weighted by the problems of the world. This child, of course, was the youthful Christ. The name Christopher itself means "carrier of Christ" in Greek. Also patron of bus drivers, motorists, porters, travelers, truck drivers; he is invoked against nightmares. Feast day, July 25.

BACTERIAL DISEASES: Agrippina, martyr. Roman (3rd century). During the persecution of Christians, Agrippina was tortured then executed when she refused to renounce her faith to Emperors Valerian or Diocletian. Her body was taken to Sicily by three women, where the afflicted have been cured at her tomb for centuries. She is invoked against evil spirits and thunderstorms. Feast day, June 23.

BAD LUCK, INVOKED AGAINST: Agricola of Avignon, bishop. French (630–700). At the age of thirty, his father, Bishop (Saint) Magnus, appointed Agricola to co-bishop Avignon, thus creating a rare father and son team in the Roman Catholic church. He is best known for a prayer that ended an invasion of storks. Also patron of good weather and rain; he is invoked against misfortune and plague. Feast day, September 2.

BAD WEATHER, INVOKED AGAINST: Eurosia, martyr. Bayonnese (8th century). According to legend, Eurosia was a maiden of noble birth, who was promised to a pagan. She sought refuge in a cave, hoping that her Moorish fiancé would give up the idea of matrimony.

The smoke from her fire caught the attention of his search party, who then dragged her from her refuge by the hair and killed her. Feast day, June 25.

BAKERS: 1) Elizabeth, Queen. Hungarian (1207–1231). Although her marriage to Ludwig IV was arranged, the two were in love and had three children. In 1227 Ludwig died while on crusade. Elizabeth and her children were kicked out of the Wartburg castle by the in-laws. She made arrangements for her children, then relinquished herself of her title. Joining the Franciscan order, she devoted herself to the care of those in need. She was counseled by a tyrant named Conrad of Marburg. He was insistent that she suffer extreme deprivation and humility for the rest of her short life, which ended at the tender age of twenty-three. Her patronage derives from a large donation of grain to Germany during a year of famine. Also patron of nursing homes and tertiaries. Canonized 1235; feast day, November 17.

2) Honortus, bishop. French (unknown dates). Died the bishop of Amiens. In 1060 his body was raised for ceremonial purposes. A number of miracles have been attributed to him, due to the unearthing. Feast day, May 16.

BANKERS: Matthew, apostle. Galilean (1st century). His name means "gift of God." Also known as Levi; no records of his early life. Tax collector turned apostle; he wrote the first Gospel between 60 and 90, which contains quotes from the Old Testament. He was martyred either in Ethiopia or Persia. Also patron of accountants, bookkeepers, customs agents, security guards, and tax collectors. Feast day, September 21.

BAPTISM: John the Baptist, martyr. Israelite (1st century). Cousin to Jesus Christ; his birth was announced by an angel to his father, Zachary. John baptized several of the apostles, including Jesus himself. He was imprisoned for condemning the incestuous relationship Herod was carrying on with his niece, Herodias, who happened to be the wife of Phillip, his half brother. Herod offered Herodias' daughter, Salome, anything she wanted. Salome requested John's head on a platter, upon her mother's prodding. Also patron of farriers; he is invoked against spasms. Feast day, June 24.

BARBERS: Cosmas and Damian, martyrs. Arabians (4th century). Known as "the holy moneyless ones." Twin physicians who took no payment from their patients, they were beheaded along with their three brothers for their Christian beliefs. Some critics feel that their legend derives from Greek mythology's Castor and Pollux. Also patrons of doctors, druggists, pharmacists, physicians, and surgeons. Feast day, September 26.

BARRELMAKERS: Abdon and Senen, martyrs. Persians (4th century). During the persecutions of the third century, these two barrelmakers aided Christian prisoners. They were caught one night recovering the remains of martyrs and were executed by Emperor Diocletian. Feast day, July 30.

BARREN WOMEN: 1) Anthony of Padua, preacher. Portuguese (1195–1231). Born Ferdinand; known as "the Wonder Worker" for his preaching savvy; the first lector in theology; Doctor of the Church; colleague of St. Francis of Assisi. A disciple once took Anthony's psalter without asking. The terrorized novice promptly returned it, claiming that he was being haunted by apparitions for his act. Also the patron of lost articles, the poor, Portugal, shipwrecks, and travelers; he is invoked against starvation. Canonized 1232; feast day, June 13.

2) Felicity and her seven sons, martyrs. Romans (2nd century). Pious legend. This young widow had seven sons. Their strong Christian faith caught the attention of Antoninus Pius, who attempted to persuade Felicity and her sons to worship pagan gods. When his promises and threats failed, Antoninus had the boys sentenced to death in seven different courts. Felicity was forced to witness each execution, then was beheaded. Also patron of children's death and heirs. Feast day, July 10.

BASKETWEAVERS: Anthony the Great, hermit. Egyptian (251–356). Founder of monasticism, first of the "white martyrs." As a hermit living in a cave, he refused the flock of naked women sent to tempt him. This caused his further retreat to a cave on Mount Kolzim. His followers wore hair shirts while making baskets and brushes to support their intellectual and spiritual search for God. Emperor Constantine was said to visit the wise hermit for counsel. Anthony was over 100 years old when he died. Also patron of amputees, brushmakers, gravediggers, and hermits; he is invoked against eczema. Feast day, January 17.

BATTLE: Michael, archangel. One of the seven archangels of God; one of the three archangels mentioned by name in the Bible. He is cited twice in the Old Testament, appearing to Moses and Abraham. In the New Testament, he contends with Satan for the body of Moses and tosses Lucifer and his cohorts from heaven. In art, he is often depicted with a scale (representing the weighing of souls) in one hand, while slaying a dragon (Satan) with the other. Also patron of the dead, grocers, mariners, paratroopers, police officers, and radiologists. Feast day, September 29.

BAVARIA: Hedwig, Queen. Bavarian (1174–1243). She and her husband, Henry I, supported a number of charities. After Henry's death, Hedwig was beset by her six children's tribulations. Hedwig found solace in a Cistercian abbey, an early endeavor of the royal couple, then committed herself to the care of the indigent. Also patron of children's death, duchesses, queens, and Silesia; she is invoked against jealousy and marital problems. Feast day, October, 16.

BEES: Ambrose, bishop. Italian (340–397). His contributions were key to the advancement of Christianity during the decline of the Roman Empire. St. Anthony converted to Christianity after hearing a sermon by Ambrose. According to legend, a swarm of bees landed on the infant Ambrose's lips, causing no injury. Also patron of chandlers and learning. Feast day, December 7.

BEGGARS: 1) Alexis, servant. Roman (5th century). Also known as the "Man of God." An autobiography was found after his death. It revealed his identity as the estranged son of a wealthy senator, whom he had served for the past seventeen years. Also patron of beltmakers. Feast day, July 17.

2) Giles, hermit. English (8th century). A forest hermit, he was wounded with an arrow while protecting a hind he had been suckling for a year. The king was so touched by the cripple's compassion, he appointed Giles as one of his advisors. Also patron of breast-feeding, hermits, horses, the physically disabled, and the woods. Feast day, September 1.

3) Benedict Joseph Labre, transient. Boulognian (18th century). He left his wealthy family to search for

God. Traveling throughout Europe for three years, he visited every pilgrimage site in his holy quest. Ending up at the Colosseum, Benedict the beggar spent his last years in intense prayer. He died in church. Also patron of the homeless, religious orders, and transients. Feast day, April 16.

BELGIUM: Joseph, carpenter. Nazarean (1st century). Descendent of David; husband to the Virgin Mary; foster father to Jesus Christ. Joseph had second thoughts about marrying Mary when he learned that she was pregnant until the angel Gabriel explained the Messiah's coming. After the birth of Christ, he was forewarned in a dream of Herod's exploits, so he took his young family to Egypt. After Herod's death, a dream directed them to return to Israel. Fearing Herod's replacement, Joseph chose to settle his family in Nazareth. Scholars believe he died before the crucifixion of Christ. Also patron of Canada, carpenters, the church, the dying, fathers, Korea, Peru, social justice, and working men. Feast days, March 19 and May 1.

BELTMAKERS: Alexis, servant. Roman (5th century). Also known as the "Man of God." An autobiography was found after his death. It revealed his identity as the estranged son of a wealthy senator, whom he had served for the past seventeen years. Also patron of beggars. Feast day, July 17.

BETRAYAL, VICTIMS OF: Flora, martyr. Spanish (9th century). Though Flora's mother was a Christian, the household was run with the strict Muslim beliefs of her father. Flora's rejection of the Islamic faith caused severe beatings by her brother and father, which worsened when she converted to Christianity. She and her best friend, Mary, chose to leave home when Flora's parents announced her engagement to a Muhammedan. The two hid in Flora's sister's home for a brief time. The fear of being associated with Christians led Flora's sister to throw them back out on the street. Flora and Mary confessed themselves to the Islamic council as Christians, and they were tortured before being beheaded. Also patron of converts and working women. Feast day, November 24.

BIRDS: Gall, hermit. Irish (7th century). The forefather of Christianity in Switzerland. Gall was once said to have exorcised the daughter of a duke. The evil spirits ascended from her mouth as a flock of blackbirds. Feast day, October 16.

BIRTH: Margaret, martyr. Antiochan (4th century). Legend. She was disowned by her father, a pagan priest, for converting to Christianity. Margaret became a shepherdess, during which time she was spotted by the governor. His failed attempts in seducing the young woman angered him to the point of incarcerating her. Margaret then revealed herself a Christian and was subjected to a number of gruesome tortures. One of these was being swallowed by a dragon whose belly was sliced open by the cross Margaret was wearing. Eventually she was beheaded. Also patron of divine intervention and pregnant women. Feast day, July 20.

BLACKSMITHS: Dunstan, bishop. English (910–988). One of the great reformers of church life in England during the tenth century. He rectified Bath and Westminster Abbey. He was advisor to King Edwy, until his accusation of the king's sexual exploits caused Dunstan's exile. A skillful metalworker and harpist. Also patron of armorers, goldsmiths, locksmiths, musicians, and silver-smiths. Feast day, May 19.

BLEEDING, INVOKED AGAINST: Rita, nun. Italian (1381–1457). An arranged marriage of eighteen years came to an end when her abusive husband was murdered in a brawl. Her two sons sought retribution for their father, but Rita would rather her sons died than become murderers. She prayed for their souls; soon after, the two became ill and died. Rita entered an Augustinian convent on her third attempt (being rejected the first two times for lacking virginity). Hearing a sermon on the crown of thorns, a "thorn-like" wound appeared on her forehead, which stayed with her for the rest of her life. Miracles were accredited to her after her death. Also patron of desperate situations and parenthood; she is invoked against infertility, and marital problems. Canonized 1900; feast day, May 22.

BLIND: 1) Odilia, abbess. Oberheiman (8th century). Her father, a nobleman, was so embarrassed by his new-born's blindness, he gave her to a commoner to raise. Miraculously, Odilia acquired her sight at age twelve, while being baptized. She founded a convent in Odilien-berg. Also patron of Alsace. Feast day, December 13.

2) Raphael, archangel. One of the seven archangels of God; one of the three archangels specified by name in the Bible. He has been venerated by both Jewish and Christian faiths. His name means "God heals." Also patron of lovers, nurses, physicians, and travelers. Feast day, September 29.

BLOOD BANKS: Januarius, martyr. Italian (3rd century). Legend. He was a bishop martyred during the Christian persecutions. For the past four centuries in Naples, a vessel containing what is said to be his blood boils when uncovered in the cathedral. Feast day, September 19.

BOATMEN: Julian the Hospitaler, innkeeper. (Unknown dates.) Pious fiction. He killed a sleeping couple in his bed, fearing adultery. The slain were not an adulterous wife and lover, but his visiting parents. His penance was to build an inn and hospital for the poor at the mouth of a river. Julian was absolved when he gave his bed to an angel, who was disguised as a leper. Also patron of circus people, ferrymen, hotel employees, and innkeepers. Feast day, February 12.

BODILY INJURY, INVOKED AGAINST: Our Lady of Lourdes, France. In 1858, the Blessed Virgin Mary appeared to a young girl named Bernadette Soubirous. The illumination was dressed in white and referred to herself as the "Immaculate Conception." On the site of her eighteen visits, a spring of curing water emerged. A church has since been built. Lourdes is one of the most popular pilgrimage sites for Catholics in the world, drawing over four million a year.

BOHEMIA: Wenceslaus, Prince. Bohemian (907–929). His grandmother, St. Ludmilla, instilled a strong Christian faith in the young prince. She was murdered by an opposing pagan party. When Wenceslaus became the ruler, he advanced the Christian faith in Bohemia as well as their neighboring countries. Wenceslaus' brother, Boleslaus, was so envious of the prince that he murdered him while en route to church. Wenceslaus' son succeeded to the throne. Also patron of Czechoslovakia. Feast day, September 28.

BOLIVIA: Our Lady of Copacabana. *"Virgen de la Candelaria."* In the late nineteenth century, a statue of the Virgin Mary was crafted by the native fishermen of Bolivia. It is housed near Lake Titicaca.

BOOKBINDERS: Peter Celestine V, pope. Italian (1210–1296). The most inept pope in history. At the age of eighty-four, this hermit was shocked to be chosen for the papacy, due to political disputes within the church. Holiness aside, he was ill-suited for the papal office; he lasted five months in the Vatican. Canonized 1313; feast day, May 19.

BOOKKEEPERS: Matthew, apostle. Galilean (1st century). His name means "Gift of God." Also known as Levi; no records of his early life. Tax collector turned apostle; he wrote the first Gospel between 60 and 90, which contains quotes from the Old Testament. He was martyred either in Ethiopia or Persia. Also patron of accountants, bankers, customs agents, security guards, and tax collectors. Feast day, September 21.

BOOKMAKERS: Columba, missionary. Irish (6th century). Some historians believe that Columba banished himself from Ireland for provoking the battle of Cooldrevne. His critics believe that this great lover of books once borrowed the first copy of St. Jerome's psalter from St. Finnian and sneakily made a copy for himself. Columba was sent before the judge, who ordered him to return the property to its rightful owner, St. Finnian. Instead of returning both books, Columba retreated to Scotland. He founded a number of monasteries in Scotland. Feast day, June 9.

BOOKSELLERS: John of God, founder. Portuguese (1495–1550). He went from soldier, to shepherd, to drifter, to bookseller. At forty, he heard a sermon by John of Avila and went mad with guilt. John of Avila visited him in his cell, where John of God confessed his sins and converted to Christianity. Building a hospital, he devoted his life to the care of the sick and needy. John died trying to save a man from drowning. He was named founder of the Brothers Hospitallers after his death. Also patron of alcoholism, heart patients, hospitals, nurses, printers, and the sick. Canonized 1690; feast day, March 8.

BORNEO: Francis Xavier, missionary. Spanish Basque (1506–1552). One of the seven founding Jesuits and considered one of the greatest missionaries; pioneer of missionary work in India and the East. He died en route to China. Also patron of Japan and foreign missions. Canonized 1602; feast day, December 3.

BOWEL DISORDERS, INVOKED AGAINST: Bonaventure of Potenza, founder. French (800–856). Bishop; builder of churches and monasteries. He left his see when a disagreement with the monks of St. Calais arose over jurisdiction, but returned before his death from an intestinal disease. Also invoked against intestinal disease. Feast day, January 7.

BOY SCOUTS: George, martyr. English (3rd century). Aside from being martyred in Palestine, this Christian knight's life is pure fiction. He is best known for a dragonslaying incident, in which he saved a princess from being sacrificed, then married her. An account of his life is found in the thirteenth-century *The Golden Legend.* Also patron of England, farmers, and soldiers. Feast day, February 21.

BOYS: Nicholas of Myra, bishop. Lycian (4th century). Better known as Saint Nick. The facts are few. He ran a monastery, was a prisoner during the time of Christian persecutions, and was present at the Council of Nicaea. The rest is myth. One tale tells of a father who was so poor he couldn't afford his three daughters' dowries. Nick tossed three bags of gold through the kitchen window, and the three daughters married soon after. Also patron of brides, children, dockworkers, Greece, merchants, pawnbrokers, spinsters, and travelers. Feast day, December 6.

BRAZIL: Immaculate Conception. In 1854, Pope Pius IX declared the Blessed Virgin Mary as born without original sin, having been immaculately conceived, and having lived a sin-free life. Also patron of Corsica, Portugal, Tanzania, and the United States.

BREAST DISEASE, INVOKED AGAINST: Agatha, martyr. Sicilian (3rd century.) Legend. Governor Quintianis used the persecution of Christians as a way of possessing her. She refused his advances and was brutally tortured. Her captor starved her, sliced off her breasts, then rolled her in hot coals and broken pottery. She died in her cell. In early paintings of this saint, her breasts displayed on a platter have been mistaken for bread. Hence, the blessing of bread on her feast day. Also patron of nurses and rape victims. Is invoked against volcanic eruptions. Feast day, February 5.

BREAST-FEEDING: Giles, hermit. English (8th century). A forest hermit, he was wounded with an arrow while protecting a hind he had been suckling for a year. The king was so touched by the cripple's compassion, he appointed Giles as one of his advisors. Also patron of beggars, hermits, horses, the physically disabled, and the woods. Feast day, September 1.

BREWERS: Augustine of Hippo, bishop, doctor. North African (354–430). He was into parties, fun, and games. Augustine kept a mistress and sired a son out of wedlock. The conversion of Augustine is attributed to the prayers of his mother, Saint Monica, and a sermon by Saint Ambrose. As a convert, he authored numerous works, *Confessions* and *City of God*, to name two. He was one of the greatest intellectuals of the Catholic church and the first philosopher of Christianity, associating the term "original sin" with Adam and Eve. Also patron of printers and theologians. Feast day, August 28.

BRICKLAYERS: Stephen, martyr. Hellenist (of the Dispersion). (1st century.) The first martyr for Christ. The Jewish council stoned Stephen to death after he denounced them. Also patron of deacons and stonemasons. Feast day, December 26.

BRIDES: 1) Nicholas of Myra, bishop. Lycian (4th century). Better known as Saint Nick. The facts are few. He ran a monastery, was a prisoner during the time of Christian persecutions, and was present at the Council of Nicaea. The rest is myth. One tale tells of a father who was so poor he couldn't afford his three daughters' dowries. Nick tossed three bags of gold through the kitchen window, and the three daughters married soon after. Also patron of boys, children, dockworkers, Greece, merchants, pawnbrokers, spinsters, and travelers. Feast day, December 6.

2) Dorothy, martyr. Cappodian (4th century). Legend. Fabricus the prefect could not talk her into being his wife, so he handed the Christian over to the authorities. While Dorothy was being escorted to her execution, a lawyer named Theophilus called out in jest that she send him some fruit from "heaven's garden." That winter, a basket with pears and roses arrived at Theophilus' door, whereupon he converted. Also patron of gardeners. Feast day, February 6.

3) Elizabeth of Portugal, Queen. Aragonian (1271–1336). Niece of Elizabeth of Hungary. King Peter III

of Aragon offered his twelve-year-old daughter's hand to King Denis of Portugal. She was constantly interceding as peacemaker between her son, Alfonso, and his father. King Denis once believed her to be endorsing her son for the throne; he then banished Elizabeth from Portugal. After the king's death, Elizabeth joined the Secular Franciscan order and moved to a convent of the Sisters of St. Claire, which she had founded in Coimbra. Also patron of tertiaries and war; she is invoked against jealousy and marital problems. Canonized 1626; feast day, July 4.

BRIDGES: John of Nepomucene, bishop and martyr. Czechoslovakian (1345–1393). Until 1961, John was believed to have been thrown from a bridge for refusing to crack the seal of the confessional, when the jealous King Wenceslaus IV demanded to know what disclosures his wife, Queen Sophia, had made to the bishop. A more logical reason for his drowning is religious and political differences. Also patron of Czechoslovakia, detraction, discretion, and silence; he is invoked against slander. Canonized 1729; feast day, May 16.

BROADCASTERS: Gabriel, archangel. Messenger of God. One of the seven archangels of God; one of the three archangels referred to by name in the Bible. Announced the birth of Jesus to Mary (Luke 1:11–21). Also patron of clerics, diplomats, messengers, postal workers, radio workers, stamp collectors, telecommunications workers, and television workers.

BROKEN BONES, INVOKED AGAINST: Stanislaus Kostka, child. Polish (1550–1568). He was subjected to constant abuse by his older brother. At the age of sixteen, Stanislaus walked 350 miles to Rome in hopes of joining the

Jesuits. He died in the Order of Francis one year later. Canonized 1726; feast day, November 13.

BRUISES, INVOKED AGAINST: Amalburga (Gudula), laywoman. German (8th century). Legend. Emperor Charlemagne was so obsessed with her beauty, he continually harassed her. When caught attempting to flee, he beat her severely. Surviving the attack, she crossed the Rhine River on a sturgeon's back. Feast day, January 8.

BRUSHMAKERS: Anthony the Great, hermit. Egyptian (251–356). Founder of monasticism, first of the "white martyrs." As a hermit living in a cave, he refused the flock of naked women sent to tempt him. This caused his further retreat to a cave on Mount Kolzim. His followers wore hair shirts while making baskets and brushes to support their intellectual and spiritual search for God. Emperor Constantine was said to visit the wise hermit for counsel. Anthony was over 100 years old when he died. Also patron of amputees, basketweavers, gravediggers, and hermits; he is invoked against eczema. Feast day, January 17.

BUILDERS: 1) Barbara, martyr. (4th century.) Religious fiction. A young woman whose pagan father locked her in a tower before leaving on a long journey. Within the walls, she converted to Christianity and had three windows built to signify the Trinity. When her father returned, he was so infuriated by his daughter's religious preference, he turned her over to the authorities. Barbara was subjected to heinous torture, yet refused to disavow her faith. The judge ordered the father to kill her himself. Atop a mountain he slew his daughter, then was immediately struck dead by a bolt of lightning. Also patron of architects, the dying, fire prevention, founders, miners, prisoners, and stonemasons. Feast day, December 4.

2) Vincent Ferrer, missionary. Spanish (1350–1419). Christ called upon this strikingly handsome man in a dream. Vincent successfully converted tens of thousands of people, including Rabbi Paul of Burgos, who became the bishop of Cartagena. He also converted St. Bernardine of Siena and St. Mary of Savoy. Vincent assisted in ending the great Western Schism by removing his support from Benedict XIII. Also patron of pavement workers and plumbers. Canonized 1455; feast day, April 5.

BURGLARY, INVOKED AGAINST: Leonard, founder. French (6th century). Legend. After assisting his godfather's, King Clovis', wife in an arduous pregnancy, the king endowed to him the land that he could cover by riding on a donkey in a day. On his new property, Leonard founded Noblac monastery and the town of Saint-Leonard. The king also released any prisoner that Leonard went to visit. Most of the former inmates sought refuge in his abbey, and many stayed on to help run it. Also patron of prisoners of war and women in labor. Feast day, November 6.

BUS DRIVERS: Christopher, Lycian (3rd century). Myth. There are a number of legends about the man martyred in Lycia. One goes like this: He was a hideous giant named Offero, who earned a living carrying travelers across the river. He carried a heavy lad one day, claiming to be weighted by the problems of the world. This child, of course, was the youthful Christ. The name Christopher itself means "carrier of Christ" in Greek. Also patron of bachelors, motorists, porters, travelers, truck drivers; he is invoked against nightmares. Feast day, July 25.

BUSINESSMEN: Homobonus, cloth worker. Italian (12th century). A wealthy merchant who went into the family's tailoring business, he donated most of his money to the needy. Homobonus died during mass. Also patron of cloth workers and tailors. Feast day, November 13.

BUSINESSWOMEN: Margaret Clitherow, martyr. English (1556–1586). This mother of three and her husband ran a successful butcher shop. She was caught hiding priests in her storeroom during the Catholic reformation of England. Margaret suffered a slow death by having weights stacked on her back, eventually crushing her to death. Canonized 1970; Feast day, March 25.

BUTCHERS: 1) Hadrian (Adrian), martyr. Roman (3rd–4th century). As a pagan military officer, he was amazed by the Christians' refusal to recant their faith. When the prefect learned that Hadrian had been baptized, he had him broken limb from limb. Also patron of soldiers. Feast day, September 8.

2) Luke, evangelist. Greek (1st century). Physician and artist. Little is known of his early life. He was the author of the third Gospel and the Acts of the Apostles, which serve as a record of the progression of early Christianity. He died in Greece at the age of 84. Also patron of artists, glassworkers, notaries, painters, physicians, and surgeons. Feast day, October 18.

BUTLERS: Adelelm, manservant. French (12th century). Legend. He left a promising military career behind to join the priesthood. Adelelm and his manservant were caught in a storm one night. Adelelm ordered his manservant to light a candle. Miraculously, the candle did not blow out in the wet wind, until they had found a refuge. Feast day, January 30.

When men wish for old age for themselves, what else do they wish for but lengthened infirmity.

—St. Augustine of Hippo

CAB DRIVERS: Fiacre, hermit. Irish (7th century). Healer; built a refuge for the sick and poor. He was once endowed by St. Faro with all the land he could clear in a single day. When the saint returned at dusk, a large field was clear and ready for planting. The first cabstand in Paris was near the Hotel Saint Fiacre. As a result, the French word for taxi is *fiacre*. Also patron of gardeners; he is invoked against hemorrhoids and syphilis. Feast day, September 1.

CABINETMAKERS: Anne, housewife. Nazarean (1st century B.C.). Grandmother of Jesus; wife of Joachim. Aside from giving birth to the Blessed Mary at the age of forty, little is known of her. The reason for her patronage to cabinetmakers is unclear. Also patron of Canada, grandmothers, housewives, and women in labor. Feast day, July 26.

CANADA: 1) Joseph, carpenter. Nazarean (1st century). Descendent of David; husband to the Virgin Mary; foster father to Jesus Christ. Joseph had second thoughts about marrying Mary when he learned that she was pregnant until the angel Gabriel explained the Messiah's coming. After the birth of Christ, he was forewarned in a dream of Herod's exploits, so he took his young family to Egypt. After Herod's death, a dream directed them to return to Israel. Fearing Herod's replacement, Joseph chose to settle his family in Nazareth. Scholars believe he died before the crucifixion of Christ. Also patron of Belgium, carpenters, the church, the dying, fathers, Korea, Peru, social justice, and working men. Feast days, March 19 and May 1.

2) Anne, housewife. Nazarean (1st century B.C.). Grandmother of Jesus; wife of Joachim. Aside from giving birth to the Blessed Mary at the age of forty, little is known of her. Also patron of cabinetmakers, grandmothers, housewives, and women in labor. Feast day, July 26.

CANCER VICTIMS: 1) Peregrine Laziosi, preacher. Italian (1260–1345). While ministering to the needy, a cancerous growth on his foot spread. The doctors decided to amputate his leg. The night before his surgery, Peregrine experienced a vision. The next morning he awoke to find the cancer had vanished. Canonized 1726; feast day, May 1.

2) Bernard of Clairvaux, theologian. French (1090–1135). At the age of twenty-three, Bernard persuaded four of his brothers and twenty-seven friends to join the Cistercian order. This powerful speaker rode with the Second Crusade of Germany and France. His written works include *On the Song of Songs* and *Rule for the Knights Templar*. The last of the fathers of the Church.

Also patron of chandlers. Canonized 1174; feast day, August 20.

CANONIST: Raymond of Peñafort, archbishop. Spanish (1175–1275). He revised the Dominican Constitution, established friaries, and helped establish the Inquisition of Catalonia. His papal decrees were the foundation of canon law until their update in 1917. Feast day, January 7.

CARPENTERS: Joseph, carpenter. Nazarean (1st century). Descendent of David; husband to the Virgin Mary; foster father to Jesus Christ. Joseph had second thoughts about marrying Mary when he learned that she was pregnant until the angel Gabriel explained the Messiah's coming. After the birth of Christ, he was forewarned in a dream of Herod's exploits, so he took his young family to Egypt. After Herod's death, a dream directed them to return to Israel. Fearing Herod's replacement, Joseph chose to settle his family in Nazareth. Scholars believe he died before the crucifixion of Christ. Also patron of Belgium, Canada, the church, the dying, fathers, Korea, Peru, social justice, and working men. Feast days, March 19 and May 1.

CARVERS: Olaf II, King. Norwegian (995–1030). This future king began his career as a Viking, taking Norway from the Swedes and the Danes. In 1016, he became the king of Norway, and he attempted to force Christianity onto his subjects. This created a retaliation by many of his subjects who, with the help of the Anglo-Danish king, ousted Olaf from power. Olaf died in battle, attempting to recoup his losses. Wood-carving was the king's favorite hobby. One Sunday he was whittling away when he was reminded by a page that it was the Sabbath. Olaf put his tools away, then thanked his servant for pointing out that menial tasks were forbidden on the Lord's day. Also patron of kings, Norway. Feast day, July 29.

CATECHISTS: Charles Borromeo, bishop/cardinal. Italian (1538–1584). A speech impediment did nothing to stop him from preaching. His uncle, Pope Pius IV, appointed this twenty-two-year-old as cardinal before he was even a priest. He was one of the predominant figures among Roman Catholic reformers in clerical education, which constantly put him at odds with the clergy and aristocracy of the time. He was the originator of Sunday schools for children. Also patron of apple orchards and seminarians. Canonized 1610; feast day, November 4.

CATHOLIC ACTION: Francis of Assisi, founder. Italian (1181–1226). Although never a priest, he is one of the dominant figures of the Christian religion. Born to a wealthy cloth merchant, Francis lived a lavish and irresponsible life. At twenty, he went to war against Perugia, where he was captured and imprisoned. After his release, Francis experienced several visions of Christ. He then renounced his inheritance and founded the Friars Minor. The first person ever to receive stigmata (five wounds, concurring with the five wounds of Christ) while praying, which never healed. He created the first Nativity scene in 1223. Also patron of animals, ecologists, Italy, merchants, and zoos. Canonized 1228; feast day, October 4.

CATHOLIC PRESS: Francis de Sales, bishop and writer. French (1567–1622). He earned a doctorate in law at the age of twenty-four. Within five years, surviving numerous assassination attempts, he managed to convert thousands of Calvinists back to Catholicism. Francis' writings include *Introduction to the Devout Life* (1609) and *Treatise on the Love of God* (1616). He was the first to receive beatification at St. Peter's. Also patron of authors, the deaf, journalists, and writers. Canonized 1877; feast day, January 24.

CATS: Gertrude of Nivelles, abbess. Flemish (626–659). When Gertrude's father died, her mother, Itta, founded a monastery at Neville. The fourteen-year-old Gertrude was appointed as the abbess and proved herself deserving of the title. Gertrude's monastic center was known for its hospitality to pilgrims and monks. At the age of thirty, Gertrude lay on her deathbed, fearing that she was unworthy of heaven. St. Ultan assured her that St. Patrick was awaiting her. She died on St. Patrick's Day. The well at her monastery was said to have repellent properties against rodents. Also patron of accommodations and the recently dead; she is invoked against rats. Feast day, March 17.

CHAMPIONS: Drausin (Drausius), bishop. Soissons (7th century). Bishop Drausin founded several religious institutions, including a chapel for nuns who had taken ill and a monastery at Rethondes. In the Middle Ages, it was believed that if one spent the night at Drausius' tomb, one would become invincible. Needless to say, entire platoons of soldiers set up camp at his tomb before battle. Feast day, March 7.

CHANDLERS: 1) Ambrose, bishop. Italian (340–397). His contributions were key to the advancement of Christianity during the decline of the Roman Empire. St. Anthony converted to Christianity after hearing a sermon by Ambrose. Also patron of bees and learning. Feast day, December 7.

2) Bernard of Clairvaux, theologian. French (1090–

1135). The last of the fathers of the Church. Also patron of cancer victims. Canonized 1174; feast day, August 20.

CHAPLAINS: John of Capistrano, preacher. Italian (1386–1456). As a lawyer, he governed Perugia. As a married man, he was faithful to his wife. John received the calling of God and walked away from it all. After being released from his wedding vows, John joined the Friars Minor. As a crusader, John opposed the Turks, his radical army resisting their threat of conquering Europe. Also patron of jurists and military chaplains. Canonized 1690; feast day, March 28.

CHASTITY: Thomas Aquinas, theologian. Neapolitan (1225–1274). His aristocratic family was so against his religious pursuits they locked him away for fifteen months. The attempt to change his mind proved futile. The greatest thinker of the Middle Ages; author of volumes of theological works, including *Summa contra Gentiles* and *Summa theologica*. Declared a Doctor of the Church in 1567. His patronage may have something to do with being raised by his widowed mother and an aunt who was a nun. Also patron of academics, colleges, pencil makers and schools. Canonized 1323; feast day, January 28.

CHARITABLE SOCIETIES: Vincent de Paul, founder. French (1580–1660). The common myth of Vincent's life is that he was captured by pirates, who then sold him into slavery in North Africa, where he escaped to France. The truth is that upon listening to the final confession of a villager, Monsieur Vincent realized the plight of the peasants. He left his comfortable position as spiritual advisor to Madame de Gondi and began to work as a minister to galley slaves. Vincent then founded the Congregation of the Missions, the Sisters of Charity, orphanages, and hospitals. His savvy with wealthy women accounted for many of his accomplishments. A charity bearing his name was established in Paris in 1833. Also patron of prisoners. Canonized 1737; feast day, September 27.

CHILD ABUSE VICTIMS: Alodia, martyr. Spanish (9th century). She, and her sister, St. Nunilo, were frequently beaten by their Muslim stepfather. The two ran away when their vows of virginity were threatened by the stepfather's attempt to marry them off to his peers. Alodia and Nunilo were reported to the authorities as Christians, apprehended, then beheaded. Also patrons of runaways. Feast day, October 22.

CHILDBIRTH: 1) Gerard Majella, laybrother. Italian (1726–1755). Healer; prophet; visionary; mind reader; ecstatic; bilocationist (able to be in two locations at the same time). Gerard was once accused of lewd behavior by a woman, which he did not challenge. Eventually, he was cleared of the charge when she admitted to lying. His mother may be responsible for his peculiar patronage. She would boast that her son "was born for heaven." Also patron of expectant mothers. Canonized 1904; feast day, October 16.

2) Raymond Nonnatus, cardinal. Spanish (1204–1240). He was taken from his dying mother by cesarian section. As a Mercedarian, he ransomed himself to the Moors in exchange for the freedom of slaves and Christian hostages. He converted within the prison walls, which angered the Muslims. His jailers realized that his ransom would exceed those of the other prisoners, so Raymond was continuously tortured for preaching. Negotiations for his release took eight months. Also patron of the falsely accused, midwives, obstetricians, and pregnant women. Canonized 1657; Feast day, August 31.

CHILDBIRTH, COMPLICATIONS IN: Ulric, bishop. Swiss (890–997). Though he was the bishop of Augsburg for fifty years, Ulric is better remembered as the first saint canonized by the papacy. It is said that pregnant women were assured a smooth delivery when they drank from his cup, hence his patronage. Feast day, July 4.

CHILDHOOD ILLNESSES, INVOKED AGAINST: Aldegonda (Aldegund), nun. Frankish (7th century). Folktale. Born into a family of saints; her parents were Walbert and Bertilia, her sister, Waudru. Her stepmother was insistent that the dedicated Christian marry. Aldegonda hid from her stepmother and fiancé in the woods and was protected by the animals of the forest. Once the search team was called off, Aldegonda joined the Benedictine order. She is also invoked against injuries. Feast day, January 30.

2) Pharaildis, housewife. Flemish (8th century). When she was of marrying age, her parents betrothed her to a man of wealth. The vow of virginity to God that Pharaildis had taken as a youth angered her hot-tempered husband. He abused her both physically and emotionally until his death. Pharaildis caused a well to spring at Braug. Its water is believed to cure children of disease. Also invoked against marital problems and physical abuse. Feast day, January 4.

CHILDREN: 1) Nicholas of Myra, bishop. Lycian (4th century). Better known as Saint Nick. The facts are few. He ran a monastery, was a prisoner during the time of Christian persecutions, and was present at the Council of Nicaea. The rest is myth. One tale tells of a father who was so poor he couldn't afford his three daughters' dowries. Nick tossed three bags of gold through the kitchen window, and the three daughters married soon after. Also patron of boys, brides, dockworkers, Greece, merchants, pawnbrokers, spinsters, and travelers. Feast day, December 6.

2) Maria Goretti, child. Italian (1890–1902). After her mother's death, Maria's father moved the family to Ferriere di Conca, where he took on work as a farmhand. Though poor, the family found room to take in another farmhand by the name of Alexander Serenelli. Maria worked the fields, as well as helped in the running of the household. Her free time was devoted to prayer. Once when Maria was cooking the evening meal, Alexander made sexual advances to her. Maria was stabbed seventeen times and died that night. On her deathbed, she said, "I forgive Alexander. I forgive him with all my heart; and I want him to be with me in heaven." A penitent Alexander attended her canonization. Also patron of rape victims. Feast day, July 6.

CHILDREN, CONVULSIVE: Scholastica, abbess. Norcian (480–543). She was the sister of St. Benedict; some historians believe they were fraternal twins. Founder of a convent near Monte Cassino, she was the first Benedictine nun. Her brother paid a visit at her convent one day. When it grew late, Benedict prepared to leave. Scholastica prayed for a storm, keeping her brother a few extra days, until she died. She is also invoked against storms. Feast day, February 10.

CHILDREN'S DEATH: 1) Clotilde, Queen. French (6th century). She gave birth to the three sons and daughter of King Clovis, before the king's death in 511. The greedy children were at constant odds with one another over control of the kingdom. The rivalry led to the murder of Clodomir, her eldest son. Clotilde quickly adopted his three children, which angered Clotaire, her youngest son. He proceeded to murder two of the small children. Clotilde managed to sneak young Saint Cloud to safety away from his uncle's wrath. Clotilde then spent the rest of her life tending to the needy. Also patron of adopted children, parenthood, queens, and widows. Feast day, June 3.

2) Hedwig, Queen. Bavarian (1174–1243). She and her husband, Henry I, supported a number of charities. After Henry's death, Hedwig was beset by her six children's tribulations. Hedwig found solace in a Cistercian abbey, an early endeavor of the royal couple, then committed herself to the care of the indigent. Also patron of Bavaria, duchesses, queens, and Silesia; is invoked against jealousy and marital problems. Feast day, October 16.

3) Felicity and her seven sons, martyrs. Romans (2nd century). Pious legend. This young widow had seven sons. Their strong Christian faith caught the attention of Antoninus Pius, who attempted to persuade Felicity and her sons to worship pagan gods. When his promises and threats failed, Antoninus had the boys sentenced to death in seven different courts. Felicity was forced to witness each execution, then was beheaded. Also patron of barren women and heirs. Feast day, July 10.

CHILDREN, SICK: Beuno, monk. Welsh (7th century). Legend. His niece, St. Winifred, rejected the advances of a chieftain's son, who then beheaded her with his sword. Beuno purportedly reattached St. Winifred's head, bringing her back to life. His tomb is believed to be a place for healing sick children. Feast day, April 21.

CHILDREN, STAMMERING: Notkar Balbulus, monk. Swiss (840–912). Notkar had a speech impediment and was nicknamed "Balbulus," which means "the stammerer." He excelled in music and is one of the originators of Gregorian chants and the liturgical sequences. Feast day, April 4.

CHILE: James the Greater, apostle. Galilean (1st century). His name James "the Greater" is to differentiate him from the other apostle, James "the Less." He and his brother John "dropped their fishing nets" at the Sea of Galilee and followed Jesus; they were witnesses to both the transfiguration and the agony of Jesus in the garden. James was beheaded in Jerusalem, the first apostle to be martyred. Also patron of Guatemala, Nicaragua, pharmacists, pilgrims, and Spain; he is invoked against arthritis and rheumatism. Feast day, July 25.

CHILLS, INVOKED AGAINST: Placid, martyr. Italian (6th century). According to legend, he, his three siblings, and thirty followers were martyred by pirates for refusing to idolize pagan gods. The document of this legend was later proved to be a forgery by Peter the Deacon. As a child, Placid was handed over to St. Benedict and lived all his days as a devout monk. St. Maurus saved the young Placid from drowning, which may or may not explain his patronage. Feast day, October 5.

CHIVALRY: Demetrius, martyr. Salonikan (unknown dates). Legend. This "soldier of God" was imprisoned for preaching the gospel. He was then lanced with a spear before his trial got underway, by the order of Emperor Maximilian. Also patron of soldiers. Feast day, October 8.

CHOIRBOYS: Dominic Savio, student. Italian (1842–1855). Visionary. One of his prophecies motivated Pope Pius IX into amending the hierarchy of England. Canonized 1954; feast day, March 9.

CHOLERA, INVOKED AGAINST: Roch (Rocco), hermit. French (1350–1380). Legend. He tended to plague sufferers in Italy, then became ill himself. Sick and alone, Roch was nourished back to health by a stray dog, who brought him food. He was then imprisoned as a spy by his unknowing uncle, the governor. After Roch's death in prison, a cross-shaped birthmark revealed his true identity. Also patron of the falsely accused and invalids; he is invoked against plagues. Feast day, March 28.

CHURCH: Joseph, carpenter. Nazarean (1st century). Descendent of David; husband to the Virgin Mary; foster father to Jesus Christ. Joseph had second thoughts about marrying Mary when he learned that she was pregnant until the angel Gabriel explained the Messiah's coming. After the birth of Christ, he was forewarned in a dream of Herod's exploits, so he took his young family to Egypt. After Herod's death, a dream directed them to return to Israel. Fearing Herod's replacement, Joseph chose to settle his family in Nazareth. Scholars believe he died before the crucifixion of Christ. Joseph was named patron to the Universal church by Pope Pius IX in 1950. Also patron of Belgium, Canada, carpenters, the dying, fathers, Korea, Peru, social justice, and working men. Feast days, March 19 and May 1.

CHURCH JANITORS: Theobald, layman. Italian (12th century). After rejecting the hand of his employer's daughter, along with a partnership in the family's business, Theobald gained employment as a janitor at the cathedral of Saint Lawrence. Also patron of bachelors and janitors. Feast day, March 9.

CIRCUS PEOPLE: Julian the Hospitaler, innkeeper. French (unknown dates). Pious fiction. He killed a sleeping couple in his bed, fearing adultery. The slain were not an adulterous wife and lover, but his visiting parents. His penance was to build an inn and hospital for the poor at the mouth of a river. Julian was absolved when he gave his bed to an angel, who was disguised as a leper.

Also patron of boatmen, ferrymen, hotel employees, and innkeepers. Feast day, February 12.

CIVIL DISORDER: Andrew Corsini, bishop. Florentine (14th century). The gifts of prophecy and healing were endowed to Andrew the day he became ordained. During a struggle between the aristocracy and peasants of Bologna, Urban V sent Andrew, who successfully acted as a go-between for the classes. Andrew died on Christmas at the age of 71. His cousin, Pope Urban VIII, canonized him in 1609. Feast day, February 4.

CLAIRVOYANCE: Agabus, prophet. Roman (1st century). After converting to Christianity, Agabus began to experience visions of the future. His predictions include the famine of 49 A.D., the incarceration of Saint Paul, and his own death. Also patron of psychics. Feast day, February 13.

CLERKS, COURTROOM: Cassian, stenographer. Tangarine (3rd century). He became a Christian after being the official recorder at the unjust trial of St. Marcellus. He threw his tablet and writing implement on the floor when the sentence was announced and was immediately put to death. Also patron of stenographers. Feast day, December 3.

CLERGY, SECULAR: Thomas Becket, martyr. English (1118–1170). Thomas' secular career peaked when he was appointed the archbishop of Canterbury. He left his illustrious position in protest of King Henry II's indulgences with the church. After performing mass one day, Thomas was found murdered in the cathedral. St. Thomas More followed a similar path some three hundred years later. Feast day, December 29.

CLERICS: 1) Gabriel Francis Possenti, priest. Italian (1838–1862). Francis' mother died, leaving this four-year-old and his twelve siblings to be raised by their father, a prominent attorney. As a young man, Francis had an eye for the ladies, until he became gravely ill. He made a promise to God that if he were to recover, he would become serious about religion. When he recovered, Francis chose to join the Society of Jesus. While having second thoughts of the vow he had made, an epidemic claimed his beloved sister. Francis then joined the order of the Passionists, who named him Gabriel of the Sorrowful Mother. He practiced severe mortification upon himself and died four years later. Feast day, February 26.

2) Gabriel, archangel. Messenger of God. One of the seven archangels of God; one of three archangels referred to by name in the Bible. Announced the birth of Jesus to Mary (Luke 1:11–21). Also patron of broadcasters, diplomats, messengers, postal workers, radio workers, stamp collectors, telecommunications workers, and television workers.

CLOTH DYERS: Lydia, laywoman. Thyatiran (1st century). Her name means "purple seller," which suits her trade as a purple cloth dyer. She is remembered as St. Paul's first convert. Feast day, August 3.

CLOTH WORKERS: Homobonus, cloth worker. Italian (12th century). A wealthy merchant who went into the family's tailoring business, he donated most of his money to the needy. Homobonus died during mass. Also patron of businessmen and tailors. Feast day, November 13.

COBBLERS: Crispin and Crispinian, martyrs. Roman (3rd century). Legend. These brothers were Christian converters by day and shoemakers by night. Their torturer, Maximian, took his own life in frustration when his attempts to execute the siblings failed. The two were then beheaded. Also patrons of leatherworkers, saddlers, shoemakers, and tanners. Feast day, October 25.

COFFEEHOUSE KEEPERS: Drogo, shepherd. Flemish (1105–1189). As a child, Drogo learned that his father died before he was born, and his mother had given her life for his. This made a great impact on the ten-year-old youth of noble lineage. While tending to sheep in his mid-forties, Drogo suffered a ruptured hernia, which disfigured him. He drilled a hole through a wall of the church to be able to attend mass without attracting attention away from the sermon. He lived his remaining forty years in prayer and penitence. Also patron of hernia sufferers, homely people, and shepherds. Feast day, April 16.

COIN COLLECTORS: Stephen the Younger, martyr. Constantinopolitan (8th century). To prove the point of how important it is to respect religious artifacts, this monk once tossed a coin with the likeness of Emperor Constantine V on the floor. He then proceeded to stomp on it, in the presence of the emperor. Stephen was sent to jail for eleven months. After his release, Stephen stood before a bewildered Constantine and chose to prove yet other points. The aggravated emperor gave up and ordered the execution of Stephen. Also patron of smelters. Feast day, November 28.

COLD WEATHER, INVOKED AGAINST: Sebald, missionary. Anglo-Saxon (8th century). Legend has it that a poor couple gave him shelter one cold winter night. Wood was scarce, and the flames of the fire burnt low. Sebald tossed icicles into the chimney, which disbursed warmth throughout the cottage. Feast day, August 19.

COLDS, INVOKED AGAINST: Maurus, founder. Roman (6th century). He was entrusted to St. Benedict at the age of twelve and grew up to become Benedict's assistant. A young St. Placid was drowning when Maurus walked on water to rescue him. He left Benedict's monastery and founded Saint-Maur-sur-Loire. Also patron of coppersmiths. Feast day, January 15.

COLIC, INVOKED AGAINST: Agapitus, martyr. Roman (3rd century). Legend. This fifteen-year-old Christian endured beatings, starvation, and burning. His patronage comes from boiling water spilled on his stomach as a final torture for his unyielding faith before being beheaded. Feast day, August 18.

COLLECTORS: Benedict (Benet) Biscop, founder. Northumbrian (628–690). Biscop Baducing was born into a noble family, then was ordained into the priesthood at the age of twenty-five. He founded two monasteries in Wearmouth, then traveled extensively. Benedict returned from each journey with impressive paintings, relics, books, and glassworks for his monasteries. He even brought home the chorus instructor from St. Peter's to teach his choir the Roman style of song. Benedict became paralyzed in his older years and died in his monastery. Feast day, January 12.

COLLEGES: Thomas Aquinas, theologian. Neapolitan (1225–1274). His aristocratic family was so against his religious pursuits they locked him away for fifteen months. The attempt to change his mind proved futile. The greatest thinker of the Middle Ages; author of volumes of theological works, including *Summa contra Gentiles* and *Summa theologica*. Declared a Doctor of the Church in 1567. Also patron of academics, chastity, pencil makers and schools. Canonized 1323; feast day, January 28.

COLOMBIA: Peter Claver, missionary. Catalonian (1580–1654). As a missionary in New Granada (Colombia), he ministered to the 300,000 African slaves brought to Cartagena to work the mines and plantations. Also patron of African Americans and slavery sufferers. Canonized 1888; feast day, September 9.

COMEDIANS: Vitus, martyr. Sicilian (3rd century). Legend. After exorcising Emperor Diocletian's son of evil spirits *(chorea)*, he found himself accused of sorcery by the emperor. Vitus was heaved into a vat of boiling water, from which he miraculously emerged unharmed. He and his two companions escaped Rome with the help of an angel and he is believed to have been martyred in the Lucanian province. Also patron of actors and dancers; he is invoked against epilepsy. Feast day, June 15.

COMMUNICATIONS PERSONNEL: Bernardine of Siena, preacher. Italian (1380–1444). "The people's preacher." At the age of twenty, he took charge of a hospital in Siena during the plague of 1400. In 1417 he set out on foot preaching and converting thousands throughout Italy; he was the second founder of the Friars of the Strict Observance. In spite of his attributes, he believed that witchcraft was running rampant and appears to have been an anti-Semite. His sermons often denounced gambling. Also patron of advertising and public relations; he is invoked against uncontrolled gambling. Canonized 1450; feast day, May 20.

COMPOSERS: Cecilia, martyr. Roman (unknown dates). Legend. On her wedding day Cecilia was unable to hear the music being performed; instead she only heard herself singing to God. Her husband, Valerian, agreed to live a life of chastity upon Cecilia's request. She, her husband, and his brother were caught burying the bodies of Christians. The others were beheaded first; her executioner botched her beheading and left her to endure a three-day death. Also patron of musicians, organ builders, poets, and singers. Feast day, November 22.

CONFESSORS: Alphonso Maria de'Liguori, theologian. Italian (1696–1787). At age sixteen, Alphonso had received his doctorate in canon and civil law. He became disillusioned with law after losing a case due to a technicality. He became a priest, then founded the Redemptorines in 1731. When not experiencing visions, ecstasies, or prophecies, he authored *Moral Theology* and *Glories of Mary*. His patronage to confessors is attributed to the large crowds he attracted to the confessionals. Also patron of moralists, professors, theologians, and vocations. Canonized 1839; feast day, August 1.

CONSTRUCTION WORKERS: Thomas, apostle. Galilee (1st century). Brother of St. James; also known as Didymus or the twin; one of the twelve apostles. He was skeptical about the resurrection of Christ (John 20:24–29), until allowed to touch the wounds in the Lord's side and hands; hence the origin of the phrase "Doubting Thomas." The legend of Thomas began after Pentecost. Thomas was assigned the conversion of India, a task he not only dreaded but refused to undertake. Christ himself failed in his attempt through a dream to talk the apostle into going to India. So, the Lord appeared to a merchant named Abban, en route to India, and arranged to have Thomas sold into slavery. Once he realized the direction that his new master was headed, Thomas gave in to the will of God. In India, he was advanced a hefty sum to build a palace for the Parthian king. Instead, he donated the money to the needy. When the king was informed of Thomas' actions, he ordered the execution of the apostle. Just then, the king's brother died and was brought back to life. He told of his glimpse of heaven, which was enough to sway the king. Thomas' patronage stems from the many churches he built during his pilgrimages. He is believed to have been martyred in India. Also patron of architects, East Indies, and India; he is invoked against doubt. Feast day, July 3.

CONVERTS: 1) Helena, empress. Bithynian (250–330). This daughter of an innkeeper married Constantius, the Roman general, in 270. They converted to Christianity. Constantine, their son, would later become the first Christian emperor of the Roman Empire. According to legend, Helena uncovered Christ's true cross while on pilgrimage through the Holy Land. Also patron of divorce and empresses. Feast day, August 18.

2) Flora, martyr. Spanish (9th century). Though Flora's mother was a Christian, the household was run with the strict Muslim beliefs of her father. Flora's rejection of the Islamic faith caused severe beatings by her brother and father, which worsened when she converted to Christianity. She and her best friend, Mary, chose to leave home when Flora's parents announced her engagement to a Muhammedan. The two hid in Flora's sister's home for a brief time. The fear of being associated with Christians led Flora's sister to throw them back out on the street. Flora and Mary confessed themselves to the Islamic council as Christians, and they were tortured before being beheaded. Also patron of victims of betrayal and working women. Feast day, November 24.

3) Vladimir, King. Russian (975–1015). He murdered his half brother, Yarapolk, ruler of Russia, then crowned himself king of Russia. He led a reign of terror until his conversion to Catholicism in 989. Giving up his

five wives and dozen concubines, Vladimir demanded that all his subjects in Kiev become baptized. This marked the beginning of Catholicism in Russia. Also patron of kings, murderers, and Russia. Feast day, July 15.

COOKS: 1) Lawrence, martyr. Spanish (3rd century). A prediction revealed that he had three days to live. The city prefect mandated the church's treasures be handed over to the emperor. Lawrence sold everything and donated the money to the poor. He returned on the third day with an array of societal misfits and said that they were the church's treasures. The prefect had him bound to a hot griddle. Lawrence asked to be flipped over at one point, claiming he was done on that side. Also patron of cutlers, glaziers, the poor, restaurateurs, and Sri Lanka. Feast day, July 29.

2) Martha, homemaker. Bethanian (1st century). A friend of Jesus; older sister of Mary and Lazarus. During one of Jesus' many visits to their home, Martha fussed away in the kitchen, while Mary listened attentively to Christ. Jesus then said to her, "Martha, Martha, thou art careful and troubled about many things; but one thing is needful; and Mary hath chosen that good part, which shall not be taken away from her" (Luke 10:41–42). Also patron of dietitians, servants, and waitpersons. Feast day, July 29.

COPPERSMITHS: Maurus, founder. Roman (6th century). He was entrusted to St. Benedict at the age of twelve and grew up to become Benedict's assistant. A young St. Placid was drowning when Maurus walked on water to rescue him. He left Benedict's monastery and founded Saint-Maur-sur-Loire. Also invoked against colds. Feast day, January 15.

CORSICA: 1) Immaculate Conception. In 1854, Pope Pius IX declared the Blessed Virgin Mary as born without original sin, having been immaculately conceived, and having lived a sin-free life. Also patron of Brazil, Portugal, Tanzania, and the United States.

2) Devota, martyr. Corsican (3rd century). This young Christian was dragged through the streets of Corsica, then pulled on a rack, yet refused to recant. It is said that a dove appeared at the moment of her death, which was followed by two men in a boat. They buried her remains on the spot where the dove landed, in Monaco. Also patron of Monaco. Feast day, January 17.

COUGHS, INVOKED AGAINST: Quentin, martyr. French (6th century). Myth. This son of a Roman senator was sentenced to death by Queen Fredegunde, when he refused her sexual advances. A prison in California bears his name. Feast day, October 4.

COUNCILMEN: Nicholas von Flue, layman. Swiss (1417–1487). After fighting in two wars, raising ten children, and holding the offices of magistrate and councilor, Nicholas received the calling from God. He left his family and lived the remainder of his life as a hermit. It is said that from that day forth, he was solely nourished by the Holy Eucharist. Also patron of spousal separation. Feast day, March 21.

COWHERDS: Gummarus, courtier. Flemish (8th century). Also known as Gomer. As a servant to the court of Pepin, Gummarus married the nefarious Guinimaria. After a number of years of persecution from this brutal woman, Gummarus paid off the money kept from the servants' wages by his wife and joined a hermitage. He founded the abbey at Lierre. Also patron of spousal separation, and unhappily married men; he is invoked against impotence. Feast day, October 11.

COWS: Perpetua, martyr. Carthaginian (3rd century). With her infant son in her arms, Perpetua was imprisoned while waiting to be baptized. In her cell, she met a slave named Felicity, who gave birth during their incarceration. The two babies were taken from the mothers who, along with three men, were thrown into an arena with wild beasts. Perpetua and Felicity were trampled by a raging cow. Feast day, March 7.

CRAMPS, INVOKED AGAINST: Pancras, martyr. Syrian (4th century). Legend. At the age of fourteen, this orphan was beheaded for his faith. Years later, a charlatan died when he lied while touching the boy's tomb. Also invoked against perjury. Feast day, May 12.

CROPS: 1) Ansovinus, bishop. Italian (9th century). This hermit's healing powers converted many followers. The granary ran low one day, while the masses were still hungry, so Ansovinus ordered the storehouse doors shut. Moments later, they swung open, spilling over with an abundance to feed all who were hungry. Also invoked against hail. Feast day, March 13.

2) Walburga, abbess. English (8th century). Medicine woman. Shortly after following her uncle, St. Boniface, to Germany, she was named abbess to the monastery in Heidenheim. Stories of Walpurgis, as she was then named, can be found in Germany's folklore. On April 30, witches honor this holy healer on what is known as Walpurgisnacht. A slippery liquid with curing powers is said to flow from near her tomb. Walburga once suppressed the voracious appetite of a child by having her consume three ears of grain. Also invoked against famine and plagues. Feast day, February 25.

CRUSADERS: Louis IX, King. French (1214–1270). Crowned king of France at the age of twelve; married Margaret, sister of Eleanor, wife of Henry III; fathered eleven children; launched France's first navy. Louis participated in two crusades: Damietta in Egypt, where the good king and his men emerged triumphant, and Mansurah, where the defeated king was taken prisoner. After six years, he was set free. Louis died of typhoid while venturing off on his third crusade, to Tunisia. Also patron of grooms, kings, and parenthood. Feast day, August 25.

CUBA: Our Lady of Charity. *"La Virgen de la Caridad."* This statue was discovered in the nets of fishermen in 1605. In 1916 Pope Benedict XV honored the Virgin of El Cobre as the patron of Cuba.

CURRIERS: Simon, apostle. (1st century.) Little is known of this apostle. He is referred to as "the Zealot," for his enthusiasm for Jewish law, prior to Christ. According to Western belief, Simon was martyred in Egypt. Feast day, October 28.

CUSTOMS AGENTS: Matthew, apostle. Galilean (1st century). His name means "Gift of God." Also known as Levi; no records of his early life. Tax collector turned apostle; he wrote the first Gospel between 60 and 90, which contains quotes from the Old Testament. He was martyred either in Ethiopia or Persia. Also patron of accountants, bankers, bookkeepers, security guards, and tax collectors. Feast day, September 21.

CUTLERS: 1) Lawrence, martyr. Spanish (3rd century). A prediction revealed that he had three days to live. The city prefect mandated the church's treasures be handed over to the emperor. Lawrence sold everything and donated the money to the poor. He returned on the third day with an array of societal misfits and said that they were the church's treasures. The prefect had him bound to a hot griddle. Lawrence asked to be flipped over at one point, claiming he was done on that side. Also patron of cooks, glaziers, the poor, restaurateurs, and Sri Lanka. Feast day, July 29.

2) Lucy, martyr. Italian (4th century). Pious myth. It is said that she was once told how pretty her eyes were by an arranged suitor. Lucy gouged them from their sockets and handed them to her horrified future husband, who promptly had her condemned for her Christian beliefs. Proving to be flame-proof when flung in the fire, Lucy was eventually stabbed in the throat. Her name translates to "light." Also patron of writers; she is invoked against eye trouble and hemorrhaging. Feast day, December 13.

CZECHOSLOVAKIA: 1) John of Nepomucene, bishop and martyr. Czechoslovakian (1345–1393). Until 1961, John was believed to have been thrown from a bridge for refusing to crack the seal of the confessional, when the jealous King Wenceslaus IV demanded to know what disclosures his wife, Queen Sophia, had made to the bishop. A more logical reason for his drowning is religious and political differences. Also patron of bridges, detraction, discretion, and silence; he is invoked against slander. Canonized 1729; feast day, May 16.

2) Wenceslaus, Prince. Bohemian (907–929). His grandmother, St. Ludmilla, instilled a strong Christian faith in the young prince. She was murdered by an opposing pagan party. When Wenceslaus became the ruler, he advanced the Christian faith in Bohemia as well as their neighboring countries. Wenceslaus' brother, Boleslaus, was so envious of the prince that he murdered him while en route to church. Wenceslaus' son succeeded to the throne. Also patron of Bohemia. Feast day, September 28.

A bird can be held by a chain or by a thread, still it cannot fly.

—St. John of the Cross

DAIRYWORKERS: Bridget (Brigid), nun. Irish (450–525). St. Patrick baptized her parents. Brigid became a nun; she founded the first convent in Ireland, a monastery, and a school of art in Kildare. Her patronage derives from a folktale in which Brigid had once turned water into milk. She then gave the dairy product to a leper, whose affliction immediately disappeared. Also patron of Ireland, nuns, and scholars. Feast day, February 1.

DANCERS: Vitus, martyr. Sicilian (3rd century). Legend. After exorcising Emperor Diocletian's son of evil spirits *(chorea)*, he found himself accused of sorcery by the emperor. Vitus was heaved into a vat of boiling water, from which he miraculously emerged unharmed. He and his two companions escaped Rome with the help of an angel and he is believed to have been martyred in the Lucanian province. Also patron of actors and comedians; he is invoked against epilepsy. Feast day, June 15.

DEACONS: Stephen, martyr. Hellenist (of the Dispersion). (1st century.) The first martyr for Christ. The Jewish council stoned Stephen to death after he denounced them. Also patron of bricklayers and stonemasons. Feast day, December 26.

DEAD, RECENTLY: Gertrude of Nivelles, abbess. Flemish (626–659). When Gertrude's father died, her mother, Itta, founded a monastery at Neville. The fourteen-year-old Gertrude was appointed as the abbess and proved herself deserving of the title. Gertrude's monastic center was known for its hospitality to pilgrims and monks. At the age of thirty, Gertrude lay on her deathbed, fearing that she was unworthy of heaven. St. Ultan assured her that St. Patrick was awaiting her. She died on St. Patrick's Day. Also patron of accommodations and cats; she is invoked against rats. Feast day, March 17.

DEAF, THE: Francis de Sales, bishop and writer. French (1567–1622). He earned a doctorate in law at the age of twenty-four. Within five years, surviving numerous assassination attempts, he managed to convert thousands of Calvinists back to Catholicism. Francis' writings include *Introduction to the Devout Life* (1609) and *Treatise on the Love of God* (1616). He was the first to receive beatification at St. Peter's. Also patron of authors, the Catholic press, journalists, and writers. Canonized 1877; feast day, January 24.

DEATH ROW INMATES: Dismas, thief. (1st century.) All that is known of this "good thief" is that he was hanged on the cross next to Jesus. Also patron of funeral directors, prisoners, thieves, and undertakers. Feast day, March 25.

DEATH SUDDEN, INVOKED AGAINST: Andrew Avellino, priest. Neapolitan (1521–1608). Sent to reform Sant Arcangelo, Andrew discovered the convent had been turned into a house of ill repute by the fallen nuns. Almost losing his life in his effort for reformation, Andrew joined the Theatines. In the midst of a sermon, he suffered an apoplectic attack and remained unconscious for the rest of his life. Some historians believe that Andrew fell into a catatonic state, was mistaken for dead, then buried. Also patron of apoplexy sufferers. Canonized 1712; feast day, November 10.

DENMARK: Ansgar, monk. French (801–865). The "Apostle of the North." He devoted his life to Christianizing Scandinavia, which then slipped back to its pagan ways upon his death. Scandinavia began to have a more prominent Christian presence two hundred years later. Also patron of Scandinavia. Feast day, February 3.

DENTISTS: Apollonia, martyr. Alexandrian (3rd century). An elderly deaconess who refused to denounce her faith during a riot against Christians. Her beating was so severe, her teeth were smashed. Saying a prayer, she flung herself into her captors' bonfire. Also patron of toothache sufferers. Feast day, February 9.

DESPERATE SITUATIONS: 1) Gregory of NeoCaesarea (Nyssa), bishop. Cappadocian (330–395). This bishop of Nyssa was accused by a corrupt governor of stealing from the church, which led to his exile for two years until his innocence was proven. He wrote a number of theological texts. Feast day, March 9.

2) Jude, apostle. (1st century.) Also known as Thaddaeus and Lebbaeus, and is referred to as the "brother of James." There is doubt among scholars that the Jude who wrote the epistle attributed to him and the Jude of

the apostles are one and the same. The former wrote of the apostles in the past tense. He may have been martyred in Persia with St. Simon. Jude's patronage derives from his letters that say one should endure difficulties, as predecessors have done. Also patron of hopeless cases. Feast day, October 28.

3) Rita, nun. Italian (1381–1457). An arranged marriage of eighteen years came to an end when her abusive husband was murdered in a brawl. Her two sons sought retribution for their father, but Rita would rather her sons died than become murderers. She prayed for their souls; soon after, the two became ill and died. Rita entered an Augustinian convent on her third attempt (being rejected the first two times for lacking virginity). Hearing a sermon on the crown of thorns, a "thornlike" wound appeared on her forehead, which stayed with her for the rest of her life. Miracles were accredited to her after her death. Also patron of parenthood; she is invoked against bleeding, infertility, and marital problems. Canonized 1900; feast day, May 22.

DETRACTION: John of Nepomucene, bishop and martyr. Czechoslovakian (1345–1393). Until 1961, John was believed to have been thrown from a bridge for refusing to crack the seal of the confessional, when the jealous King Wenceslaus IV demanded to know what disclosures his wife, Queen Sophia, had made to the bishop. A more logical reason for his drowning is religious and political differences. Also patron of bridges, Czechoslovakia, discretion, and silence; he is invoked against slander. Canonized 1729; feast day, May 16.

DIABOLIC POSSESSION, INVOKED AGAINST: 1) Quirnus, bishop. Danubian (4th century). Pious legend. As he tried to escape the persecution of Christians, Quirnus was apprehended. The magistrate Maximus offered

Quirnus the position of priest to Jupiter if he would recant his faith. Exclaiming that he was already a priest, Quirnus insisted that the magistrate put him to death. Not having the proper authority, Maximus sent him before Amantius, who sentenced him to death by drowning. Quirnus was thrown, praying, into the Raab River, with a rock tied to him. Also invoked against obsession. Feast day, June 4.

2) Bruno, founder. German (1033–1101). This professor of theology at Rheims had a falling-out with the archbishop. He handed in his resignation, then founded the Carthusian order in the Grande Chartreuse, near Grenoble. Pope Urban II had been one of his students back at the university and called Bruno back to act as his councilor. He never returned to his order. Feast day, October 6.

3) Dymphna, martyr. Irish (7th century). Folktale. She and her confessor ran away from her incestuous father, a pagan chieftain. In Belgium, the two lived as hermits in an oratory they had built, until her father and his men hunted them down. The confessor was murdered and Dymphna was beheaded for refusing to return home. Many have been cured at Dymphna's tomb. Also patron of epileptics and runaways; she is invoked against mental disorders and sleepwalking. Feast day, May 15.

DIETITIANS: Martha, homemaker. Bethanian (1st century). A friend of Jesus; older sister of Mary and Lazarus. During one of Jesus' many visits to their home, Martha fussed away in the kitchen, while Mary listened attentively to Christ. Jesus then said to her, "Martha, Martha, thou art careful and troubled about many things; but one thing is needful; and Mary hath chosen that good part, which shall not be taken away from her" (Luke 10:

41–42). Also patron of cooks, servants, and waitpersons. Feast day, July 29.

DIPLOMATS: Gabriel, archangel. Messenger of God. One of the seven archangels of God; one of the three archangels referred to by name in the Bible. Announced the birth of Jesus to Mary (Luke 1:11–21). Also patron of clerics, messengers, postal workers, radio workers, stamp collectors, telecommunications workers, and television workers.

DISASTERS, INVOKED AGAINST: Genevieve, nun. French (420–500). After receiving the call of God at the age of seven, Genevieve predicted the invasion of Attila the Hun in 451. The sparing of Paris from the barbarians' invasion was attributed to her prayers. In 1129, Genevieve's relics were raised and an epidemic of ergot poisoning miraculously ceased. Also patron of the women's army corps; she is invoked against plagues. Feast day, January 3.

DISCRETION: John of Nepomucene, martyr. Czechoslovakian (1345–1393). Until 1961, John was believed to have been thrown from a bridge for refusing to crack the seal of the confessional, when the jealous King Wenceslaus IV demanded to know what disclosures his wife, Queen Sophia, had made to the bishop. A more logical reason for his drowning is religious and political differences. Also patron of bridges, Czechoslovakia, detraction, and silence; he is invoked against slander. Canonized 1729; feast day, May 16.

DIVINE INTERVENTION: Margaret, martyr. Antiochan (4th century). Legend. She was disowned by her father, a pagan priest, for converting to Christianity. Margaret became a shepherdess, during which she was spotted by the governor. His failed attempts in seducing the young woman angered him to the point of incarcerating her. Margaret then revealed herself a Christian and was subjected to a number of gruesome tortures. One of these was being swallowed by a dragon whose belly was sliced open by the cross Margaret was wearing. Eventually she was beheaded. Also patron of birth and pregnant women. Feast day, July 20.

DIVORCE: 1) Fabiola, founder. Roman (3rd century). After divorcing her abusive husband, she remarried. This prevented her from receiving the Sacraments of the church. Fabiola performed public penance, then founded the first Christian hospital. Pope St. Siricus pardoned Fabiola her sins, after her second husband died. Also patron of infidelity and widows; she is invoked against physical abuse. Feast day, December 27.

2) Helena, empress. Bithynian (250–330). This daughter of an innkeeper married Constantius, the Roman general, in 270. They converted to Christianity. Constantine, their son, would later become the first Christian emperor of the Roman Empire. According to legend, Helena uncovered Christ's true cross while on pilgrimage through the Holy Land. It is believed that Constantius divorced Helena to marry a woman of status. Also patron of converts and empresses. Feast day, August 18.

DIZZINESS, INVOKED AGAINST: Avertinus, hermit. French (12th century). Prior to his martyrdom, while St. Thomas of Canterbury was in Touraine, he promoted his companion, Avertinus, to deacon. Avertinus then became a hermit. Accounts of his patronages can be seen in the *ex votos* of his church in Tours. Also invoked against headaches. Feast day, May 5.

DOCKWORKERS: Nicholas of Myra, bishop. Lycian (4th century). Better known as Saint Nick. The facts are few. He ran a monastery, was a prisoner during the time of Christian persecutions, and was present at the Council of Nicaea. The rest is myth. One tale tells of a father who was so poor he couldn't afford his three daughters' dowries. Nick tossed three bags of gold through the kitchen window, and the three daughters married soon after. Also patron of boys, brides, children, Greece, merchants, pawnbrokers, spinsters, and travelers. Feast day, December 6.

DOCTORS: 1) Luke, evangelist. Greek (1st century). Physician, artist. Little is known of his early life. Author of the third Gospel and the Acts of the Apostles, which serve as a record of the progression of early Christianity. He died in Greece at the age of 84. Also patron of artists, butchers, glassworkers, notaries, painters, physicians, and surgeons. Feast day, October 18.

2) Cosmas and Damian, martyrs. Arabians (4th century). Known as "the holy moneyless ones." Twin physicians who took no payment from their patients, they were beheaded along with their three brothers for their Christian beliefs. Some critics feel that their legend derives from Greek mythology's Castor and Pollux. Also patrons of barbers, druggists, pharmacists, physicians, and surgeons. Feast day, September 26.

3) Pantaleon, martyr. Bithynian (4th century). Pious legend. This respected man of medicine lived a privileged life as the personal physician to Emperor Galerius. When the emperor learned that Pantaleon had converted to Christianity, he had him sentenced to death. The six attempts to execute the convert (burning, molten lead, being thrown to the lions, drowning, the wheel, and stabbing) all failed. Once Pantaleon was confident that

he had proved his theological point, he bowed his head and allowed the haggard executioner to behead him. Also patron of endurance and tuberculosis sufferers. Feast day, July 27.

DOGS: Hubert, bishop. French (8th century). He put an end to idol worship in his diocese. The story of Hubert's conversion to Christianity is remarkably similar to Eustachius' conversion. He was on the trail of a stag, which turned to face him. Between the animal's antlers was the mark of a crucifix. His patronage to dogs came about when people suffering from rabies were cured at his grave. Also patron of hunters and rabies sufferers. Feast day, November 3.

DOMESTIC HELP: Zita, servant. Italian (1218–1278). Legend has it that this servant of the Fatinelli family would take bits of food from her rich employers to give to the poor. One day she was caught by the mistress while leaving the house with her apron stuffed with leftovers. When forced to disclose the contents, roses spilled out onto the floor. Also patron of housekeepers, maids, and servants. Canonized 1696; feast day, April 27.

DOMINICAN REPUBLIC: Our Lady of Grace. This title was bestowed upon the Blessed Virgin Mary by the people of the Dominican Republic. In Luke 1:28, she is referred to by the Archangel Gabriel as "full of grace," which is recited in the beginning of the "Hail Mary." Also patron of motorcyclists.

DOUBT, INVOKED AGAINST: Thomas, apostle. Galilean (1st century). Brother of St. James; also known as Didymus or the twin; one of the twelve apostles. He was skeptical about the resurrection of Christ (John 20:24–29), until allowed to touch the wounds in the Lord's side and hands; hence the origin of the phrase "Doubting Thomas." The legend of Thomas began after Pentecost. Thomas was assigned the conversion of India, a task he not only dreaded but refused to undertake. Christ himself failed in his attempt through a dream to talk the apostle into going to India. So, the Lord appeared to a merchant named Abban, en route to India, and arranged to have Thomas sold into slavery. Once he realized the direction that his new master was headed, Thomas gave in to the will of God. In India, he was advanced a hefty sum to build a palace for the Parthian king. Instead, he donated the money to the needy. When the king was informed of Thomas' actions, he ordered the execution of the apostle. Just then, the king's brother died and was brought back to life. He told of his glimpse of heaven, which was enough to sway the king. Thomas' patronage stems from the many churches he built during his pilgrimages. He is believed to have been martyred in India. Also patron of architects, construction workers, East Indies, and India. Feast day, July 3.

DOVES: David (Dewi), bishop. Welsh (6th century). This third son of King Sant and St. Non was ordained, then founded twelve monasteries. According to the legend, David was about to give a sermon in Brefi. The ground beneath him swelled enough for him to be visible from the back of the crowd. Just then a dove landed on David's shoulder. Also patron of Wales. Feast day, March 1.

DRAPERS: Ursula, martyr. German (unknown dates). Myth. According to the chiseled words on a stone in Cologne, a group of Christian maidens were martyred in the fourth century. Four hundred years later, the tales of the women flowered into this legend. Ursula was the Christian daughter of a British king, whose wedding date to a pagan prince had been set. In an attempt to postpone the nuptials, she boarded a ship with her ladies-in-waiting. They set out for a pilgrimage to Rome. In Cologne, Ursula and her maidens (numbering anywhere from a dozen to a thousand) were attacked by the Huns. Ursula rejected the chieftain's marriage proposal and all of the women were murdered. Also patron of schoolgirls and young women. Feast day, October 21.

DROUGHT, INVOKED AGAINST: 1) Swithun (Swithin), bishop. English (9th century). On July 15th, 971, his relics were transferred to Winchester Cathedral. The heavy rain that followed initiated the belief that if it rains on July 15, expect another forty days of rain. Also patron of rain. Feast day, July 15.

2) Godberta, nun. German (6th century). It is said that in the midst of a crowd, the bishop St. Eloi placed his ring on her finger and proclaimed her married to the church. She is best remembered for extinguishing a blazing fire by making the sign of the cross. Also invoked against epidemics. Feast day, April 5.

DROWNING, INVOKED AGAINST: Adjutor, monk. French (12th century). Knight and the Lord of Vernon-sur-Seine. While sailing to his first crusade in 1095, he was captured by Muslims but managed to escape. Back in France, he became a monk. Adjutor's final years were devoted to prayer and meditation; he died at Tiron. Also patron of swimmers and yachtsmen. Feast day, April 30.

DRUG ADDICTION: Maximilian Kolbe, priest. Polish (1894–1941). Imprisoned in Auschwitz for his anti-Nazi publications. He traded places with a young married man, who was to be slaughtered in retribution for an escaped prisoner. Maximilian was killed by means of a carbonic acid injection. Also patron of political prisoners. Canonized 1982; feast day, August 14.

DRUGGISTS: 1) James the Less, apostle. Galilean (1st century). One of the twelve apostles; one of the "four brothers" of the Lord. After Christ's resurrection, James headed the Church of Jerusalem. He was martyred when thrown from a temple, then stoned to death. Also patron of fullers and hatters. Feast day, May 3.

2) Cosmas and Damian, martyrs. Arabians (4th century). Known as "the holy moneyless ones." Twin physicians who took no payment from their patients, they were beheaded along with their three brothers for their Christian beliefs. Some critics feel that their legend derives from Greek mythology's Castor and Pollux. Also patrons of barbers, doctors, pharmacists, physicians, and surgeons. Feast day, September 26.

DUCHESSES: Hedwig, Queen. Bavarian (1174–1243). She and her husband, Henry I, supported a number of charities. After Henry's death, Hedwig was beset by her six children's tribulations. Hedwig found solace in a Cistercian abbey, an early endeavor of the royal couple, then committed herself to the care of the indigent. Also patron of Bavaria, children's death, queens, and Silesia; she is invoked against jealousy and marital problems. Feast day, October 16.

DUKES: Henry II, emperor. Bavarian (11th century). Good King Henry and his wife, St. Cunegund, were childless. Unwarranted rumors after the couple's death claim the two had taken a vow of celibacy. They were cofounders of schools and reformers of the church. Henry died with the title of emperor of the Holy Roman Empire. Also invoked against sterility. Feast day, July 15.

DYERS: Maurice, officer. Egyptian (3rd century). Legend. As officer in the Theban Legion, Maurice encouraged his Christian platoon to refuse Maximian Herculius' request to worship pagan gods. Maximian ordered the execution of every tenth man, which proved to be an ineffective deterrent. A second, then third decimation began. Eventually, the entire unit was put to death. Also patron of infantrymen, knife sharpeners, swordsmiths, and weavers; he is invoked against gout. Feast day, September 22.

DYING: 1) Barbara, martyr. (4th century.) Religious fiction. A young woman whose pagan father locked her in a tower before leaving on a long journey. Within the walls, she converted to Christianity and had three windows built to signify the Trinity. When her father returned, he was so infuriated by his daughter's religious preference, he turned her over to the authorities. Barbara was subjected to heinous torture, yet refused to disavow her faith. The judge ordered the father to kill her himself. Atop a mountain he slew his daughter, then was immediately struck dead by a bolt of lightning. Also patron of architects, builders, fire prevention, founders, miners, prisoners, and stonemasons. Feast day, December 4.

2) Joseph, carpenter. Nazarean (1st century). Descendent of David; husband to the Virgin Mary; foster father to Jesus Christ. Joseph had second thoughts about marrying Mary when he learned that she was pregnant until the angel Gabriel explained the Messiah's coming. After the birth of Christ, he was forewarned in a dream of Herod's exploits, so he took his young family to Egypt. Upon Herod's death, a dream directed them to return to Israel. Fearing Herod's replacement, Joseph chose to settle his family in Nazareth. Scholars believe he died before the crucifixion of Christ. Also patron of

Belgium, Canada, carpenters, the church, fathers, Korea, Peru, social justice, and working men. Feast days, March 19 and May 1.

DYSENTERY SUFFERERS: Matrona, Portuguese (unknown dates). Roman martyrology. All that is known of this daughter of royalty is that she suffered from dysentery. A vision ordered her to go to Italy, where she was cured. Feast day, March 15.

Hope always draws the soul from the beauty that is seen to what is beyond, always kindles the desire for the hidden through what is perceived.

—St. Gregory of NeoCaesarea (Nyssa)

EARACHE SUFFERERS: Polycarp, martyr. Smyrnian (69–155). A council in Smyrna ordered him to swear on God's name, but the eighty-six-year-old refused. So this bishop of fifty years was ordered burned to death, during the persecution of Marcus Aurelius. As Polycarp prayed in silence, the flames encircled him, without harming him. The guards then punctured his throat with a sword. The first feast day of the Catholic Church was held in his honor. His patronage is from his saying once that he would rather stop hearing than "listen to arguments for heretical doctrines." Feast day, February 23.

EARTHQUAKES, INVOKED AGAINST: Emygdius, martyr. Trier (4th century). Pious legend. After smashing pagan idols, he was forced to flee to Rome. Emygdius' ability to evangelize created such a stir that the newly appointed bishop was beheaded. Feast day, August 9.

EAST INDIES: Thomas, apostle. Galilean (1st century). Brother of St. James; also known as Didymus or the twin; one of the twelve apostles. He was skeptical about the resurrection of Christ (John 20:24–29), until allowed to touch the wounds in the Lord's side and hands; hence the origin of the phrase "Doubting Thomas." The legend of Thomas began after Pentecost. Thomas was assigned the conversion of India, a task he not only dreaded but refused to undertake. Christ himself failed in his attempt through a dream to talk the apostle into going to India. So, the Lord appeared to a merchant named Abban, en route to India, and arranged to have Thomas sold into slavery. Once he realized the direction that his new master was headed, Thomas gave in to the will of God. In India, he was advanced a hefty sum to build a palace for the Parthian king. Instead, he donated the money to the needy. When the king was informed of Thomas' actions, he ordered the execution of the apostle. Just then, the king's brother died and was brought back to life. He told of his glimpse of heaven, which was enough to sway the king. Thomas' patronage stems from the many churches he built during his pilgrimages. He is believed to have been martyred in India. Also patron of architects, construction workers, and India; he is invoked against doubt. Feast day, July 3.

ECOLOGISTS: Francis of Assisi, founder. Italian (1181–1226). Although never a priest, he is one of the dominant figures of Christian religion. Born to a wealthy cloth merchant, Francis lived a lavish and irresponsible life. At twenty, he went to war against Perugia, where he was captured and imprisoned. After his release, Francis experienced several visions of Christ. He then renounced his inheritance and founded the Friars Minor. The first person ever to receive stigmata (five wounds, concurring with the five wounds of Christ) while praying, which never healed. He created the first Nativity scene in 1223. Also patron of animals, Catholic action, Italy, merchants, and zoos. Canonized 1228; feast day, October 4.

ECUADOR: Immaculate/Sacred Heart of Mary. In 1942, Pope Pius XII sanctified the holiness of Mary's heart, which has since been revered as the embodiment of purity and mercy. In order to achieve the Sacred Heart one must follow the code of the decent Christian: go to mass, recite the rosary, and receive communion, all of which must be done on a regular basis. Also patron of Angola, Lesotho, and the Philippines.

ECUMENISTS: Cyril and Methodius, monk and bishop. Greeks (826–869, 815–885). "Apostles of the Slavs." These brothers translated the Bible into Slavonic, were the inventors of the Glagotithic alphabet, and founded Slavonic literature. Also patrons of Moravia. Canonized 1980; feast day, February 14.

ECZEMA SUFFERERS: Anthony the Great, hermit. Egyptian (251–356). Founder of monasticism, first of the "white martyrs." As a hermit living in a cave, he refused the flock of naked women sent to tempt him. This caused his further retreat to a cave on Mount Kolzim. His followers wore hair shirts while making baskets and brushes to support their intellectual and spiritual search for God. Emperor Constantine was said to visit the wise hermit for counsel. Anthony was over 100 years old when he died. Also patron of amputees, basketweavers, brushmakers, gravediggers, and hermits. Feast day, January 17.

EDITORS: 1) John Bosco, founder. Italian (1815–1888). He and his mother established a refuge for boys. Their "boys town" offered education and apprenticeships in various trades for homeless and exploited youths. He then opened the Daughters of Mary of Christians for neglected girls. John authored three books to help finance his centers. Also patron of apprentices and laborers. Canonized 1934; feast day, January 31.

2) John the Divine, apostle. Galilean (1st century). Brother of James. Christ called the siblings "sons of thunder." John was referred to as the "disciple whom Jesus loved" (John 21:20–24). Christ, on the cross, left his mother in John's care (John 19:25–27). He was eventually exiled to the island of Patmos. He was the author of the fourth Gospel, three biblical epistles, and the book of the Revelation. Also patron of art dealers, Asia Minor, friendship, and publishers. Feast day, December 27.

EL SALVADOR: Our Lady of Peace. In 1966, Mary was anointed as the "Queen of Peace" in El Salvador. This belief goes back to the early centuries of Christianity, when the holiest of women was prayed to for preventing war and destruction.

ELOQUENCE: Catherine, martyr. Alexandrian (4th century). Pious legend. This woman of noble birth chose to study philosophy rather than relish in her beauty. Her conversion to Christianity was prompted by a hermit's dream. She then converted Emperor Maxentius' wife, an officer, and two hundred soldiers. In retaliation, the emperor gathered fifty pagan scholars, then challenged her to a religious debate. After a long and heated exchange, Catherine's words swayed all of the fifty scholars to convert. Maxentius had Catherine tied to a wheel, which immediately broke into pieces. She was then beheaded. Also patron of maidens, philosophers, preachers, spinners, single women, and students. Feast day, November 25.

EMBROIDERERS: Rose of Lima, mystic. Peruvian (1586–1617). The daughter of Spaniards, Isabel de Flores y del Oliva (Rose) has the distinction of being the first saint born in the New World. Instead of marrying into comfort, Rose helped support her family by doing laundry and embroidery for others. When old enough, she joined the Dominicans as a tertiary. She applied harsh penance to herself; she experienced visions and stigmata (five wounds concurring with the five wounds of Christ). Since her death, Rose has been attributed with saving Lima from countless local earthquakes. Also patron of Central and South America. Canonized 1671; feast day, August 23.

EMERGENCIES: Expiditus. (Unknown dates.) Absolutely no facts are known about this saint. An unreliable story claims the relics of an unknown saint were sent to a convent in France, with the word *spedito* across the lid. The nuns mistook this for the word *expedite*, which they thought must be the holy deceased's name. But, a Saint Expeditus is named in the eighteenth century, so one can only wonder. Also patron of solutions; he is invoked against procrastination. Feast day, April 19.

EMIGRANTS: Frances Xavier Cabrini, nun. Italian (1850–1917). Mother Cabrini arrived in New York and immediately began to aid the Italian emigrants. She founded hospitals, schools, orphanages, and the Sisters of the Sacred Heart, which has since spread throughout the Americas and back to Europe. She became a citizen in 1909 and was the first American citizen canonized. Frances' uncorrupted body has been enshrined in Manhattan. Also patron of hospital administrators. Canonized 1946; feast day, November 13.

EMPRESSES: 1) Helena, Empress. Bithynian (250–330). This daughter of an innkeeper married Constantius, the Roman general, in 270. Constantine, their son, would later become the first Christian emperor of the Roman Empire. According to legend, Helena uncovered Christ's true cross while on pilgrimage through the Holy Land. Also patron of converts and divorce. Feast day, August 18.

2) Adelaide, Empress. Burgundian (931–991). A first marriage to Lothair, the king of Italy, was brief. Lothair died shortly after the birth of their daughter Emma. Adelaide was then kidnaped by Berengarius, who tried to force the young queen to marry his son. Adelaide refused and was thrown in the dungeon of a castle on Lake Garda. Otto the Great of Germany rescued Adelaide and defeated Berengarius' army. The two were wed on Christmas, which united the German and Italian empires. The couple raised their five children, along with Emma and Otto's son Rudolph. In 962, Otto became emperor of Rome. Empress Adelaide founded monasteries, convents, and donated generously to the needy. Also patron of parenthood, princesses, second marriages, and step-parents. Feast day, December 16.

ENDURANCE: Pantaleon, martyr. Bithynian (4th century). Pious legend. This respected man of medicine lived a privileged life as the personal physician to Emperor Galerius. When the emperor learned that Pantaleon had converted to Christianity, he had him sentenced to death. The six attempts to execute the convert (burning, molten lead, being thrown to the lions, drowning, the wheel, and stabbing) all failed. Once Pantaleon was confident that he had proved his theological point, he bowed his head and allowed the haggard executioner to behead him. Also patron of doctors and tuberculosis. Feast day, July 27.

ENGAGED COUPLES: Valentine, martyr. Roman (3rd century). He was beheaded and buried on February 14. It is said that birds began to pair at the moment of his death. Also patron of greetings and lovers. Feast day, February 14.

ENGINEERS: Ferdinand III, King. Castilian (1198–1252). Married Princess Beatrice; fathered ten children. He and King Alfonso, his father, teamed up to drive the Moors out of Spain. He was the founder of the University of Salamanca and the cathedral of Burgos, and reformer of the canon code of laws. Also patron of governors, magistrates, parenthood, and rulers. Canonized 1671; feast day, May 30.

ENGLAND: George, martyr. English (3rd century). Aside from being martyred in Palestine, this Christian knight's life is pure fiction. He is best known for a dragonslaying incident, in which he saved a princess from being sacrificed, then married her. An account of his life is found in the thirteenth-century *The Golden Legend*. Also patron of Boy Scouts, farmers, and soldiers. Feast day, February 21.

EPIDEMICS, INVOKED AGAINST: Godberta, nun. German (6th century). It is said that in the midst of a crowd, the bishop St. Eloi placed his ring on her finger and proclaimed her married to the church. She is best remembered for extinguishing a blazing fire by making the sign of the cross. Also invoked against droughts. Feast day, April 5.

EPILEPTICS: 1) Dymphna, martyr. Irish (7th century). Folktale. She and her confessor ran away from her incestuous father, a pagan chieftain. In Belgium, the two lived as hermits in an oratory they had built, until her father and his men hunted them down. The confessor was murdered and Dymphna was beheaded for refusing to return home. Many have been cured at Dymphna's tomb. Also patron of runaways; she is invoked against mental disorders, diabolic possession, and sleepwalking. Feast day, May 15.

2) Vitus, martyr. Sicilian (3rd century). Legend. After exorcising Emperor Diocletian's son of evil spirits (*chorea*), he found himself accused of sorcery by the emperor. Vitus was heaved into a vat of boiling water, from which he miraculously emerged unharmed. He and his two companions escaped Rome with the help of an angel and he is believed to have been martyred in the Lucanian province. Also patron of actors, comedians, and dancers. feast day, June 15.

EUCHARISTIC CONGRESSES AND SOCIETIES: Paschal Baylon, laybrother. Spanish (1540–1592). Superior devotion in helping the poor and sick. Canonized 1690; feast day, May 17.

EUROPE: Benedict of Nursia, monk. Italian (480–547). Accredited as the father of Western monasticism. At fourteen, he left his noble family and sister, St. Scholastica, to further his studies in Rome; at twenty, he chose the life of a hermit and moved into a cave; at thirty, he had founded a dozen monasteries. Benedict's book of holy rules became the model for monastic life throughout Europe for centuries. After a poisoning attempt by a jealous monk named Florentius, who found his methods too fastidious, Benedict left the position of abbot. He systemized a dozen monasteries, establishing Western monasticism. Patron of monks and speleologists; he is invoked against poison and witchcraft. Feast day, March 21.

EVIL SPIRITS, INVOKED AGAINST: Agrippina, martyr. Roman (3rd century). During the persecution of Christians, Agrippina was tortured then executed when she refused to renounce her faith to Emperors Valerian or Diocletian. Her body was taken to Sicily by three women, where the afflicted have been cured at her tomb for centuries. She is invoked against bacterial diseases and thunderstorms. Feast day, June 23.

EXPECTANT MOTHERS: Gerard Majella, laybrother. Italian (1726–1755). Healer; prophet; visionary; mind reader; ecstatic; bilocationist (able to be in two locations at the same time). Gerard was once accused of lewd behavior by a woman, which he did not challenge. Eventually, he was cleared of the charge when she admitted to lying. His mother may be responsible for his peculiar patronage. She would boast that her son "was born for heaven." Also patron of childbirth. Canonized 1904; feast day, October 16.

EXPOSURE, INVOKED AGAINST: Valerian, bishop. African (5th century). King Arian of Genseric demanded the church's valuables but Bishop Valerian refused. The bishop was then evicted from his home. The king decreed that anyone who attempted to feed or house the eighty-six-year-old transient would be punished for their efforts. Valerian froze to death one night in winter. Also patron of victims of freezing. Feast day, December 15.

EYE TROUBLE, INVOKED AGAINST: 1) Herve (Harvey), abbott. English. (6th century). Pious myth. This musician was born blind and is said to have wandered the countryside converting people with song. One of his most popular miracles occurred one day while plowing. A wolf killed and ate his beast of burden. No sooner had Harvey said "Amen," when the wolf strapped on the harness and finished plowing the field. Another story tells of a fox that stole a chicken farm from his coop and returned the bird alive. Also invoked against foxes and wolves. Feast day, June 17.

2) Lucy, martyr. Italian (4th century). Pious myth. It is said that she was once told how pretty her eyes were by an arranged suitor. Lucy gouged them from their sockets and handed them to her horrified future husband, who promptly had her condemned for her Christian beliefs. Proving to be flame-proof when flung in the fire, Lucy was eventually stabbed in the throat. Her name translates to "light." Also patron of cutlers and writers; she is invoked against hemorrhaging. Feast day, December 13.

Poor human reason when it trusts in itself substitutes the strangest absurdities for the highest divine concepts.

—St. John Chrysostom

FALSELY ACCUSED: 1) Raymond Nonnatus, cardinal. Spanish (1204–1240). He was taken from his dying mother by cesarian section. As a Mercedarian, he ransomed himself to the Moors in exchange for the freedom of slaves and Christian hostages. He converted within the prison walls, which angered the Muslims. His jailers realized that his ransom would exceed those of the other prisoners, so Raymond was continuously tortured for preaching. Negotiations for his release took eight months. Also patron of childbirth, midwives, obstetricians, and pregnant women. Canonized 1657; feast day, August 31.

2) Roch (Rocco), hermit. French (1350–1380). Legend. He tended to plague sufferers in Italy, then became ill himself. Sick and alone, Roch was nourished back to health by a stray dog, who brought him food. He was

then imprisoned as a spy by his unknowing uncle, the governor. After Roch's death in prison, a cross-shaped birthmark revealed his true identity. Also patron of invalids; he is invoked against cholera and plagues. Feast day, March 28.

FAMINE, INVOKED AGAINST: 1) Domitian, bishop. French (6th century). Once his seat as bishop was taken away, Domitian took to the road. He built churches and converted thousands. In the final year of a great famine, Domitian implored the rich to share their grain, promising a bountiful harvest the following autumn. Feast day, May 7.

2) Walburga, abbess. English (8th century). Medicine woman. Shortly after following her uncle, St. Boniface, to Germany, she was named abbess to the monastery in Heidenheim. Stories of Walpurgis, as she was then named, can be found in Germany's folklore. On April 30 witches honor this holy healer on what is known as Walpurgisnacht. A slippery liquid with curing powers is said to flow from near her tomb. Also patron of crops; she is invoked against plagues. Feast day, February 25.

FARMERS: 1) George, martyr. English (3rd century). Aside from being martyred in Palestine, this Christian knight's life is pure fiction. He is best known for a dragon-slaying incident, in which he saved a princess from being sacrificed, then married her. An account of his life is found in the thirteenth-century *The Golden Legend*. Also patron of Boy Scouts, England, and soldiers. Feast day, February 21.

2) Isidore the Farmer, layman. Spanish (1070–1130). A hired hand who worked miracles and shared what little he had with those few who were less fortunate. Also patron of laborers. Canonized 1622; feast day, May 10.

FARRIERS: 1) Eligius (Eloi), bishop. French (588–660). As a metalsmith, he crafted two thrones for King Choltar II with the portions of gold and jewels provided to him for one. He was then appointed as the master of the mint and used his influence to help the sick and homeless. Also patron of garage workers, jewelers, and steel workers. Feast day, December 1.

2) John the Baptist, martyr. Israelite (1st century). Cousin to Jesus Christ; his birth was announced by an angel to his father, Zachary. John baptized several of the apostles, including Jesus himself. He was imprisoned for condemning the incestuous relationship Herod was carrying on with his niece, Herodias, who happened to be the wife of Phillip, his half brother. Herod offered Herodias's daughter, Salome, anything she wanted. Salome requested John's head on a platter, upon her mother's prodding. Also patron of baptism; he is invoked against spasms. Feast day, June 24.

FATHERS: Joseph, carpenter. Nazarean (1st century). Descendent of David; husband to the Virgin Mary; foster father to Jesus Christ. Joseph had second thoughts about marrying Mary when he learned that she was pregnant until the angel Gabriel explained the Messiah's coming. After the birth of Christ, he was forewarned in a dream of Herod's exploits, so he took his young family to Egypt. Upon Herod's death, a dream directed them to return to Israel. Fearing Herod's replacement, Joseph chose to settle his family in Nazareth. Scholars believe he died before the crucifixion of Christ. Pope Leo XII invoked Joseph as the patron of fathers in 1899. Also patron of Belgium, Canada, carpenters, the church, the dying, Korea, Peru, social justice, and working men. Feast days, March 19 and May 1.

FERRYMEN: Julian the Hospitaler, innkeeper. (Unknown dates.) Pious fiction. He killed a sleeping couple in his bed, fearing adultery. The slain were not an adulterous wife and lover, but his visiting parents. His penance was to build an inn and hospital for the poor at the mouth of a river. Julian was absolved when he gave his bed to an angel, who was disguised as a leper. Also patron of boatmen, circus people, hotel employees, and innkeepers. Feast day, February 12.

FEVER SUFFERERS: 1) Antoninus of Florence, archbishop. Italian (1389–1405). Founded the friary of San Marco; healer of the sick; theologian. Canonized 1523; feast day, May 10.

2) Albert of Trapani, friar. Italian (17th century). This Carmelite friar tirelessly tended to the plague sufferers of Sicily. Also patron of jaundice sufferers. Feast day, August 8.

FIELDWORKERS: Notburga, servant. Austrian (1264–1313). Religious myth. After being fired for giving food to the poor, the one-eyed Notburga was hired as a farmhand. One Saturday afternoon, Notburga's boss noticed that one of his fieldworkers was knocking off a bit early. Notburga explained that she had to go to church. Her employer became irritated with the Christian and ordered her back to work. Notburga simply threw her sickle in the air, where it stayed until her boss gave in. Feast day, September 14.

FINLAND: Henry of Uppsala, martyr. English (12th century). This bishop was companion to King Eric of Sweden during the battles against Finnish pirates. Henry remained in Finland as a missionary. A disgruntled convert by the name of Lalli murdered Henry for inflicting an extreme penance upon the man for a previous murder. Feast day, January 19.

FIREFIGHTERS: Florian, martyr. Austrian (4th century). This officer relinquished himself to the governor as a Christian. He was beaten, set on fire, and cast into the River Enns with a rock tied to him. Also invoked against floods. Feast day, May 4.

FIRE PREVENTION: 1) Catherine of Siena, mystic. Italian (1347–1380). The twenty-fourth of twenty-five children; one of the great Christian mystics; suffered the pain of stigmata without the visible marks; worked tirelessly with leprosy patients; Doctor of the Church. She persuaded Pope Gregory XI to leave Avignon, which returned the papacy to Rome after 68 years. Dictated *Dialogue*, since she was illiterate. Also patron of Italy, nursing homes, and spinsters. Canonized 1461; feast day, April 29.

2) Barbara, martyr. (4th century.) Religious fiction. A young woman whose pagan father locked her in a tower before leaving on a long journey. Within the walls, she converted to Christianity and had three windows built to signify the Trinity. When her father returned, he was so infuriated by his daughter's religious preference, he turned her over to the authorities. Barbara was subjected to heinous torture, yet refused to disavow her faith. The judge ordered the father to kill her himself. Atop a mountain he slew his daughter, then was immediately struck dead by a bolt of lightning. Also patron of architects, builders, dying, founders, miners, prisoners, and stonemasons. Feast day, December 4.

FIRST HOLY COMMUNICANTS: Tarsicius, martyr. Roman (3rd or 4th century). An angry mob beat him to death while he was carrying the Eucharist to Christian prisoners. Feast day, August 15.

FISHERMEN: 1) Andrew, apostle. Bethsaidan (1st century). Son of Jonah. This fisherman was the first called by Jesus Christ, who then recruited his brother Peter; he was a witness to the Feeding of the Five thousand (John 6:8–9). After the resurrection of Christ, Andrew made his way to Greece and was crucified in Achaia. Also patron of Greece, Russia, and Scotland. Feast day, November 30.

2) Peter, apostle. Bethsaidan (1st century). Son of Jonah; brother of Andrew; first pope; witness of the transfiguration and the agony of Jesus in the garden. Peter once walked on water, then sank when he hesitated; denied the Lord three times; asked to be hanged upside down when crucified in Rome. Peter's birth name was Simon, but Jesus gave him the distinction of *Kephas*, which is Aramaic for "rock." The representation of Peter as the gatekeeper of the pearly gates stems from Christ once symbolically endowing the "keys to the kingdom" to his chief apostle. Also patron of longevity and the papacy. Feast day, June 29.

FISHMONGERS: Magnus, Prince. Scottish (12th century). This prisoner of the Norwegian king, Magnus the Barefoot, escaped to Scotland where Malcolm III harbored him. After Magnus the Barefoot's death, Prince Magnus was reinstated along with his cousin, Haakon, to co-rule the Orkney Islands. But Haakon was a jealous man, with no intention of sharing the throne with his well-received cousin. Haakon struck and killed Magnus. Feast day, April 16.

FLIGHT ATTENDANTS: Bona, pilgrim. Pisa (1156–1207). At the age of fourteen, Bona set off to visit her father, who was a soldier on crusade in Jerusalem. On her way back home, she was captured and taken prisoner by pirates in the Mediterranean. Bona was then rescued and returned home. She guided many on the thousand-mile pilgrimage, making the trip nine times before she took ill. Bona died at home. Also patron of travelers. Feast day, May 29.

FLOODS, INVOKED AGAINST: Florian, martyr. Austrian (4th century). This officer relinquished himself to the governor as a Christian. He was beaten, set on fire, and cast into the River Enns with a rock tied to him. Also patron of firemen. Feast day, May 4.

FLORISTS: Therese of Lisieux, nun. French (1873–1897). Also known as "The Little Flower." She and her five sisters became Carmelite nuns. Author of *The Story of a Soul,* Therese wrote that she would "let fall a shower of roses" (miracles) when she passed on. Dying of tuberculosis on September 30, she kept her word. Also patron of aviators, foreign missions, and France. Canonized 1925; feast day, October 1.

FOOT TROUBLE, INVOKED AGAINST: Victor of Marseilles, martyr. Gaulish (3rd century). Pious legend. When Emperor Maximian discovered that his favorite Roman guard was a Christian, Victor was subjected to a number of tortures. As he was being stretched on a rack for refusing to worship pagan deities, Jesus Christ appeared to Victor. That night, God sent his angels to his cell, causing the conversion of three prison guards. The next day, Emperor Maximian had the new converts beheaded. Victor was brought before the emperor again. Maximian ordered the battered man to offer incense to Jupiter. Victor kicked the statue, which enraged Maximian. The Christian's foot was ordered to be hacked off before he was crushed in a mill. The grindstone broke about halfway through the execution, yet a partially pulverized Victor still lived on. One of his executioners drew a sword and beheaded him. Also patron of millers and torture victims. Feast day, July 21.

FORESTERS: John Gualbert, abbott. Florentine (11th century). The thought of Christ on the cross incited him to spare his brother Hugh's murderer. John then became a monk and built his own monastery in Vallombrosa, from the wood of a nearby forest. Ironically, he is patron of foresters. Also patron of park services. Canonized 1193; feast day, July 12.

FOUNDATIONS: Antony Claret, archbishop. Catalonian (19th century). Antonio Maria Claret y Clara worked with his father, a cloth weaver, by day, and studied Latin and religion by night. At twenty-five, Antony was ordained and eventually was named archbishop of Cuba. His sermons (numbering 10,000 in his lifetime) were so powerful that an assassination attempt was made by a jealous man over his mistress' reconversion to Catholicism. Antony is responsible for establishing a museum of natural history, a laboratory of science, schools of language and music, and other institutions. Antony published 200 religious books and pamphlets, many of which are housed in the Libreria Religiosa, in Barcelona, another of his foundations. Feast day, October 24.

FOUNDERS: Barbara, martyr. (4th century.) Pious legend. A young woman whose pagan father locked her in a tower before leaving on a long journey. Within the walls, she converted to Christianity and had three windows built to signify the Trinity. When her father returned, he was so infuriated by his daughter's religious preference, he turned her over to the authorities. Barbara was subjected to heinous torture, yet refused to disavow her faith. The judge ordered the father to kill her himself. Atop a mountain he slew his daughter, then was immediately struck dead by a bolt of lightning. Also patron of architects, builders, dying, fire prevention, prisoners, and stonemasons. Feast day, December 4.

FOUNDLINGS: Holy Innocents. According to Matthew (2:16–18), Herod feared the new king had been born in Bethlehem, so he ordered that all male infants be slain. They are considered the first martyrs for Christ. Also patrons of babies. Feast day, December 28.

FOXES, INVOKED AGAINST: Herve (Harvey), abbott. English (6th century). Pious myth. This musician was born blind and is said to have wandered the countryside converting people with song. One of his most popular miracles occurred one day while plowing. A wolf killed and ate his beast of burden. No sooner had Harvey said "Amen," when the wolf strapped on the harness and finished plowing the field. Another story tells of a fox that stole a chicken from his coops and returned the bird alive. Also invoked against eye trouble and wolves. Feast day, June 17.

FLOUR INDUSTRY WORKERS: Arnulf, bishop. Flemish (1040–1087). He was a soldier in the armies of Robert and Henry I of France before he received his calling. While at Saint-Medard, Arnulf was named bishop of Soissons. In art, Arnulf stands with a baker's shovel, hence his patronage. Also patron of millers. Feast day, August 15.

FRANCE: 1) Our Lady of the Assumption. In 1950, Pope Pius XII surmised that since the Blessed Virgin Mary was born without original sin ("revealed by God and defined as dogma" by Pope Pius IX in 1854), she was elevated (body and soul) to heaven upon her death. Also patron of India, Malta, Paraguay, and South Africa.

2) Joan of Arc, soldier. French (1412–1431). Known in France as Jean La Pucelle. At the age of fourteen, this daughter of a peasant farmer began hearing voices directing her to her destiny of saving France from English rule. After a panel of theologians found Joan to be sane, King Charles VII provided her with an army which defeated the English, who had been invaders of their native soil. She was captured and sold to the British. King Charles did not lift a finger to save her. Since the English could not openly admit that she had defeated them, they drummed up the charge of heresy and witchcraft, then burned her at the stake. Joan was nineteen years old when she died. Also patron of soldiers. Canonized 1920; feast day, May 30.

3) Therese of Lisieux, nun. French (1873–1897). Also known as "The Little Flower." She and her five sisters became Carmelite nuns. Author of *The Story of a Soul*, Therese wrote that she would "let fall a shower of roses" (miracles) when she passed on. Dying of tuberculosis on September 30, she kept her word. Also patron of aviators, florists, and foreign missions. Canonized 1925; feast day, October 1.

4) Denis, martyr. Italian (3rd century). Also known as Dionysius. He and two companions were sent by St. Clement to convert Gaul, where the three were beheaded. It is said that the headless Denis stood up, collected his head, and walked to an abbey, which was immediately named after him. Also invoked against headaches. Feast day, October 9.

FREEMASONS: Four Crowned Martyrs, martyrs. Yugoslavians (3rd century). Castorius, Claudius, Nicostratus, and Simpronian were skilled carvers who declined to sculpt a pagan statue for the Roman Emperor Diocletian. They were weighted with lead, then drowned in the river. Also patrons of sculptors. Feast day, November 8.

FREEZING, VICTIMS OF: 1) Sebald, missionary. Anglo-Saxon (8th century). Legend has it that a poor couple gave him shelter one cold winter night. Wood was scarce, and the flames of the fire burnt low. Sebald tossed icicles into the chimney which disbursed warmth throughout the cottage. Also patron of cold weather. Feast day, August 19.

2) Valerian, bishop. African (5th century). King Arian of Genseric demanded the church's valuables but Bishop Valerian refused. The bishop was then evicted from his home. The king decreed that anyone who attempted to feed or house the eighty-six-year-old transient would be punished for their efforts. Valerian froze to death one night in winter. Also invoked against exposure. Feast day, December 15.

FRIENDSHIP: John the Divine, apostle. Galilean (1st century). Brother of James. Christ called the siblings "sons of thunder." John was referred to as the "disciple whom Jesus loved" (John 21:20–24). Christ, on the cross, left his mother in John's care (John 19:25–27). He was eventually exiled to the island of Patmos. He was the author of the fourth Gospel, three biblical epistles, and the book of the Revelation. Also patron of art dealers, Asia Minor, editors, and publishers. Feast day, December 27.

FULLERS: 1) Anastasius, martyr. Aquileian (4th century). Of noble birth, Anastasius came across the writings of St. Paul, where he stated that there is wisdom in working with one's own hands. Anastasius became a clothes fuller (one who shrinks and thickens clothes) and was martyred during Emperor Diocletian's persecution of Christians. Feast day, September 7.

2) James the Less, apostle. Galilean (1st century). One of the twelve apostles; one of the "four brothers" of the Lord. After Christ's resurrection, James headed the Church of Jerusalem. He was martyred when thrown from a temple, then stoned to death. Also patron of druggists and hatters. Feast day, May 3.

FUNERAL DIRECTORS: 1) Dismas, thief. (1st century.) All that is known of this "good thief" is that he was hanged on the cross next to Jesus. Also patron of death row inmates, prisoners, thieves, and undertakers. Feast day, March 25.

2) Joseph of Arimathea, disciple. Arimathean (1st century). He witnessed Christ's crucifixion, then laid Christ's body in a tomb. His name is cited in the four gospels. Legend has it that he obtained the holy grail from the last supper. Feast day, March 17.

FURRIERS: James the Greater, apostle. Galilean (1st century). His name James "the Greater" is to differentiate him from the other apostle, James "the Less." He and his brother John "dropped their fishing nets" at the Sea of Galilee and followed Jesus; they witnessed both the transfiguration and the agony of Jesus in the garden. James was beheaded in Jerusalem, the first apostle to be martyred. Also patron of Chile, Guatemala, Nicaragua, pharmacists, pilgrims, and Spain; he is invoked against arthritis and rheumatism. Feast day, July 25.

Be not anxious about what you have, but about what you are.

—St. Gregory the Great

GALLSTONES, INVOKED AGAINST: Albinus, martyr. Albanian (3rd century). He fled his homeland of Albania when it was conquered by the Arians. St. Ambrose appointed him bishop and assigned him and St. Ursus to Gaul, where they were beheaded. Also invoked against kidney disease. Feast day, June 21.

GAMBLING, UNCONTROLLED: Bernardine of Siena, preacher. Italian (1380–1444). "The people's preacher." At the age of twenty, he took charge of a hospital in Siena during the plague of 1400. In 1417 he set out on foot preaching and converting thousands throughout Italy. He was the second founder of the Friars of the Strict Observance. In spite of his attributes, he believed that witchcraft was running rampant and appears to have been an anti-Semite. His sermons often denounced gambling. Also patron of advertising, communications personnel, and public relations. Canonized 1450; feast day, May 20.

GARAGE WORKERS: Eligius (Eloi), bishop. French (588–660). As a metalsmith, he crafted two thrones for King Choltar II with the portions of gold and jewels provided to him for one. He was then appointed as the master of the mint and used his influence to help the sick and homeless. Also patron of farriers, jewelers, and steel workers. Feast day, December 1.

GARDENERS: 1) Dorothy, martyr. Cappodian (4th century). Legend. Fabricus the prefect could not talk her into being his wife, so he handed the Christian over to the authorities. While Dorothy was being escorted to her execution, a lawyer named Theophilus called out in jest that she send him some fruit from "heaven's garden." That winter, a basket with pears and roses arrived at Theophilus' door, whereupon he converted. Also patron of brides. Feast day, February 6.

2) Phocas, martyr. Paphlagonian (unknown dates). Legend. As an innkeeper and market gardener near Sinope, Phocas would give his excess crops to the poor. According to the story, he lodged the soldiers that were sent to kill him. The next morning Phocas revealed himself as the Christian they were to assassinate. Sensing their apprehension, Phocas insisted that they slay him. Once the uncomfortable moment passed, the soldiers beheaded their gracious host. They then buried him in a grave that Phocas had prepared for himself during the night. Also patron of agricultural workers. Feast day, September 22.

3) Fiacre, hermit. Irish (7th century). Healer; built a refuge for the sick and poor. He was once endowed by St. Faro with all the land he could clear in a single day. When the saint returned at dusk, a large field was clear

and ready for planting. The first cabstand in Paris was near the Hotel Saint Fiacre. As a result, the French word for taxi is *fiacre*. Also patron of cab drivers; he is invoked against hemorrhoids and syphilis. Feast day, September 1.

GERMANY: Boniface, martyr. English (680–754). This "Apostle of Germany" was actually an Englishman by the name of Winfrid. As Boniface, he successfully expanded Christianity in Germany. He also founded a monastery in Fulda. Feast day, June 5.

GIBRALTAR: Our Lady of Europe. On May 31, 1979, the citizens of Gibraltar paid tribute to the Blessed Virgin Mary by presenting her with this title.

GIRLS: Agnes, martyr. Roman (4th century). At the age of eleven, the governor's son failed in his attempt to court Agnes, who had pledged herself to God. He denounced her as a Christian, then had his father send her to a house of prostitution. She maintained her purity through prayer and a miracle. She was then tortured and stabbed in the throat. Feast day, January 21.

GLANDULAR DISORDERS, INVOKED AGAINST: Cadoc, abbot. Welsh (6th century). This son of Saints Gwladys and Gundleus was tutored by St. Tatheus. He then founded the monastery of Nant Carfan. The tales of South Wales tell of Cadoc being shuttled to Rome on a cloud. He was appointed bishop shortly before he was martyred while saying mass. Feast day, September 25.

GLASS PAINTERS: James Grissinger, laybrother. German (1407–1491). As a young man, James was recruited as a mercenary by the military in Naples. Becoming disillusioned with his work, James joined the Dominican order. There, he spent the better half of his life painting images on the windows of churches. Feast day, October 11.

GLASSWORKERS: Luke, evangelist. Greek (1st century). Physician and artist. Little is known of his early life. He was the author of the third Gospel and the Acts of the Apostles, which serve as a record of the progression of early Christianity. He died in Greece at the age of 84. Also patron of artists, butchers, notaries, painters, physicians, and surgeons. Feast day, October 18.

GLAZIERS: Lawrence, martyr. Spanish (3rd century). A prediction revealed that he had three days to live. The city prefect mandated the church's treasures be handed over to the emperor. Lawrence sold everything and donated the money to the poor. He returned on the third day with an array of societal misfits and said that they were the church's treasures. The prefect had him bound to a hot griddle. Lawrence asked to be flipped over at one point, claiming he was done on that side. Also patron of cooks, cutlers, the poor, restaurateurs, and Sri Lanka. Feast day, July 29.

GOLDSMITHS: Dunstan, bishop. English (910–988). One of the great reformers of church life in England during the tenth century. He rectified Bath and Westminster Abbey. He was advisor to King Edwy, until his accusation of the king's sexual exploits caused Dunstan's exile. A skillful metalworker and harpist. Also patron of armorers, blacksmiths, locksmiths, musicians, and silversmiths. Feast day, May 19.

GOOD WEATHER: Agricola of Avignon, bishop. French (630–700). At the age of thirty, his father, Bishop (Saint) Magnus, appointed Agricola to co-bishop Avignon, thus creating a rare father and son team in the Roman Catholic church. He is best known for a prayer that ended an invasion of storks. Also patron of rain; he is invoked against bad luck, misfortune, and plague. Feast day, September 2.

GOUT: Maurice, officer. Egyptian (3rd century). Legend. As officer in the Theban Legion, Maurice encouraged his Christian platoon to refuse Maximian Herculius' request to worship pagan gods. Maximian ordered the execution of every tenth man, which proved to be an ineffective deterrent. A second, then third decimation began. Eventually, the entire unit was put to death. Also patron of dyers, infantrymen, knife sharpeners, swordsmiths, and weavers. Feast day, September 22.

GOVERNORS: Ferdinand III, King. Castilian (1198–1252). Married Princess Beatrice; fathered ten children. He and King Alfonso, his father, teamed up to drive the Moors out of Spain. He was the founder of the University of Salamanca and the cathedral of Burgos, and reformer of the canon code of laws. Also patron of engineers, magistrates, parenthood, and rulers. Canonized 1671; feast day, May 30.

GRANDMOTHERS: Anne, housewife. Nazarean (1st century B.C.). Grandmother of Jesus; wife of Joachim. Aside from giving birth to the Blessed Mary at the age of forty, little is known of her. Also patron of cabinetmakers, Canada, housewives, and women in labor. Feast day, July 26.

GRAVEDIGGERS: Anthony the Great, hermit. Egyptian (251–356). Founder of monasticism, first of the "white martyrs." As a hermit living in a cave, he refused the flock of naked women sent to tempt him. This caused his further retreat to a cave on Mount Kolzim. His followers wore hair shirts while making baskets and brushes to support their intellectual and spiritual search for God.

Emperor Constantine was said to visit the wise hermit for counsel. Anthony was over 100 years old when he died. Also patron of amputees, basketweavers, brushmakers, and hermits; he is invoked against eczema. Feast day, January 17.

GREECE: 1) Nicholas of Myra, bishop. Lycian (4th century). Better known as Saint Nick. The facts are few. He ran a monastery, was a prisoner during the time of Christian persecutions, and was present at the Council of Nicaea. The rest is myth. One tale tells of a father who was so poor he couldn't afford his three daughters' dowries. Nick tossed three bags of gold through the kitchen window, and the three daughters married soon after. Also patron of boys, brides, children, dockworkers, merchants, pawnbrokers, spinsters, and travelers. Feast day, December 6.

2) Andrew, apostle. Bethsaidan (1st century). Son of Jonah. This fisherman was the first called by Jesus Christ, who then recruited his brother Peter; he was a witness to the Feeding of the Five thousand (John 6:8–9). After the resurrection of Christ, Andrew made his way to Greece and was crucified in Achaia. Also patron of fishermen, Russia, and Scotland. Feast day, November 30.

GREETINGS: Valentine, martyr. Roman (3rd century). He was beheaded and buried on February 14. It is said that birds began to pair at the moment of his death. Also patron of engaged couples and lovers. Feast day, February 14.

GROCERS: Michael, archangel. One of the seven archangels of God; one of the three archangels mentioned by name in the Bible. He is cited twice in the Old Testament, appearing to Moses and Abraham. In the New Testament, he contends with Satan for the body of

Moses and tosses Lucifer and his cohorts from heaven. In art, he is often depicted with a scale (representing the weighing of souls) in one hand, while slaying a dragon (Satan) with the other. Also patron of battle, the dead, mariners, paratroopers, police officers, and radiologists. Feast day, September 29.

GROOMS: Louis IX, King. French (1214–1270). Crowned king of France at the age of twelve; married Margaret, sister of Eleanor, wife of Henry III; fathered eleven children; launched France's first navy. Louis participated in two crusades: Damietta in Egypt, where the good king and his men emerged triumphant, and Mansurah, where the defeated king was taken prisoner. After six years, he was set free. Louis died of typhoid while venturing off on his third crusade, to Tunisia. Also patron of crusaders, kings, and parenthood. Feast day, August 25.

GUATEMALA: James the Greater, apostle. Galilean (1st century). His name James "the Greater" is to differentiate him from the other apostle, James "the Less." He and his brother John "dropped their fishing nets" at the Sea of Galilee and followed Jesus; they were witnesses to both the transfiguration and the agony of Jesus in the garden. James was beheaded in Jerusalem, the first apostle to be martyred. Also patron of Chile, furriers, Nicaragua, pharmacists, pilgrims, and Spain; he is invoked against arthritis and rheumatism. Feast day, July 25.

GUARDIANS: Mamas, martyr. Cappadocian (3rd century). This shepherd was mentioned by both Saints Gregory and Basil as being martyred under Emperor Aurelian. The legends have since varied: one has him stoned to death as a child, while another says he was burned to death as a very old man. Feast day, August 17.

No wonder you have so few friends, since this is the way you treat them.

—St. Teresa of Avila

(This prayer to God was overheard by her driver after their carriage had overturned.)

HAIL, INVOKED AGAINST: Ansovinus, bishop. Italian (9th century). This hermit's healing powers converted many followers. The granary ran low one day, while the masses were still hungry, so Ansovinus ordered the storehouse doors shut. Moments later, they swung open, spilling over with an abundance to feed all who were hungry. Also patron of crops. Feast day, March 13.

HAIRSTYLISTS (MEN): Martin de Porres, laybrother. Peruvian (1579–1639). A barber-surgeon apprentice before joining the laybrothers. He attended to the African slaves brought into Peru, was founder of an orphanage and a foundling hospital, and experienced bilocation and aerial flights. Also patron of health workers, interracial justice, public education, and race relations. Canonized 1962; feast day, November 3.

HAIRSTYLISTS (WOMEN): Mary Magdalen. Magdalene (1st century). She is known for washing Christ's feet with her tears, which she dried with her hair, then anointed with perfume. There is no reference that the repentant adulteress in the New Testament was actually Mary. Christ cast seven devils out of her (Mark 16:9; Luke 8:2), she was present at the crucifixion (Matthew 27:56; Mark 15:40; John 19:25), and was the first to see Christ after his resurrection (Matthew 28:9; Mark 16:9; John 20:1–18). Also patron of perfumers and repentant prostitutes. Feast day, July 22.

HANGINGS, INVOKED AGAINST: Colman, martyr. Irish (11th century). Roman martyrology has a list of 300 saints named Colman. While on a pilgrimage to Jerusalem, Colman was stopped by the suspicious Viennese who, fearing he was a Moravian spy, tried and hanged Colman. After his death, his body showed no sign of decay. The miracles which have since occurred at his grave have confirmed his holiness. Also patron of Austria and horned cattle. Feast day, October 13.

HANGOVERS, INVOKED AGAINST: Bibliana, martyr. Roman (4th century). After being beaten to death for her Christian beliefs, the young woman was laid to rest with her martyred mother and sister. The plants that grew over their grave are believed to remedy hangovers. Feast day, December 2.

HARVESTS, CORN: Medard, bishop. French (470–560). Medard was appointed to the dioceses of Tournai and Noyan after the attack by the Huns. According to local belief, if it rains on Medard's feast day, expect forty more days of wet weather. If it's sunny on his feast day, the next forty will be as well. This legend is remarkably similar to St. Swithun's. Also patron of vintages. Feast day, June 8.

HATTERS: James the Less, apostle. Galilean (1st century). One of the twelve Apostles; one of the "four brothers" of the Lord. After Christ's resurrection, James headed the Church of Jerusalem. He was martyred when thrown from a temple, then stoned to death. Also patron of druggists and fullers. Feast day, May 3.

HAYMAKERS: Gervase and Protase, martyrs. Milanese (1st century). Myth. St. Ambrose was led to the skeletons of these brothers through a dream. They are believed to be the first martyrs of Milan. Feast day, June 19.

HEADACHES, INVOKED AGAINST: 1) Denis, martyr. Italian (3rd century). Also known as Dionysius. He and two companions were sent by St. Clement to convert Gaul, where the three were beheaded. It is said that the headless Denis stood up, collected his head, and walked to an abbey, which was immediately named after him. Also patron of France. Feast day, October 9.

2) Avertinus, hermit. French (12th century). Prior to his martyrdom, while St. Thomas of Canterbury was in Touraine, he promoted his companion, Avertinus, to deacon. Avertinus then became a hermit. Accounts of his patronages can be seen in the *ex votos* of his church in Tours. Also invoked against dizziness. Feast day, May 5.

3) Teresa of Avila, nun. Spanish (1515–1582). She was forced to leave the convent because of her failing health. Teresa then founded sixteen convents, several reform monasteries, and authored several books, including *The Interior Castle*. She was the first woman to be de-

clared a Doctor of the Church. Also patron of heart attack sufferers. Canonized 1622; feast day, October 15.

HEALERS: Bridget of Sweden, Princess. Swedish (1303–1373). Mystic, prophet; wife of Ulf Gudmarrson; mother of eight, including St. Catherine. She reformed much of the lapsed attitude in the convents, cared for the sick, and was the founder of a monastery in Vadstena. For some reason, Bridget was canonized three times. Also patron of Sweden; she is invoked against miscarriages. Canonized 1391; feast day, July 23.

HEALTH WORKERS: Martin de Porres, laybrother. Peruvian (1579–1639). A barber-surgeon apprentice before joining the laybrothers. He attended to the African slaves brought into Peru, was founder of an orphanage and a foundling hospital, and experienced bilocation and aerial flights. Also patron of hairstylists (men), interracial justice, public education, and race relations. Canonized 1962; feast day, November 3.

HEART ATTACK SUFFERERS: Teresa of Avila, nun. Spanish (1515–1582). She was forced to leave the convent because of her failing health. Teresa then founded sixteen convents, several reform monasteries, and authored several books, including *The Interior Castle*. She was the first woman to be declared a Doctor of the Church. Also invoked against headaches. Canonized 1622; feast day, October 15.

HEART PATIENTS: John of God, founder. Portuguese (1495–1550). He went from soldier, to shepherd, to drifter, to bookseller. At forty, he heard a sermon by John of Avila and went mad with guilt. John of Avila visited him in his cell, where John of God confessed his sins and converted to Christianity. Building a hospital, he devoted his life to the care of the sick and needy.

John died trying to save a man from drowning. He was named founder of the Brothers Hospitallers after his death. Also patron of alcoholism, booksellers, hospitals, nurses, printers, and the sick. Canonized 1690; feast day, March 8.

HEIRS: Felicity and her seven sons, martyrs. Romans (2nd century). Pious legend. This young widow had seven sons. Their strong Christian faith caught the attention of Antoninus Pius, who attempted to persuade Felicity and her sons to worship pagan gods. When his promises and threats failed, Antoninus had the boys sentenced to death in seven different courts. Felicity was forced to witness each execution, then was beheaded. Also patron of barren women and children's death. Feast day, July 10.

HEMORRHAGING, INVOKED AGAINST: Lucy, martyr. Italian (4th century). Pious myth. It is said that she was once told how pretty her eyes were by an arranged suitor. Lucy gouged them from their sockets and handed them to her horrified future husband, who promptly had her condemned for her Christian beliefs. Proving to be flame-proof when flung into the fire, Lucy was eventually stabbed in the throat. Her name translates to "light." Also patron of cutlers and writers; she is invoked against eye trouble. Feast day, December 13.

HEMORRHOIDS, INVOKED AGAINST: Fiacre, hermit. Irish (7th century). Healer; built a refuge for the sick and poor. He was once endowed by St. Faro with all the land he could clear in a single day. When the saint returned at dusk, a large field was clear and ready for planting. The first cabstand in Paris was near the Hotel Saint Fiacre. As a result, the French word for taxi is *fiacre*. Also patron of cab drivers and gardeners; he is invoked against syphilis. Feast day, September 1.

HERMITS: 1) Giles, hermit. English (8th century). A forest hermit, he was wounded with an arrow while protecting a hind he had been suckling for a year. The king was so touched by the cripple's compassion, he appointed Giles as one of his advisors. Also patron of beggars, breast-feeding, horses, the physically disabled, and the woods. Feast day, September 1.

2) Anthony the Great, hermit. Egyptian (251–356). Founder of monasticism, first of the "white martyrs." As a hermit living in a cave, he refused the flock of naked women sent to tempt him. This caused his further retreat to a cave on Mount Kolzim. His followers wore hair shirts while making baskets and brushes to support their intellectual and spiritual search for God. Emperor Constantine was said to visit the wise hermit for counsel. Anthony was over 100 years old when he died. Also patron of amputees, basketweavers, brushmakers, and gravediggers; he is invoked against eczema. Feast day, January 17.

HERNIA SUFFERERS: 1) Conrad, hermit. Italian (14th century). While hunting one day, Conrad set fire to some bushes in an attempt to flush out the wild game. The winds shifted, causing the fire to spread to the village, which caused Conrad to panic and run home. He had decided not to take responsibility for his actions, until he learned that an old man had been accused of the disaster. The man's execution was set for the following morning. Conrad disclosed the truth to his wife, then turned himself in. He was ordered to compensate all of the victims of the fire and pay a heavy fine. Conrad and his wife obliged, then donated what little was left to charity. His wife joined the Poor Clares, and Conrad a hermitage, where he lived for many years. His patronage is due to the high recovery rate of hernia sufferers at his tomb. Feast day, February 19.

2) Drogo, shepherd. Flemish (1105–1189). As a child, Drogo learned that his father died before he was born, and his mother had given her life for his. This left a great impact on the ten-year-old youth of noble lineage. While tending to sheep in his mid-forties, Drogo suffered a ruptured hernia, which disfigured him. He drilled a hole through a wall of the church to be able to attend mass without attracting attention away from the sermon. He lived his remaining forty years in prayer and penitence. Also patron of coffeehouse keepers, homely people, and shepherds. Feast day, April 16.

HOLLAND: Willibrord, missionary. English (658–739). "The Apostle of the Frisians." Willibrord's father chose to live as a hermit, sending the seven-year-old youth to an Irish monastery. At the age of twenty, he was ordained. Venturing off to Holland, Willibrord significantly influenced Christianity there. Feast day, November 7.

HOME BUILDERS: Our Lady of Loretto. In 1291, the Blessed Virgin Mary's home in Nazareth was suddenly found in the town of Loretto, Italy. Researchers have confirmed that the stones of the abode match those of first-century homes in Nazareth. Some say it was placed there by divine intervention, while others feel it was hauled over by the military to protect the holy house from the Muslims. Also patron of lampmakers.

HOMELESS: 1) Benedict Joseph Labre, transient. Boulognian (18th century). He left his wealthy family to search for God. Traveling throughout Europe for three years, he visited every pilgrimage site in his holy quest. Ending up at the Colosseum, Benedict the beggar spent his last years in intense prayer. He died in church. Also patron of beggars, religious orders, and transients. Feast day, April 16.

2) Margaret of Cortona, mystic. Italian (1247–1297). At the age of seven, Margaret's mother suddenly died. Her father remarried a woman who was cruel to the girl. When old enough, Margaret left the farm and moved in with a knight. She was the mistress of the castle for nine years, and she bore a son before her lover's murder. She publicly confessed, then served her penance. Margaret's father turned the two away from his home. It was at this time that Margaret joined the Franciscan tertiaries and began to experience visions and healing powers. She devoted the rest of her life to the neglected. Also patron of midwives, single mothers, and tertiaries. Canonized 1728; feast day, February 22.

HOMELY PEOPLE: 1) Drogo, shepherd. Flemish (1105–1189). As a child, Drogo learned that his father died before he was born, and his mother had given her life for his. This made a great impact on the ten-year-old youth of noble lineage. While tending to sheep in his mid-forties, Drogo suffered a ruptured hernia, which disfigured him. He drilled a hole through a wall of the church to be able to attend mass without attracting attention away from the sermon. He lived his remaining forty years in prayer and penitence. Also patron of coffeehouse keepers, hernia sufferers, and shepherds. Feast day, April 16.

HOPELESS CASES: Jude, apostle. (1st century.) Also known as Thaddaeus and Lebbaeus, and is referred to as the "brother of James." There is doubt among scholars that the Jude who wrote the epistle attributed to him and the Jude of the apostles are one and the same. The former wrote of the apostles in the past tense. He may have been martyred in Persia with St. Simon. Jude's patronage derives from his letters that say one should endure difficulties, as predecessors have done. Also patron of desperate situations. Feast day, October 28.

HORNED CATTLE: Colman, martyr. Irish (11th century). Roman martyrology has a list of 300 saints named Colman. While on a pilgrimage to Jerusalem, Colman was stopped by the suspicious Viennese who, fearing he was a Moravian spy, had Colman tried and hanged. After death, his body showed no sign of decay. The miracles which have since occurred at his grave have confirmed his holiness. Also patron of Austria; he is invoked against hangings. Feast day, October 13.

HORSEMEN: Martin of Tours, bishop. Hungarian (316–397). One night, this soldier came upon a peasant shivering in the doorway. He tore his cape in half and covered the old man with it. Through a dream, Martin saw Christ wearing the half-cloak and awoke a converted man. After his baptism, Martin advanced to the battlefield as a conscientious objector. Martin then left the military to begin his work as one of the forefathers of monasticism, where he and his followers practiced mortification and penance. The people of Tours elected an uneager Martin as their bishop. Leaving his monastery in the countryside, Bishop Martin took his place at the see wearing his animal skins. The oldest church in England is named after him. Also patron of the impoverished and tailors. Feast day, November 8.

HORSES: 1) Hippolytus, martyr. Roman (3rd century). Pious legend. After assisting in the burial of a martyr, this newly baptized soldier was taken before the emperor. Hippolytus was sentenced to be strapped by the ankles to two wild horses. The emperor's men cast the horses in the direction of the harshest landscape, then set the animals free. His fellow Christians followed behind, collecting the fragmented remains of their friend. Hippolytus means "loosed horse." Feast day, August 13.

2) Giles, hermit. English (8th century). A forest hermit, he was wounded with an arrow while protecting a hind he had been suckling for a year. The king was so touched by the cripple's compassion, he appointed Giles as one of his advisors. Also patron of beggars, breastfeeding, hermits, the physically disabled, and the woods. Feast day, September 1.

HOSPITAL ADMINISTRATORS: 1) Basil the Great, bishop. Cappadocian (329–379). Born into a family of saints (both parents, two siblings, and his paternal grandmother), he instituted the first monastery in Asia Minor. Also regarded as the father of Eastern monasticism. Doctor of the Church. Feast day, January 2.

2) Frances Xavier Cabrini, nun. Italian (1850–1917). Mother Cabrini arrived in New York and immediately began to aid the Italian emigrants. She founded hospitals, schools, orphanages, and the Sisters of the Sacred Heart, which has since spread throughout the Americas and back to Europe. She became a citizen in 1909 and was the first American citizen canonized. Also patron of emigrants. Canonized 1946; feast day, November 13.

HOSPITALS: 1) Camillus de Lellis, founder. Italian (1550–1614). A festering inflammation on his foot kept him from joining the Capuchin order. He became a hospital director and was ordained. Camillus then founded the Servants of the Sick, a lay order of male nurses, which organized the first military ambulance task force. Also patron of infirmarians, nurses, and the sick. Feast day, July 14.

2) John of God, founder. Portuguese (1495–1550). He went from soldier, to shepherd, to drifter, to bookseller. At forty, he heard a sermon by John of Avila and went mad with guilt. John of Avila visited him in his cell, where John of God confessed his sins and converted to Christianity. Building a hospital, he devoted his life to the care of the sick and needy. John died trying to save a man from drowning. He was named founder of the Brothers Hospitallers after his death. Also patron of alcoholism, booksellers, heart patients, nurses, printers, and the sick. Canonized 1690; feast day, March 8.

HOTEL EMPLOYEES: Julian the Hospitaler, innkeeper. (Unknown dates.) Pious fiction. He killed a sleeping couple in his bed, fearing adultery. The slain were not an adulterous wife and lover, but his visiting parents. His penance was to build an inn and hospital for the poor at the mouth of a river. Julian was absolved when he gave his bed to an angel, who was disguised as a leper. Also patron of boatmen, circus people, ferrymen, and innkeepers. Feast day, February 12.

HOUSEKEEPERS: Zita, servant. Italian (1218–1278). Legend has it that this servant of the Fatinelli family would take bits of food from her rich employers to give to the poor. One day she was caught by the mistress while leaving the house with her apron stuffed with leftovers. When forced to disclose the contents, roses spilled out onto the floor. Also patron of domestic help, maids and servants. Canonized 1696; feast day, April 27.

HOUSEWIVES: 1) Anne, housewife. Nazarean (1st century B.C.). Grandmother of Jesus; wife of Joachim. Aside from giving birth to the Blessed Mary at the age of forty, little is known of her. Also patron of cabinetmakers, Canada, grandmothers, and women in labor. Feast day, July 26.

2) Monica, mother. Tagastian (331–387). She was married to Patricius, a pagan alcoholic with a bad temper, and converted him to Christianity. With some persistence she also converted her son Augustine, who later became the most distinguished of the Catholic church's intellectuals. Also patron of alcoholism, infidelity, married women, and mothers. Feast day, August 27.

HUNGARY: Stephen, King. Hungarian (975–1038). At the age of twenty-six, Stephen was crowned Hungary's first king. Having been baptized at the age of ten with his father, Duke Geza, King Stephen set out to convert his subjects. He built churches, monasteries, and restructured the government. When his health was to fail him, his son, Emeric, was to be crowned the second king of Hungary. Unfortunately, the young prince was fatally wounded while hunting in 1031. Canonized 1083; feast day, August 16.

HUNTERS: 1) Eustachius (Eustace), martyr. Roman (1st century). Pious legend. One of the fourteen "Holy Helpers." He was a general with Emperor Trajan's army. Eustachius converted to Christianity while hunting a stag with the shape of a crucifix between its antlers. He and his family were burnt to death for refusing to denounce their Christian faith. Also patron of torture victims. Feast day, September 20.

2) Hubert, bishop. French (8th century). He put an end to idol worship in his diocese. The story of Hubert's

conversion to Christianity is remarkably similar to Eustachius' conversion. He was on the trail of a stag, which turned to face him. Between the animal's antlers was the mark of a crucifix. Also patron of dogs and rabies sufferers. Feast day, November 3.

The more we indulge ourselves in soft living and pampered bodies, the more rebellious they will become against the spirit.

—St. Rita of Cascia

ICELAND: Thorlac Thorhallsson, bishop. Icelandic (1133–1193). Receiving the call of God at a very young age, Thorlac became a deacon at fifteen; was ordained at the age of eighteen. Returning from his studies in England, Thorlac founded a monastery in Thykkvíboer. He was selected as the patron of Iceland in 1984. Canonized 1198; feast day, December 23.

ILLEGITIMATE CHILDREN: John-Francis Regis, missionary. French (1507–1640). This Jesuit was not only a profound preacher, but the founder of orphanages and improver of prison conditions. He also established a lace factory as a form of skilled labor for repentant prostitutes. John-Francis worked intensely with the neglected until, suffering from exhaustion, he died at the age of thirty-three. Also patron of lacemakers and medical social workers. Canonized 1737; feast day, June 16.

IMPOTENCE, INVOKED AGAINST: Winwaloe, monk. English (6th century). An unusual statue of this English monk is said to be housed at a church in the city of Brest. The antique figurine was carved with an erect penis. For over a millennium believers have chipped off pieces in a faithful attempt to remedy their deficiencies. Amazingly, its length has not diminished one bit. Feast day, March 3.

2) Gummarus, courtier. Flemish (8th century). Also known as Gomer. As a servant to the court of Pepin, Gummarus married the nefarious Guinimaria. After a number of years of persecution from this brutal woman, Gummarus paid off the money kept from the servants' wages by his wife and joined a hermitage. He founded the abbey at Lierre. Also patron of cowherds, spousal separation, and unhappily married men. Feast day, October 11.

IMPOVERISHED: Martin of Tours, bishop. Hungarian (316–397). One night, this soldier came upon a peasant shivering in the doorway. He tore his cape in half and covered the old man with it. Through a dream, Martin saw Christ wearing the half-cloak and awoke a converted man. After his baptism, Martin advanced to the battlefield as a conscientious objector. Martin then left the military to begin his work as one of the forefathers of monasticism, where he and his followers practiced mortification and penance. The people of Tours elected an uneager Martin as their bishop. Leaving his monastery in the countryside, Bishop Martin took his place at the see wearing his animal skins. The oldest church in England is named after him. Also patron of horsemen and tailors. Feast day, November 8.

INDIA: 1) Our Lady of the Assumption. In 1950, Pope Pius XII surmised that since the Blessed Virgin Mary was born without original sin ("revealed by God as defined as dogma" by Pope Pius IX in 1854), she was elevated (body and soul) to heaven upon her death. Also patron of France, Malta, Paraguay, and South Africa.

2) Thomas, apostle. Galilean (1st century). Brother of St. James; also known as Didymus or the twin; one of the twelve apostles. He was skeptical about the resurrection of Christ (John 20:24–29), until allowed to touch the wounds in the Lord's side and hands; hence the origin of the phrase "Doubting Thomas." The legend of Thomas began after Pentecost. Thomas was assigned the conversion of India, a task he not only dreaded but refused to undertake. Christ himself failed in his attempt through a dream to talk the apostle into going to India. So, the Lord appeared to a merchant named Abban, en route to India, and arranged to have Thomas sold into slavery. Once he realized the direction that his new master was headed, Thomas gave in to the will of God. In India, he was advanced a hefty sum to build a palace for the Parthian king. Instead, he donated the money to the needy. When the king was informed of Thomas' actions, he ordered the execution of the apostle. Just then, the king's brother died and was brought back to life. He told of his glimpse of heaven, which was enough to sway the king. Thomas' patronage stems from the many churches he built during his pilgrimages. He is believed to have been martyred in India. Also patron of architects, construction workers, and East Indies; he is invoked against doubt. Feast day, July 3.

INFANTRYMEN: Maurice, officer. Egyptian (3rd century). Legend. As officer in the Theban Legion, Maurice encouraged his Christian platoon to refuse Maximian Herculius' request to worship pagan gods. Maximian ordered the execution of every tenth man, which proved to be an ineffective deterrent. A second, then third decimation began. Eventually, the entire unit was put to death. Also patron of dyers, knife sharpeners, swordsmiths, and weavers; he is invoked against gout. Feast day, September 22.

INFANTS: 1) Wite, mother. Breton (unknown dates). Religious myth. Also known as Candida, Gwen, and Whyte. It is said that after she gave birth to triplets, a third breast appeared. Feast day, June 1.

2) Nicholas of Tolentino, preacher. Italian (1245–1305). This only child of older parents joined the Augustinians; a dream then directed him to the city of Tolentino. There, he helped neglected children and criminals until his death. According to a Saxon myth, Nicholas once retrieved the body of a man who had drowned the week before, resuscitating him long enough to administer his last rites. Also patron of lost souls and mariners. Feast day, September 10.

INFERTILITY, INVOKED AGAINST: Rita, nun. Italian (1381–1457). An arranged marriage of eighteen years came to an end when her abusive husband was murdered in a brawl. Her two sons sought retribution for their father, but Rita would rather her sons died than become murderers. She prayed for their souls; soon after, the two became ill and died. Rita entered an Augustinian convent on her third attempt (being rejected the first two times for lacking virginity). Hearing a sermon on the crown of thorns, a "thorn-like" wound appeared on her forehead, which stayed with her for the rest of her life. Miracles were accredited to her after her death. Also patron of desperate situations and parenthood; she is invoked against bleeding and marital problems. Canonized 1900; feast day, May 22.

INFIDELITY: 1) Monica, mother. Tagaste (331–387). She was married to Patricius, a pagan alcoholic with a bad temper, and converted him to Christianity. With some persistence she also converted her son Augustine, who later became the most distinguished of the Catholic church's intellectuals. Also patron of alcoholism, housewives, married women, and mothers. Feast day, August 27.

2) Fabiola, founder. Roman (3rd century). After divorcing her abusive husband, she remarried. This prevented her from receiving the Sacraments of the church. Fabiola performed public penance, then founded the first Christian hospital. Pope St. Siricus pardoned Fabiola her sins after her second husband died. Also patron of divorce and widows; she is invoked against physical abuse. Feast day, December 27.

3) Gengulphus, knight. Burgundian (8th century). Also known as Gengulf; one of King Pepin the Short's compatriots. Upon learning of his wife's infidelity, Gengulphus left her, moving to a castle in Avalon. He devoted his time to prayer and aiding the less fortunate. He was murdered while he slept, by his wife's lover. Also patron of knights and spousal separation. Feast day, May 11.

INFIRMARIANS: Camillus de Lellis, founder. Italian (1550–1614). A festering inflammation on his foot kept him from joining the Capuchin order. He became a hospital director and was ordained. Camillus then founded the Servants of the Sick, a laity of male nurses. His order organized the first military ambulance task force. Also patron of hospitals, nurses, and the sick. Feast day, July 14.

INJURIES, INVOKED AGAINST: Aldegonda (Aldegund), nun. Frankish (7th century). Folktale. Born into a family of saints; her parents were Walbert and Bertilia, her sister, Waudru. Her stepmother was insistent that the dedicated Christian marry. Aldegonda hid from her stepmother and fiancé in the woods and was protected by the animals of the forest. Once the search team was called off, Aldegonda joined the Benedictine order. Also invoked against childhood illness. Feast day, January 30.

INNKEEPERS: Julian the Hospitaler, innkeeper. (Unknown dates.) Pious fiction. He killed a sleeping couple in his bed, fearing adultery. The slain were not an adulterous wife and lover, but his visiting parents. His penance was to build an inn and hospital for the poor at the mouth of a river. Julian was absolved when he gave his bed to an angel, who was disguised as a leper. Also patron of boatmen, circus people, ferrymen, and hotel employees. Feast day, February 12.

INNOCENCE: Hallvard, martyr. Norwegian (11th century). Religious folktale. One day this son of a landowner was about to take his boat out for a leisurely day of fishing. A frantic woman burst from the wilderness and told a startled Hallvard that she had wrongly been accused of stealing, then asked for his aid. As the two rowed away, the mob reached the shore. They insisted that the woman be returned; Hallvard continued rowing. Both were then shot with arrows by her pursuers. Also patron of virtue. Feast day, May 15.

INSANITY, INVOKED AGAINST: Fillan, monk. Irish (8th century). Son of St. Kentigerna. Near St. Andrews Monastery, he lived the life of a hermit. Moving to Gledochart, Fillan built a church. For centuries after his death, the insane were dipped in the waters of his fountains, where many made miraculous recoveries. Feast day, January 19.

INTERRACIAL JUSTICE: Martin de Porres, laybrother. Peruvian (1579–1639). A barber-surgeon apprentice before joining the laybrothers. He attended to the African slaves brought into Peru, was founder of an orphanage and a foundling hospital, and experienced bilocation and aerial flights. Also patron of hairstylists (men), health workers, public education, and race relations. Canonized 1962; feast day, November 3.

INTESTINAL DISEASE, INVOKED AGAINST: 1) Elmo (Erasmus), martyr. Italian (4th century). Legend. One legend has him surviving unharmed Emperor Diocletian's order of execution by bonfire during the Christian persecutions. Another has him tortured to death by having his intestines pulled from him by a windlass. The electrical discharge on a ship's masthead, which sometimes occurs before or after a storm, is believed to be a sign that St. Elmo is protecting the vessel. Also patron of sailors; he is invoked against appendicitis and seasickness. Feast day, June 2.

2) Bonaventure of Potenza, founder and bishop. French (800–856). Builder of churches and monasteries. He left his see when a disagreement with the monks of St. Calais arose over jurisdiction, but returned before his death from an intestinal disease. Also invoked against bowel disorders. Feast day, January 7.

INVALIDS: Roch (Rocco), hermit. French (1350–1380). Legend. He tended to plague sufferers in Italy, then became ill himself. Sick and alone, Roch was nourished back to health by a stray dog, who brought him food. He was then imprisoned as a spy by his unknowing uncle, the governor. After Roch's death in prison, a cross-shaped birthmark revealed his true identity. Also patron of the falsely accused; he is invoked against cholera and plagues. Feast day, March 28.

IRELAND: 1) Patrick, bishop. Romano-Briton (389–461). It's difficult to separate the myth from the man. At the age of sixteen, he was abducted from his homeland of Kilpatrick and enslaved in Ireland. After six years of working as a herdsman, he escaped to Gaul, where he was ordained. Returning to Ireland, Patrick carried on the work of St. Pallidius in the successful conversion of much of Ireland. Though the snake is one of his emblems (the other being a shamrock), scholars have ruled out that the creatures were ever native to Irish soil. Also patron of snakes. Feast day, March 17.

2) Bridget (Brigid), nun. Irish (450–525). St. Patrick baptized her parents. Brigid became a nun; she founded the first convent in Ireland, a monastery, and a school of art in Kildare. Also patron of dairyworkers, nuns, and scholars. Feast day, February 1.

3) Columban, missionary. Irish (540–615). Europe acquired a most persuasive monk from Ireland; he founded monasteries in France, Germany, Switzerland, and Italy. In France, he refused to baptize the illegitimate children of King Thierry II; he and all of the other Irish monks were deported. On his way back to Ireland, Columban's ship was thrown off course by a storm, and he was taken in by King Theodebert II of Neustria. Again he founded monasteries. Thierry then defeated Theodebert's army, and once again Columban found himself forced to flee. This time he went to Italy, where he received a warm greeting from King Agilulf. Once again he founded monasteries. Columban left behind a number of sermons and poems. Also patron of poets. Feast day, November 23.

ITALY: Francis of Assisi, founder. Italian (1181–1226). Although never a priest, he is one of the dominant figures of the Christian religion. Born to a wealthy cloth merchant, Francis lived a lavish and irresponsible life. At twenty, he went to war against Perugia, where he was captured and imprisoned. After his release, Francis experienced several visions of Christ. He then renounced his inheritance and founded the Friars Minor. The first person ever to receive stigmata (five wounds, concurring with the five wounds of Christ) while praying, which never healed. He created the first Nativity scene in 1223. Also patron of animals, Catholic action, ecologists, merchants, and zoos. Canonized 1228; feast day, October 4.

2) Catherine of Siena, mystic. Italian (1347–1380). The twenty-fourth of twenty-five children; one of the great Christian mystics; suffered the pain of stigmata without the visible marks; worked tirelessly with leprosy patients; Doctor of the Church. She persuaded Pope Gregory XI to leave Avignon, which returned the papacy to Rome after 68 years. Dictated *Dialogue*, since she was illiterate. Also patron of fire prevention, nursing homes, and spinsters. Canonized 1461; feast day, April 29.

If we wish to keep peace with our neighbor, we should never remind anyone of his natural defects.

—St. Philip Neri

JANITORS: Theobald, layman. Italian (12th century). After rejecting the hand of his employer's daughter, along with a partnership in the family's business, Theobald gained employment as a janitor at the cathedral of Saint Lawrence. Also patron of bachelors and church janitors. Feast day, March 9.

JAPAN: 1) Peter Baptist, martyr. Spanish (1545–1597). He led a group of missionaries into Japan, where they were joined by St. Paul Miki and St. Leo Karasuma. The twenty-six men and boys were martyred. They were hanged on crucifixes, then stabbed, under the order of Emperor Toyotomi Hideyoshi, at Nagasaki. Canonized 1862; feast day, February 6.

2) Francis Xavier, missionary. Spanish Basque (1506–1552). One of the seven founding Jesuits and considered one of the greatest missionaries; pioneer of missionary work in India and the East. He died en route to China.

Also patron of Borneo and foreign missions. Canonized 1602; feast day, December 3.

JAUNDICE SUFFERERS: Albert of Trapani, friar. Italian (17th century). This Carmelite friar tirelessly tended to the plague sufferers of Sicily. Also patron of fever sufferers. Feast day, August 8.

JEALOUSY, INVOKED AGAINST: 1) Elizabeth of Portugal, queen. Aragonian (1271–1336). Niece of Elizabeth of Hungary. King Peter III of Aragon offered his twelve-year-old daughter's hand to King Denis of Portugal. She was constantly interceding as peacemaker between her son, Alfonso, and his father. King Denis once believed her to be endorsing her son for the throne; he then banished Elizabeth from Portugal. After the king's death, Elizabeth joined the Secular Franciscan order and moved to a convent of the Sisters of St. Claire, which she had founded in Coimbra. Also patron of brides, tertiaries, and war; she is invoked against marital problems. Canonized 1626; feast day, July 4.

2) Hedwig, Queen. Bavarian (1174–1243). She and her husband, Henry I, supported a number of charities. After Henry's death, Hedwig was beset by her six children's tribulations. Hedwig found solace in a Cistercian abbey, an early endeavor of the royal couple, then committed herself to the care of the indigent. Also patron of Bavaria, children's death, duchesses, queens, and Silesia; she is invoked against marital problems. Feast day, October 16.

JEWELERS: Eligius (Eloi), bishop. French (588–660). As a metalsmith, he crafted two thrones for King Choltar II with the portions of gold and jewels provided to him for one. He was then appointed as the master of the mint and used his influence to help the sick and homeless.

Also patron of farriers, garage workers, and steel workers. Feast day, December 1.

JOURNALISTS: Francis de Sales, bishop, writer. French (1567–1622). He earned a doctorate in law at the age of twenty-four. Within five years, surviving numerous assassination attempts, he managed to convert thousands of Calvinists back to Catholicism. Francis' writings include *Introduction to the Devout Life* (1609) and *Treatise on the Love of God* (1616). He was the first to receive beatification at St. Peter's. Also patron of authors, the Catholic press, the deaf, and writers. Canonized 1877; feast day, January 24.

JURISTS: 1) John of Capistrano, preacher. Italian (1386–1456). As a lawyer, he governed Perugia. As a married man, he was faithful to his wife. John received the calling of God and walked away from it all. After being released from his wedding vows, John joined the Friars Minor. As a crusader, John opposed the Turks, his radical army resisting their threat of conquering Europe. Also patron of chaplains and military chaplains. Canonized 1690; feast day, March 28.

2) Ivo Kermartin (Yves), priest. Breton (1253–1303). He studied law in Paris and Orleans. As an attorney, he represented the poor free of charge. At the age of thirty, Ivo was appointed diocesan judge and proved himself to be incorruptible. He became a priest in 1284, aiding his parishioners in both spiritual and legal matters. Also patron of lawyers. Canonized 1347; feast day, May 19.

. . . Occupy your minds with good thoughts, or the enemy will find the bad ones. Unoccupied they cannot be.

—St. Thomas More

KIDNAPING VICTIMS: Arthelius, young woman. Constantinopolitan (544–560). Pious myth. Emperor Justinian had chosen this young woman as his bride. Her family sent her to live with her uncle, before the emperor could be alerted. On her way to Benevento, Arthelius' beauty caught the eye of three bandits, who abducted her. After three days of prayer, Arthelius escaped. She made it to Benevento, where she was greeted by the entire village. She died at the age of sixteen, during a fast. Feast day, March 3.

KIDNEY DISEASE, INVOKED AGAINST: Albinus, martyr. Albanian (3rd century). He left his homeland of Albania when it was conquered by the Arians. St. Ambrose appointed him bishop and assigned him and St. Ursus to Gaul, where they were beheaded. Also invoked against gallstones. Feast day, June 21.

KINGS: 1) Vladimir, King. Russian (975–1015). He murdered his half brother, Yarapolk, ruler of Russia, then crowned himself king of Russia. He led a reign of terror until his conversion to Catholicism in 989. Giving up his five wives and dozen concubines, Vladimir demanded that all his subjects in Kiev become baptized. This marked the beginning of Catholicism in Russia. Also patron of converts, murderers, and Russia. Feast day, July 15.

2) Louis IX, King. French (1214–1270). Crowned king of France at the age of twelve; married Margaret, sister of Eleanor, wife of Henry III; fathered eleven children; launched France's first navy. Louis participated in two crusades: Damietta in Egypt, where the good king and his men emerged triumphant, and Mansurah, where the defeated king was taken prisoner. After six years, he was set free. Louis died of typhoid while venturing off on his third crusade, to Tunisia. Also patron of crusaders, grooms, and parenthood. Feast day, August 25.

3) Olaf II, King. Norwegian (995–1030). This future king began his career as a Viking, taking Norway from the Swedes and the Danes. In 1016, he became the king of Norway, and he attempted to force Christianity onto his subjects. This created a retaliation by many of his subjects who, with the help of the Anglo-Danish king, ousted Olaf from power. Olaf died in battle, attempting to recoup his losses. Also patron of carvers and Norway. Feast day, July 29.

KNIFE SHARPENERS: Maurice, officer. Egyptian (3rd century). Legend. As officer in the Theban Legion, Maurice encouraged his Christian platoon to refuse Maximian Herculius' request to worship pagan gods. Maximian ordered the execution of every tenth man, which proved to be an ineffective deterrent. A second, then third decimation began. Eventually, the entire unit was put to death. Also patron of dyers, infantrymen, swordsmiths, and weavers; he is invoked against gout. Feast day, September 22.

KNIGHTS: Gengulphus, knight. Burgundian (8th century). Also known as Gengulf; one of King Pepin the Short's compatriots. Upon learning of his wife's infidelity, Gengulphus left her, moving to a castle in Avalon. He devoted his time to prayer and aiding the less fortunate. He was murdered while he slept, by his wife's lover. Also patron of infidelity and spousal separation. Feast day, May 11.

KOREA: 1) Blessed Virgin Mary. (1st century.) Mother of God. The second holiest person (Christ, her son, is first); daughter of Anne and Joachim; born free of original sin; wife of Joseph; impregnated by the Holy Spirit; mother of Jesus; witness to Christ's first miracle in Cana, where he turned water into wine (John 2:1–11); was present when Christ was nailed to the cross (John 19:25–27); prayed for her son after his death (Acts 1:12–14). Her body was raised to heaven upon her death, where it was reunited with her soul. Mary is the most sought-after saint in heaven. She has appeared with messages and prophesies and is venerated throughout the world. Also patron of mothers and virgins. Feast day, August 15.

2) Joseph, carpenter. Nazarean (1st century). Descendent of David; husband to the Virgin Mary; foster father to Jesus Christ. Joseph had second thoughts about marrying Mary when he learned that she was pregnant until the angel Gabriel explained the Messiah's coming. After the birth of Christ, he was forewarned in a dream of Herod's exploits, so he took his young family to Egypt. After Herod's death, a dream directed them to

return to Israel. Fearing Herod's replacement, Joseph chose to settle his family in Nazareth. Scholars believe he died before the crucifixion of Christ. Also patron of Belgium, Canada, carpenters, the church, the dying, fathers, Peru, social justice, and working men. Feast days, March 19 and May 1.

Anger is a kind of temporary madness.

—St. Basil

LABORERS: 1) Isidore the Farmer, layman. Spanish (1070–1130). A hired hand who worked miracles and shared what little he had with those few who were less fortunate. Also patron of farmers. Canonized 1622; feast day, May 10.

2) John Bosco, founder. Italian (1815–1888). He and his mother established a refuge for boys. Their "boys town" offered education and apprenticeships in various trades for homeless and exploited youths. He then opened the Daughters of Mary of Christians for neglected girls. He authored three books to help finance his centers. Also patron of apprentices and editors. Canonized 1934; feast day, January 31.

LACEMAKERS: John-Francis Regis, missionary. French (1507–1640). This Jesuit was not only a profound preacher, but the founder of orphanages and improver of prison conditions. He also established a lace factory as a form of skilled labor for repentant prostitutes. John-

Francis worked intensely with the neglected until, suffering from exhaustion, he died at the age of thirty-three. Also patron of illegitimate children and medical social workers. Canonized 1737; feast day, June 16.

LAMPMAKERS: Our Lady of Loretto. In 1291, the Blessed Virgin Mary's home in Nazareth was suddenly found in the town of Loretto, Italy. Researchers have confirmed that the stones of the abode match those of first-century homes in Nazareth. Some say it was placed there by divine intervention, while others feel it was hauled over by the military, to protect the holy house from the Muslims. Also patron of home builders.

LAUNDRESSES: 1) Veronica, laywoman. (1st century.) According to tradition, Veronica is the woman who wiped Christ's perspiration when he was carrying the cross to his crucifixion. The name Veronica actually means *vera icon* or "true image." Feast day, July 12.

2) Hunna, matron. Alsace (7th century). This wife of a nobleman chose to fill her hours by serving the destitute. They affectionately referred to her as "the Holy Washerwoman," a name she earned by doing their laundry. Canonized 1520; feast day, April 15.

LAWSUITS: Agia, widow. Flemish (7th century). Pious myth. Upon her demise, this wealthy woman bequeathed her entire fortune to a prisoner by the name of Mons. When her family contested the will, Agia ominously testified on behalf of Mons from her grave. Feast day, April 18.

LAWYERS: 1) Thomas More, martyr. English (1478–1535). Writer, lawyer. Opposed King Henry VIII's divorce of Catherine of Aragon; he was imprisoned for not signing the Act of Succession, which acknowledged Henry and Anne Boleyn's child as England's heir. He was then accused of treason and eventually beheaded. Also patron of adopted children. Canonized 1935; feast day, June 22.

2) Ivo Kermartin (Yves), priest. Breton (1253–1303). He studied law in Paris and Orleans. As an attorney, he represented the poor free of charge. At the age of thirty, Ivo was appointed diocesan judge and proved himself to be incorruptible. He became a priest in 1284, aiding his parishioners in both spiritual and legal matters. Canonized 1347; feast day, May 19.

3) Genesius, martyr. Roman (3rd century). Legend. This comedian converted to Christianity while performing a farce of Christian baptism on stage for the Emperor Diocletian in Rome. For refusing the emperor's order to recant, Genesius was tortured, then beheaded while still on stage. Also patron of actors, printers, secretaries, and stenographers. Feast day, August 25.

LEARNING: Ambrose, bishop. Italian (340–397). His contributions were key to the advancement of Christianity during the decline of the Roman Empire. St. Anthony converted to Christianity after hearing a sermon by Ambrose. Also patron of bees and chandlers. Feast day, December 7.

LEATHERWORKERS: Crispin and Crispinian, martyrs. Roman (3rd century). Legend. These brothers were Christian converters by day and shoemakers by night. Their torturer, Maximian, took his own life in frustration when his attempts to execute the siblings failed. The two were then beheaded. Also patrons to cobblers, saddlers, shoemakers, and tanners. Feast day, October 25.

LECTORS: 1) Pollio, martyr. Roman (4th century). As a church lector during the times of Christian persecutions,

Pollio was charged with verbally defying the Emperor Diocletian's orders. He was then burnt at the stake. Feast day, April 28.

2) Sabas, martyr. Romanian (4th century). According to legend, Sabas was a cantor in Sansalas who, along with fifty other disciples, was martyred for refusing to eat food that had been dedicated to pagan gods. His public outburst against the practice was the cause of his drowning. Feast day, April 12.

LEG DISORDERS, INVOKED AGAINST: Servatius, bishop. Armenian (4th century). This native Armenian gave refuge to St. Athanasius while he was in exile. Servatius foresaw the invasion of the Huns seventy years before Attila devastated Gaul, then died shortly after he returned from a penitential trip to Rome. His staff, cup, and a key, presented to him by St. Peter's apparition, are kept in Maestricht. Also patron to successful enterprises; he is invoked against vermin. Feast day, May 13.

LESOTHO: Immaculate/Sacred Heart of Mary. In 1942, Pope Pius XII sanctified the holiness of Mary's heart, which has since been revered as the embodiment of purity and mercy. In order to achieve the Sacred Heart one must follow the code of the decent Christian: go to mass, recite the rosary, and receive communion, all of which must be done on a regular basis. Also patron of Angola, Ecuador, and the Philippines.

LIBERAL ARTS: Catherine of Bologna, visionary. French (1413–1463). Also known as Catherine de Virgi. She is probably best remembered for her vision on Christmas Day of the infant Jesus cradled in Mary's arms, still a popular subject for artists. Died the prioress of the new

Poor Clares' Corpus Christi Convent. Also patron of art. Canonized 1712; feast day, March 9.

LIBRARIES: Jerome, scholar. Dalmatian (342–420). Best known for translating the Bible from Hebrew and Greek to Latin. The Vulgate volume was the primary biblical source for Roman Catholicism until 1979, when Pope John Paul II updated it with the New Vulgate. Feast day, September 30.

LIES, INVOKED AGAINST: Felix, priest. Nolan (3rd century). All that is known of Felix comes from a poem by Paulinus, one hundred years after his death. After Felix escaped the Emperor Decius' tyranny, Felix went in search of Bishop Maximus of Nola, who had gone into hiding. He found the dying man and carried him to a safe refuge. The emperor's soldiers had been tipped off that Felix was back and went to arrest him. He hid in an abandoned dwelling, where a spider spun its web across the entrance, fooling the mob. Felix rejected an offer of the see after Bishop Maximus died and lived his days out in piety. Feast day, January 14.

LIGHTHOUSE KEEPERS: Venerius, bishop. Italian (5th century). As the second bishop of Milan, Venerius assisted the Council of Carthage in 401. According to Pope John XXIII, "because the radiance of his life shone out," Venerius was honored with this particular patronage. Canonized 1961; feast day, September 13.

LINGUISTS: Gotteschalc, Prince. German (11th century). This student of St. Michael broke with Christianity when he learned of his father Uto's death. While avenging his father, Gotteschalc was captured and imprisoned by Saxons. Upon his release, he returned to his native land and was confirmed once again to Christianity. Also patron of princes. Feast day, June 7.

LITHUANIA: Casimir, Prince. Polish (1458–1484). Also known as the "Peace Maker." King Casimir ordered the young prince to seize Hungary. Casimir's refusal left the king with no choice but to imprison his thirteenth child. Prince Casimir never wavered, praying to the Blessed Virgin Mary for hours on end. He died after his release in Lithuania. Also patron of Poland and princes. Canonized 1522; feast day, March 4.

LOCKSMITHS: Dunstan, bishop. English (910–988). One of the great reformers of church life in England during the tenth century. He rectified Bath and Westminster Abbey. He was advisor to King Edwy, until his accusation of the king's sexual exploits caused Dunstan's exile. A skillful metalworker and harpist. Also patron of armorers, blacksmiths, goldsmiths, musicians, and silversmiths. Feast day, May 19.

LONGEVITY: Peter, apostle. Bethsaidan (1st century). Son of Jonah; brother of Andrew; first pope; witness of the transfiguration and the agony of Jesus in the garden. Peter once walked on water, then sank when he hesitated; denied the Lord three times; asked to be hanged upside down when crucified in Rome. The representation of Peter as the gatekeeper of the pearly gates stems from Christ once symbolically endowing the "keys to the kingdom" to his chief apostle. Also patron of fishermen and the papacy. Feast day, June 29.

LOST ARTICLES: Anthony of Padua, preacher. Portuguese (1195–1231). Born Ferdinand; known as "the Wonder Worker" for his preaching savvy; the first lector in theology; Doctor of the Church; colleague of St.

Francis of Assisi. A disciple once took Anthony's psalter without asking. The terrorized novice promptly returned it, claiming that he was being haunted by apparitions for his act. Also the patron of barren women, the poor, Portugal, shipwrecks, and travelers; he is invoked against starvation. Canonized 1232; feast day, June 13.

LOST SOULS: Nicholas of Tolentino, preacher. Italian (1245–1305). This only child of older parents joined the Augustinians; a dream then directed him to the city of Tolentino. There, he helped neglected children and criminals until his death. According to a Saxon myth, Nicholas once retrieved the body of a man who had drowned the week before, resuscitating him long enough to administer his last rites. Also patron of infants and mariners. Feast day, September 10.

LOVERS: 1) Raphael, archangel. One of the seven archangels of God; one of the three archangels specified by name in the Bible. He has been venerated by both Jewish and Christian faiths. His name means "God heals." Also patron of the blind, nurses, physicians, and travelers. Feast day, September 29.

2) Valentine, martyr. Roman (3rd century). He was beheaded and buried on February 14. It is said that birds began to pair at the moment of his death. Also patron of engaged couples and greetings. Feast day, February 14.

LUNATICS: Christina the Astonishing, laywoman. Flemish (1150–1224). At the age of twenty-one, Christina had a seizure which appeared to kill her. During her funeral mass, Christina opened her eyes, then flew to the rafters of the cathedral. She landed on the altar and spoke of her journey through heaven, hell, purgatory, and back. Christina believed she was released from the afterlife to pray for the souls in purgatory. It is said that Christina was never the same, being repulsed by the scent of people. She would hide in small spaces, such as cupboards or ovens. Christina died in St. Catherine's convent some years later. Also patron of therapists. Feast day, July 24.

He who loves himself, loves all men.

—St. Anthony the Great

MADMEN: Romanus, founder. French (5th century). With a book on hermits, some seeds and a few utensils, Romanus found a secluded spot to build his monastery. He then sent for his brother, St. Lupicinus, who was followed by a number of disciples. Together, they built a monastery in Condat, Lueconne, and a convent in La Beaume, to which their sister was appointed abbess. Romanus' patronage stems from curing two madmen while on pilgrimage to Valais. Feast day, February 28.

MAGISTRATES: Ferdinand III, King. Castilian (1198–1252). Married Princess Beatrice; fathered ten children. He and King Alfonso, his father, teamed up to drive the Moors out of Spain. He was the founder of the University of Salamanca and the cathedral of Burgos, and reformer of the canon code of laws. Also patron of engineers, governors, parenthood, and rulers. Canonized 1671; feast day, May 30.

MAIDENS: Catherine, martyr. Alexandrian (4th century). Religious legend. This woman of noble birth chose to study philosophy rather than relish her beauty. Her conversion to Christianity was prompted by a hermit's dream. She then converted Emperor Maxentius' wife, an officer, and two hundred soldiers. In retaliation, the emperor gathered fifty pagan scholars, then challenged her to a religious debate. After a long and heated exchange, Catherine's words swayed all of the fifty scholars to convert. Maxentius had Catherine tied to a wheel, which immediately broke into pieces. She was then beheaded. Also patron of eloquence, philosophers, preachers, single women, spinners, and students. Feast day, November 25.

MAIDS: Zita, servant. Italian (1218–1278). Legend has it that this servant of the Fatinelli family would take bits of food from her rich employers to give to the poor. One day she was caught by the mistress while leaving the house with her apron stuffed with leftovers. When forced to disclose the contents, roses spilled out onto the floor. Also patron of domestic help, housekeepers, and servants. Canonized 1696; feast day, April 27.

MALTA: 1) Paul, apostle. Roman (1st century). "The Great Apostle." A tentmaker by trade, Paul was a Jew named Saul who was one of the tormenters of the early Christians, until Christ's voice from heaven asked him why he was persecuting "His people." After converting, Paul traveled to Jerusalem, where he was welcomed by the apostles. From there, Paul ventured on three crucial missionary trips throughout Europe and Asia Minor. He converted thousands and authored fourteen New Testament letters. Paul and St. Peter were arrested in Rome. Paul was beheaded, and St. Peter was crucified upside down during Emperor Nero's persecutions of Christians.

Paul was once shipwrecked on Malta while en route to Rome, yet managed to board another vessel, continuing on to his destination and his martyrdom. Also patron of public relations and tentmakers; he is invoked against snake bites. Feast day, June 29.

2) Our Lady of the Assumption. In 1950, Pope Pius XII surmised that since the Blessed Virgin Mary was born without original sin (Pope Pius IX, 1854), she was elevated (body and soul) to heaven upon her death. Also patron of France, India, Paraguay, and South Africa.

MARBLE WORKERS: Clement I, martyr. Roman (1st–2nd century). The third pope (Peter was the first, Cletus was the second). When Emperor Trajan banished Clement from Rome, he was forced to work the quarries in Russia. It is said that during a water shortage in the mines, a spring suddenly flowed from the earth, quenching the prisoners' thirst. Clement founded seventy-five churches in his absence from Rome. He was martyred when thrown into the Black Sea with an anchor tied to him. Also patron of stonecutters. Feast day, November 23.

MARINERS: 1) Cuthbert, bishop. Northumbrian (7th century). This orphan grew up to be a soldier. He left the battle against the Mercians to become a monk. While a hermit on the Farne Islands, Cuthbert was called by St. Eata to be bishop of Lindisfarne. There he miraculously cured plague sufferers until his own death. Feast day, March 20.

2) Michael, archangel. One of the seven archangels of God; one of the three archangels mentioned by name in the Bible. He is cited twice in the Old Testament, appearing to Moses and Abraham. In the New Testament, he contends with Satan for the body of Moses and tosses Lucifer and his cohorts from heaven. In art, he is

often depicted with a scale (representing the weighing of souls) in one hand, while slaying a dragon (Satan) with the other. Also patron of battle, the dead, grocers, paratroopers, police officers, and radiologists. Feast day, September 29.

3) Nicholas of Tolentino, preacher. Italian (1245–1305). This only child of older parents joined the Augustinians; a dream then directed him to the city of Tolentino. There, he helped neglected children and criminals until his death. According to a Saxon myth, Nicholas once retrieved the body of a man who had drowned the week before, resuscitating him long enough to administer his last rites. Also patron of infants and lost souls. Feast day, September 10.

MARITAL PROBLEMS, INVOKED AGAINST: 1) Elizabeth of Portugal, queen. Aragonian (1271–1336). Niece of Elizabeth of Hungary. King Peter III of Aragon offered his twelve-year-old daughter's hand to King Denis of Portugal. She was constantly interceding as peacemaker between her son, Alfonso, and his father. King Denis once believed her to be endorsing her son for the throne; he then banished Elizabeth from Portugal. After the king's death, Elizabeth joined the Secular Franciscan order and moved to a convent of the Sisters of St. Claire, which she had founded in Coimbra. Also patron of brides, tertiaries, and war; she is invoked against jealousy. Canonized 1626; feast day, July 4.

2) Rita, nun. Italian (1381–1457). An arranged marriage of eighteen years came to an end when her abusive husband was murdered in a brawl. Her two sons sought retribution for their father, but Rita would rather her sons died than become murderers. She prayed for their souls; soon after, the two became ill and died. Rita entered an Augustinian convent on her third attempt (be-

ing rejected the first two times for lacking virginity). Hearing a sermon on the crown of thorns, a "thornlike" wound appeared on her forehead, which stayed with her for the rest of her life. Miracles were accredited to her after her death. Also patron of desperate situations and parenthood; she is invoked against bleeding and infertility. Canonized 1900; feast day, May 22.

3) Pharaildis, housewife. Flemish (8th century). When she was of marrying age, her parents betrothed her to a man of wealth. The vow of virginity to God that Pharaildis had taken as a youth angered her hottempered husband. He constantly abused her both physically and emotionally until his death. Pharaildis once caused a well to spring at Braug. Its water is believed to cure children of disease. Also invoked against childhood diseases and physical abuse. Feast day, January 4.

4) Hedwig, Queen. Bavarian (1174–1243). She and her husband, Henry I, supported a number of charities. After Henry's death, Hedwig was beset by her six children's tribulations. Hedwig found solace in a Cistercian abbey, an early endeavor of the royal couple, then committed herself to the care of the indigent. Also patron of Bavaria, children's death, duchesses, queens, and Silesia; she is invoked against jealousy. Feast day, October 16.

MARRIED WOMEN: Monica, mother. Tagastean (331–387). She was married to Patricius, a pagan alcoholic with a bad temper, and converted him to Christianity. With some persistence she also converted her son Augustine, who later became the most distinguished of the Catholic church's intellectuals. Also patron of alcoholism, housewives, infidelity, and mothers. Feast day, August 27.

MEDICAL SOCIAL WORKERS: John-Francis Regis, missionary. French (1507–1640). This Jesuit was not only a profound preacher, but the founder of orphanages and improver of prison conditions. He also established a lace factory as a form of skilled labor for repentant prostitutes. John-Francis worked intensely with the neglected until, suffering from exhaustion, he died at the age of thirty-three. Also patron of illegitimate children and lacemakers. Canonized 1737; feast day, June 16.

MEDICAL TECHNICIANS: Albert the Great, theologian. German (1206–1280). "The Universal Doctor." A great intellectual of the medieval church; mentor to St. Thomas Aquinas; believed the earth to be round; a pioneer of natural sciences. Also patron of scientists. Canonized 1931; feast day, November 15.

MENTAL DISORDERS, INVOKED AGAINST: Dymphna, martyr. Irish (7th century). Folktale. She and her confessor ran away from her incestuous father, a pagan chieftain. In Belgium, the two lived as hermits in an oratory they had built, until her father and his men hunted them down. The confessor was murdered and Dymphna was beheaded for refusing to return home. Many have been cured at Dymphna's tomb. Also patron of epileptics and runaways; she is invoked against diabolic possession and sleepwalking. Feast day, May 15.

MERCHANTS: 1) Francis of Assisi, founder. Italian (1181–1226). Although never a priest, he is one of the dominant figures of Christian religion. Born to a wealthy cloth merchant, Francis lived a lavish and irresponsible life. At twenty, he went to war against Perugia, where he was captured and imprisoned. After his release, Francis experienced several visions of Christ. He then renounced his inheritance and founded the Friars Minor. The first person ever to receive stigmata (five wounds, concurring with the five wounds of Christ) while praying, which never healed. Also patron of animals, Catholic action, ecologists, Italy, and zoos. He created the Nativity scene in 1223. Canonized 1228; feast day, October 4.

2) Nicholas of Myra, bishop. Lycian (4th century). Better known as Saint Nick. The facts are few. He ran a monastery, was a prisoner during the time of Christian persecutions, and was present at the Council of Nicaea. The rest is myth. One tale tells of a father who was so poor he couldn't afford his three daughters' dowries. Nick tossed three bags of gold through the kitchen window, and the three daughters married soon after. Also patron of boys, brides, children, dockworkers, Greece, pawnbrokers, spinsters, and travelers. Feast day, December 6.

MESSENGERS: Gabriel, archangel. Messenger of God. One of the seven archangels of God; one of the three archangels referred to by name in the Bible. Announced the birth of Jesus to Mary (Luke 1:11–21). Also patron of broadcasters, clerics, diplomats, postal workers, radio workers, stamp collectors, telecommunications workers, and television workers.

MEXICO: Our Lady of Guadalupe. Tepeyac, Mexico. In the winter of 1531, Juan Diego was walking on a hillside where he was visited by the Virgin Mary. Declaring herself as the "Mother of the true God who gives life," she instructed Juan to build a church in her honor. Juan explained Mary's request to Bishop Juan de Zumarraga, who asked for a sign as proof of her appearance. When Juan returned to the hill, he found it covered with roses in full bloom. Juan filled his *tilma* (shawl) at Mary's request, then took the bundle back to the bishop's residence. Juan opened the tilma, letting the roses spill onto the floor, and there on the cloth emerged the likeness of an olive-complexioned Virgin Mary. Also patron of North America.

MIDWIVES: 1) Margaret of Cortona, mystic. Italian (1247–1297). At the age of seven, Margaret's mother suddenly died. Her father remarried a woman who was cruel to the girl. When old enough, Margaret left the farm and moved in with a knight. She was the mistress of the castle for nine years, and she bore a son before her lover's murder. She publicly confessed, then served her penance. Margaret's father turned the two away from his home. It was at this time that Margaret joined the Franciscan tertiaries and began to experience visions and healing powers. She devoted the rest of her life to the neglected. Also patron of the homeless, single mothers, and tertiaries. Canonized 1728; feast day, February 22.

2) Raymond Nonnatus, cardinal. Spanish (1204–1240). He was taken from his dying mother by cesarian section. As a Mercedarian, he ransomed himself to the Moors in exchange for the freedom of slaves and Christian hostages. He converted within the prison walls, which angered the Muslims. His jailers realized that his ransom would exceed those of the other prisoners, so Raymond was continuously tortured for preaching. Negotiations for his release took eight months. Also patron of the falsely accused, childbirth, obstetricians, and pregnant women. Canonized 1657; feast day, August 31.

MIGRAINE SUFFERERS: Gereon, soldier. Roman (3rd century). Similar to the story of St. Maurice and his legion, Gereon and his soldiers refused to worship pagan gods before battle. All 290 of the "Golden Saints," as they are known, were martyred under Emperor Maximian's order. Feast day, October 10.

MILITARY: Theodore Tiro, martyr (4th century). Pious myth. After he refused to worship pagan idols, his battalion turned in the young recruit. Theodore admitted to his faith in one God, but was released from the charges. He found himself before the emperor a second time, after torching a pagan idol; his punishment was a severe flogging. An angel came down from heaven and nursed his wounds. He was summoned to a third and final trial before the emperor. This time he was sentenced to an execution by fire. Feast day, November 9.

MILITARY CHAPLAINS: John of Capistrano, preacher. Italian (1386–1456). As a lawyer, he governed Perugia. As a married man, he was faithful to his wife. John received the calling of God and walked away from it all. After being released from his wedding vows, John joined the Friars Minor. As a crusader, John opposed the Turks, his radical army resisting their threat of conquering Europe. Also patron of chaplains and jurists. Canonized 1690; feast day, March 28.

MILLERS: 1) Victor of Marseilles, martyr. Gaulish (3rd century). Pious legend. When Emperor Maximian discovered that his favorite Roman guard was a Christian, Victor was subjected to a number of tortures. As he was being stretched on a rack for refusing to worship pagan deities, Jesus Christ appeared to Victor. That night, God sent his angels to his cell, causing the conversion of three prison guards. The next day, Emperor Maximian had the new converts beheaded. Victor was brought before the emperor again. Maximian ordered the battered man to offer incense to Jupiter. Victor kicked the statue, which enraged Maximian. The Christian's foot was ordered to be hacked off before he was crushed in a mill. The grindstone broke about halfway through the execution, yet a partially pulverized Victor still lived on. One of his executioners drew a sword and beheaded him. Also patron of torture victims; he is invoked against foot trouble. Feast day, July 21.

2) Arnulf, bishop. Flemish (1040–1087). He was a soldier in the armies of Robert and Henry I of France before he received his calling. While at Saint-Medard, Arnulf was named bishop of Soissons. In art, Arnulf stands with a baker's shovel, hence his patronage. Also patron of flour industry workers. Feast day, August 15.

MINERS: Barbara, martyr. (4th century.) Religious fiction. A young woman whose pagan father locked her in a tower before leaving on a long journey. Within the walls, she converted to Christianity and had three windows built to signify the Trinity. When her father returned, he was so infuriated by his daughter's religious preference, he turned her over to the authorities. Barbara was subjected to heinous torture, yet refused to disavow her faith. The judge ordered the father to kill her himself. Atop a mountain he slew his daughter, then was immediately struck dead by a bolt of lightning. Also patron of architects, builders, dying, fire prevention, founders, prisoners, and stonemasons. Feast day, December 4.

MISCARRIAGES, INVOKED AGAINST: 1) Dorothy of Montau, mystic. Prussian (14th century). In the twenty-five years of her marriage to Albert, Dorothy gave birth nine times. Only the youngest of her children survived to adulthood. When her disdainful husband died, Dorothy moved into a hermit's cell. There she healed and counseled visitors in the last year of her life. Also patron of Prussia. Feast day, October 30.

2) Bridget of Sweden, Princess. Swedish (1303–1373). Mystic, prophet; wife of Ulf Gudmarrson; mother of eight, including St. Catherine. She reformed

much of the lapsed attitude in the convents, cared for the sick, and was the founder of a monastery in Vadstena. For some reason, Bridget was canonized three times. Also patron of healers and Sweden. Canonized 1391; feast day, July 23.

MISFORTUNE, INVOKED AGAINST: Agricola of Avignon, bishop. French (630–700). At the age of thirty, his father, Bishop (Saint) Magnus, appointed Agricola to co-bishop Avignon, thus creating a rare father and son team in the Roman Catholic church. He is best known for a prayer that ended an invasion of storks. Also patron of good weather and rain; he is invoked against bad luck and plague. Feast day, September 2.

MISSIONS, FOREIGN: 1) Francis Xavier, missionary. Spanish Basque (1506–1552). One of the seven founding Jesuits and considered one of the greatest missionaries; pioneer of missionary work in India and the East. He died en route to China. Also patron of Borneo and Japan. Canonized 1602; feast day, December 3.

2) Therese of Lisieux, nun. French (1873–1897). Also known as "The Little Flower." She and her five sisters became Carmelite nuns. Author of *The Story of a Soul,* Therese wrote that she would "let fall a shower of roses" (miracles) when she passed on. Dying of tuberculosis on September 30, she kept her word. Also patron of aviators, florists, and France. Canonized 1925; feast day, October 1.

MISSIONS, PARISH: 1) Leonard of Port Maurice, priest. Italian (1676–1751). This Jesuit student became a Franciscan of the Strict Observance, then directed the missions of Italy. Feast day, November 26.

2) Benedict the Black, laybrother. Sicilian (1526–1589). While still a youth, Benedict's master freed him

from slavery. Benedict was harassed one afternoon by a group of adolescents for being the son of slaves, yet he never lost his composure. This was witnessed by the head of the Franciscan hermits, who then persuaded Benedict to join the order. Eventually, he became the superior before it disbanded. He was then assigned as cook to another order, where once again Benedict became its superior. He then asked to be reduced to cook status at yet another community. Also patron of African Americans. Feast day, April 4.

MONACO: Devota, martyr. Corsican (3rd century). This young Christian was dragged through the streets of Corsica, then pulled on a rack, yet refused to recant. It is said that a dove appeared at the moment of her death, which was followed by two men in a boat. They buried her remains on the spot where the dove landed, in Monaco. Also patron of Corsica. Feast day, January 17.

MONKS: Benedict of Nursia, monk. Italian (480–547). Accredited as the father of Western monasticism. At fourteen, he left his noble family and sister, St. Scholastica, to further his studies in Rome; at twenty, he chose the life of a hermit and moved into a cave; at thirty, he had founded a dozen monasteries. Benedict's book of holy rules became the model for monastic life throughout Europe for centuries. After a poisoning attempt by a jealous monk named Florentius, who found his methods too fastidious, Benedict left the position of abbot. He systemized a dozen monasteries, establishing Western monasticism. Also patron of Europe and speleologists; he is invoked against poison and witchcraft. Feast day, March 21.

MORAVIA: Cyril and Methodius, monk and bishop. Greeks (826–869, 815–885). "Apostles of the Slavs."

These brothers translated the Bible into Slavonic, were the inventors of the Glagotithic alphabet, and founded Slavonic literature. Also patrons of ecumenists. Canonized 1980; feast day, February 14.

MOTHERS: 1) Blessed Virgin Mary. (1st century.) Mother of God. The second holiest person (Christ, her son, is first); daughter of Anne and Joachim; born free of original sin; wife of Joseph; impregnated by the Holy Spirit; mother of Jesus; witness to Christ's first miracle in Cana, where he turned water into wine (John 2:1–11); was present when Christ was nailed to the cross (John 19:25–27); prayed for her son after his death (Acts 1:12–14). Her body was raised to heaven upon her death, where it was reunited with her soul. Mary is the most sought-after saint in heaven. She has appeared with messages and prophesies and is venerated throughout the world. Also patron of Korea and virgins. Feast day, August 15.

2) Monica, mother. Tagaste (331–387). She was married to Patricius, a pagan alcoholic with a bad temper, and converted him to Christianity. With some persistence she also converted her son Augustine, who later became the most distinguished of the Catholic church's intellectuals. Also patron of alcoholism, housewives, infidelity, and married women. Feast day, August 27.

MOTORCYCLISTS: Our Lady of Grace. This title was bestowed upon the Blessed Virgin Mary by the people of the Dominican Republic. In Luke 1:28, she is referred to by the Archangel Gabriel as "full of grace," which is recited in the beginning of the "Hail Mary." Also patron of the Dominican Republic.

MOTORISTS: 1) Christopher, martyr. Lycian (3rd century). Myth. There are a number of legends about the man martyred in Lycia. One goes like this: He was a hideous giant named Offero, who earned a living carrying travelers across the river. He carried a heavy lad one day, claiming to be weighted by the problems of the world. This child, of course, was the youthful Christ. The name Christopher itself means "carrier of Christ" in Greek. Also patron of bachelors, bus drivers, porters, travelers, and truck drivers; he is invoked against nightmares. Feast day, July 25.

2) Frances of Rome, activist. Roman (1384–1440). Devoted her life to plague victims; founded a hospital and the Oblates of Mary. Canonized 1608; feast day, March 9.

MOUNTAINEERS: Bernard of Montijoix, priest. Italian (996–1081). He devoted his forty years as a priest to the residence of the Alps. Builder of schools and churches; best known for Great and Little Bernard, two shelters on mountain passes created for travelers of all religions and origins. Also patron of alpinists and skiers. Feast day, May 28.

MURDERERS: Vladimir, King. Russian (975–1015). He murdered his half brother, Yarapolk, ruler of Russia, then crowned himself king of Russia. He led a reign of terror until his conversion to Catholicism in 989. Giving up his five wives and dozen concubines, Vladimir demanded that all his subjects in Kiev become baptized. This marked the beginning of Catholicism in Russia. Also patron of converts, kings, and Russia. Feast day, July 15.

MUSICIANS: 1) Cecilia, martyr. Roman (unknown dates). Legend. On her wedding day Cecilia was unable to hear the music being performed; instead she only heard herself singing to God. Her husband, Valerian, agreed to live a life of chastity upon Cecilia's request.

She, her husband, and his brother were caught burying the bodies of Christians. The others were beheaded first; her executioner botched her beheading and left her to endure a three-day death. Also patron of composers, organ builders, poets, and singers. Feast day, November 22.

2) Dunstan, bishop. English (910–988). One of the great reformers of church life in England during the tenth century. He rectified Bath and Westminster Abbey. He was advisor to King Edwy, until his accusation of the king's sexual exploits caused Dunstan's exile. A skillful metalworker and harpist. Also patron of armorers, blacksmiths, goldsmiths, locksmiths, and silversmiths. Feast day, May 19.

3) Gregory the Great, pope. Roman (540–604). Originator of the Gregorian chants; Doctor of the Church. His "height of embarrassment," as he put it, occurred when Gregory was named pope in 590. He converted England to Christianity, initiated medieval papacy, and authored fourteen books. Also patron of popes, singers, and teachers. Canonized 604; feast day, September 3.

4) Odo, abbot. French (10th century). Founder and reformer of monasticism; accomplished musician; composer of hymns. His most famous is a hymn to St. Martin. Feast day, November 18.

MYSTICS: John of the Cross, theologian. Castilian (1542–1591). Born Juan de la Cruz. He began to write poetry while imprisoned for attempting to reform his Carmelite order. Authored *The Dark Night of the Soul*, *Spiritual Canticle*, and *Living Flame of Love*. Canonized 1726; feast day, March 8.

Fear is a greater evil than evil itself.

—St. Francis de Sales

NAIL MAKERS: Cloud, hermit. French (6th century). As a lad, Cloud and his two brothers were next in line for the Frankish throne. Their jealous uncles abducted the boys and stabbed Cloud's brothers. Somehow, the eight-year-old managed to escape to Provence. Years later, Cloud became a hermit, declining his birthright as king. Upon his return to Paris, Cloud forgave his uncles and founded a monastery. Feast day, September 7.

NAVAL OFFICERS: Francis of Paola, founder. Italian (1416–1507). At the age of fifteen, Francis chose the life of a hermit; at the age of twenty, he founded his own order, the Minims. He founded a monastery in Plessis, France. Francis' nautical patronages emanate from a tale in which Francis once placed his shawl on the water of an Italian channel and navigated the cloth home. Also patron of seamen. Canonized 1519; feast day, April 2.

NEARSIGHTEDNESS: Clarus, abbot. French (7th century). Clarus means "brightness," a name given to this child for his insight. As the archbishop of Vienne, Clarus became the advisor to a convent in which his mother and sister were nuns. Feast day, January 1.

NEW ZEALAND: Our Lady Help of Christians. In 1964, Pope Paul VI venerated the Blessed Virgin Mary as the protector of Australia and New Zealand.

NICARAGUA: James the Greater, apostle. Galilean (1st century). His name James "the Greater" is to differentiate him from the other apostle, James "the Less." He and his brother John "dropped their fishing nets" at the Sea of Galilee and followed Jesus; they were witnesses to both the transfiguration and the agony of Jesus in the garden. James was beheaded in Jerusalem, the first apostle to be martyred. Also patron of Chile, furriers, Guatemala, pharmacists, pilgrims, and Spain; he is invoked against arthritis and rheumatism. Feast day, July 25.

NIGHTMARES, INVOKED AGAINST: Christopher, martyr. Lycian (3rd century). Legend. There are a number of legends about the man martyred in Lycia. One goes like this: He was a hideous giant named Offero, who earned a living carrying travelers across the river. He carried a heavy lad one day, claiming to be weighted by the problems of the world. This child, of course, was the youthful Christ. The name Christopher itself means "carrier of Christ" in Greek. Also patron of bachelors, bus drivers, motorists, porters, and travelers. Feast day, July 25.

NORWAY: Olaf II, King. Norwegian (995–1030). This future king began his career as a Viking, taking Norway from the Swedes and the Danes. In 1016, he became the king of Norway, and he attempted to force Christianity onto his subjects. This created a retaliation by many of his subjects who, with the help of the Anglo-Danish king, ousted Olaf from power. Olaf died in battle, attempting to recoup his losses. Also patron of kings and carvers. Feast day, July 29.

NOTARIES: 1) Luke, evangelist. Greek (1st century). Physician and artist. Little is known of his early life. He was the author of the third Gospel and the Acts of the Apostles, which serve as a record of the progression of early Christianity. He died in Greece at the age of 84. Also patron of artists, butchers, glassworkers, painters, physicians, and surgeons. Feast day, October 18.

2) Mark, apostle. (1st century.) Cousin of St. Barnabas. He authored the principles of Peter's teachings, better known as the first Gospel, around 70. He was martyred in Alexandria by means of strangulation. Feast day, April 25.

NUNS: Bridget (Brigid), nun. Irish (450–525). St. Patrick baptized her parents. Brigid became a nun; she founded the first convent in Ireland, a monastery, and a school of art in Kildare. Also patron of dairyworkers, Ireland, and scholars. Feast day, February 1.

NURSES: 1) Agatha, martyr. Sicilian (3rd century). Legend. Governor Quintianis used the persecution of Christians as a way of possessing her. She refused his advances and was brutally tortured. Her captor starved her, sliced off her breasts, then rolled her in hot coals and broken pottery. She died in her cell. In early paintings of this saint, her breasts displayed on a platter have been mistaken for bread. Hence, the blessing of bread on her feast day. Also patron of rape victims, and volcanic eruptions, she is invoked against breast disease. Feast day, February 5.

2) Camillus de Lellis, founder. Italian (1550–1614). A festering inflammation on his foot kept him from joining the Capuchin order. He became a hospital director and was ordained. Camillus then founded the Servants of the Sick, a lay order of male nurses, which organized the first military ambulance task force. Also patron of hospitals, infirmarians, and the sick. Feast day, July 14.

3) John of God, founder. Portuguese (1495–1550). He went from soldier, to shepherd, to drifter, to bookseller. At forty, he heard a sermon by John of Avila and went mad with guilt. John of Avila visited him in his cell, where John of God confessed his sins and converted to Christianity. Building a hospital, he devoted his life to the care of the sick and needy. John died trying to save a man from drowning. He was named founder of the Brothers Hospitallers after his death. Also patron of alcoholism, booksellers, heart patients, hospitals, printers, and the sick. Canonized 1690; feast day, March 8.

4) Raphael, archangel. One of the seven archangels of God; one of the three archangels specified by name in the Bible. He has been venerated by both Jewish and Christian faiths. His name means "God heals." Also patron of the blind, lovers, physicians, and travelers. Feast day, September 29.

NURSING HOMES: 1) Catherine of Siena, mystic. Italian (1347–1380). The twenty-fourth of twenty-five children; one of the great Christian mystics; suffered the pain of stigmata without the visible marks; worked tirelessly with leprosy patients; Doctor of the Church. She persuaded Pope Gregory XI to leave Avignon, which returned the papacy to Rome after 68 years. Dictated *Dialogue*, since she was illiterate. Also patron of fire prevention, Italy, and spinsters. Canonized 1461; feast day, April 29.

2) Elizabeth, Queen. Hungarian (1207–1231). Although her marriage to Ludwig IV was arranged, the two were in love and had three children. In 1227 Ludwig died while on crusade. Elizabeth and her children were kicked out of the Wartburg castle by the in-laws. She made arrangements for her children, then relinquished herself of her title. Joining the Franciscan order, she devoted herself to the care of those in need. She was counseled by a tyrant named Conrad of Marburg. He was insistent that she suffer extreme deprivation and humility for the rest of her short life, which ended at the tender age of twenty-three. Also patron of bakers and tertiaries. Canonized 1235; feast day, November 17.

NURSING MOTHERS: Concordia, martyr. Roman (3rd century). Legend. By the order of the emperor, this nurse to Hippolytus, along with seventeen other Christian servants, were beaten to death with lead-filled whips, all because they attended a Christian funeral. He was sentenced to death by having his feet tied to two wild horses, which were then set free. Feast day, August 13.

Nothing is sweeter than the calm of conscience: nothing safer than the purity of soul, which yet no one can bestow on itself because it is properly the gift of another.

—St. Columban

OBSESSION, INVOKED AGAINST: Quirnus, bishop. Danubian (4th century). Pious legend. As he tried to escape the persecution of Christians, Quirnus was apprehended. The magistrate Maximus offered Quirnus the position of priest to Jupiter if he would recant his faith. Exclaiming that he was already a priest, Quirnus insisted that the magistrate put him to death. Not having the proper authority, Maximus sent him before Amantius, who sentenced him to death by drowning. Quirnus was thrown, praying, into the Raab River, with a rock tied to him. Also invoked against diabolical possession. Feast day, June 4.

OBSTETRICIANS: Raymond Nonnatus, cardinal. Spanish (1204–1240). He was taken from his dying mother by cesarian section. As a Mercedarian, he ransomed himself to the Moors in exchange for the freedom of slaves and Christian hostages. He converted within the prison walls, which angered the Muslims. His jailers realized that his ransom would exceed those of the other prisoners, so Raymond was continuously tortured for preaching. Negotiations for his release took eight months. Also patron of childbirth, the falsely accused, midwives, and pregnant women. Canonized 1657; feast day, August 31.

ORATORS: 1) John Chrysostom, preacher. Antiochan (347–407). One of the four Greek Doctors of the Church. An eminent speaker, he was exiled for denouncing the Empress Eudoxia's plethoric lifestyle as well as her vanity. Chrysostom means "golden mouth." He authored ninety homilies on Matthew, eighty-eight on John, and thirty-two on Romans. Also patron of preachers. Feast day, September 13.

2) Philip Neri, priest. Italian (1515–1595). Arriving in Rome during its religious low point of 1527, Philip roomed in the attic of an officer's home. He earned his keep by tutoring the officer's son and spent the rest of his time devouring books on philosophy and religion. After a couple of years, Philip took to the streets of post-Renaissance Rome. He would stand on the corner and chat with those passing by. The response of the citizens was so favorable that Philip became ordained and reformed the failing churches of Rome. On May 25, 1595, Philip heard confessions all day. When he was through, he announced to his parish that "Last of all, we must die." He passed away around midnight. Also patron of Rome. Canonized 1622; feast day, May 26.

ORGAN BUILDERS: Cecilia, martyr. Roman (unknown dates). Legend. On her wedding day Cecilia was unable to hear the music being performed; instead she only heard herself singing to God. Her husband, Valerian, agreed to live a life of chastity upon Cecilia's request. She, her husband, and his brother were caught burying the bodies of Christians. The others were beheaded first; her executioner botched her beheading and left her to endure a three-day death. Also patron of composers, musicians, poets, and singers. Feast day, November 22.

ORPHANS: Jerome Emiliani, founder. Italian (1481–1537). A prisoner of war set free after praying to the Virgin Mary, who then devoted his life to the care of orphans. Founder of several orphanages, a home for reformed prostitutes, and the Order of the Samashi; introduced the catechism system of teaching. Jerome died while tending to the sick. Also patron of abandoned children. Canonized 1767; feast day, February 8.

Pride makes us hate our equals because they are our equals; our inferiors from fear that they may equal us; our superiors because they are above us.

—St. John Vianney

PAIN, INVOKED AGAINST: Madron, monk. English (6th century). This missionary's well has healed pilgrims suffering from body aches for centuries. Feast day, May 17.

PAINTERS: Luke, evangelist. Greek (1st century). Physician and artist. Little is known of his early life. He was the author of the third Gospel and the Acts of the Apostles, which serve as a record of the progression of early Christianity. He died in Greece at the age of 84. Also patron of artists, butchers, glassworkers, notaries, physicians, and surgeons. Feast day, October 18.

PAPACY: Peter, apostle. Bethsaidan (1st century). Son of Jonah; brother of Andrew; first pope; witness of the transfiguration and the agony of Jesus in the garden. Peter once walked on water, then sank when he hesitated; denied the Lord three times; asked to be hanged upside down when crucified in Rome. The representation of Peter as the gatekeeper of the pearly gates stems from Christ once symbolically endowing the "keys to the kingdom" to his chief apostle. Also patron of fishermen and longevity. Feast day, June 29.

PARAGUAY: Our Lady of the Assumption. In 1950, Pope Pius XII surmised that since the Blessed Virgin Mary was born without original sin (Pope Pius IX, 1854), she was elevated (body and soul) to heaven upon her death. Also patron of France, India, Malta, and South Africa.

PARALYZED: Osmund, bishop. Norman (11th century). He prepared the Domesday survey and collected literature for Salisbury Cathedral library. Osmund was canonized in 1457. No English canonizations took place after Osmund for nearly 500 years (John Fisher and Thomas More, 1935). Feast day, December 4.

PARATROOPERS: Michael, archangel. One of the seven archangels of God; one of the three archangels mentioned by name in the Bible. He is cited twice in the Old Testament, appearing to Moses and Abraham. In the New Testament, he contends with Satan for the body of Moses and tosses Lucifer and his cohorts from heaven. In art, he is often depicted with a scale (representing the weighing of souls) in one hand, while slaying a dragon (Satan) with the other. Also patron of battle, the dead, grocers, mariners, police officers, and radiologists. Feast day, September 29.

PARENTHOOD: 1) Adelaide, Empress. Burgundian (931–991). A first marriage to Lothair, the king of Italy, was brief. Lothair died shortly after the birth of their daughter Emma. Adelaide was then kidnaped by Berengarius, who tried to force the young queen to marry his son. Adelaide refused and was thrown in the dungeon of a castle on Lake Garda. Otto the Great of Germany rescued Adelaide and defeated Berengarius' army. The two were wed on Christmas, which united the German and Italian empires. The couple raised their five children, along with Emma and Otto's son Rudolph. In 962, Otto became emperor of Rome. Empress Adelaide founded monasteries, convents, and donated generously to the needy. Also patron of empresses, princesses, second marriages, and step-parents. Feast day, December 16.

2) Clotilde, Queen. French (6th century B.C.). She gave birth to the three sons and daughter of King Clovis, before the king's death in 511. The greedy children were at constant odds with one another over control of the kingdom. The rivalry led to the murder of Clodomir, her eldest son. Clotilde quickly adopted his three children, which angered Clotaire, her youngest son. He proceeded to murder two of the small children. Clotilde managed to sneak young Saint Cloud to safety away from his uncle's wrath. Clotilde then spent the rest of her life tending to the needy. Also patron of adopted children, the death of children, queens, and widows. Feast day, June 3.

3) Ferdinand III, King. Castilian (1198–1252). Married Princess Beatrice; fathered ten children. He and King Alfonso, his father, teamed up to drive the Moors out of Spain. He was the founder of the University of Salamanca and the cathedral of Burgos, and reformer of the canon code of laws. Also patron of engineers, governors, magistrates, and rulers. Canonized 1671; feast day, May 30.

4) Louis IX, King. French (1214–1270). Crowned king of France at the age of twelve; married Margaret, sister of Eleanor, wife of Henry III; fathered eleven children; launched France's first navy. Louis participated in

two crusades: Damietta in Egypt, where the good king and his men emerged triumphant, and Mansurah, where the defeated king was taken prisoner. After six years, he was set free. Louis died of typhoid while venturing off on his third crusade, to Tunisia. Also patron of crusaders, grooms, and kings. Feast day, August 25.

5) Rita, nun. Italian (1381–1457). An arranged marriage of eighteen years came to an end when her abusive husband was murdered in a brawl. Her two sons sought retribution for their father, but Rita would rather her sons died than become murderers. She prayed for their souls; soon after, the two became ill and died. Rita entered an Augustinian convent on her third attempt (being rejected the first two times for lacking virginity). When she heard a sermon on the crown of thorns, a "thorn-like" wound appeared on her forehead, which stayed with her for the rest of her life. Miracles were accredited to her after her death. Also patron of desperate situations; she is invoked against bleeding, infertility, and marital problems. Canonized 1900; feast day, May 22.

PARK SERVICES: John Gualbert, abbott. Florentine (11th century). The thought of Christ on the cross incited him to spare his brother Hugh's murderer. John then became a monk and built his own monastery in Vallombrosa, from the wood of a nearby forest. Ironically, he is also patron of foresters. Canonized 1193; feast day, July 12.

PAVEMENT WORKERS: Vincent Ferrer, missionary. Spanish (1350–1419). Christ called upon this strikingly handsome man in a dream. Vincent successfully converted tens of thousands of people, including Rabbi Paul of Burgos, who became the bishop of Cartagena. He also converted St. Bernardine of Siena and St. Mary of Savoy.

Vincent assisted in ending the great Western Schism by removing his support from Benedict XIII. Also patron of builders and plumbers. Canonized 1455; feast day, April 5.

PAWNBROKERS: Nicholas of Myra, bishop. Lycian (4th century). Better known as Saint Nick. The facts are few. He ran a monastery, was a prisoner during the time of Christian persecutions, and was present at the Council of Nicaea. The rest is myth. One tale tells of a father who was so poor he couldn't afford his three daughters' dowries. Nick tossed three bags of gold through the kitchen window, and the three daughters married soon after. Also patron of boys, brides, children, dockworkers, Greece, merchants, spinsters, and travelers. Feast day, December 6.

PEACE: Irene, martyr. Roman (3rd century). Legend. She and her two sisters, Agape and Chionia, were imprisoned for refusing to eat sacrificial meat. It was then learned that the three had been hiding Christian Scriptures. Governor Dulcitius had her sisters burnt at the stake. Irene was sent to a house of ill repute, but remained pure. The governor then had her stripped of her clothing and chained to a column. She was shot with arrows. Feast day, April 3.

PENCIL MAKERS: Thomas Aquinas, theologian. Neapolitan (1225–1274). His aristocratic family was so against his religious pursuits they locked him away for fifteen months. The attempt to change his mind proved futile. The greatest thinker of the Middle Ages; author of volumes of theological works, including *Summa contra Gentiles* and *Summa theologica*. Declared a Doctor of the Church in 1567. Also patron of academics, chastity, colleges, and schools. Canonized 1323; feast day, January 28.

PERFUMERS: Mary Magdalen. Magdalene (1st century). She is known for washing Christ's feet with her tears, which she dried with her hair, then anointed with perfume. There is no reference that the repentant adulteress in the New Testament was actually Mary. Christ cast seven devils out of her (Mark 16:9; Luke 8:2); she was present at the crucifixion (Matthew 27:56; Mark 15:40; John 19:25); and was the first to see Christ after his resurrection (Matthew 28:9; Mark 16:9; John 20:1–18). Also patron of hairstylists for women and repentant prostitutes. Feast day, July 22.

PERJURY, INVOKED AGAINST: Pancras, martyr. Syrian (4th century). Legend. At the age of fourteen, this orphan was beheaded for his faith. Years later, a charlatan died when he lied while touching the boy's tomb. Also invoked against cramps. Feast day, May 12.

PERU: Joseph, carpenter. Nazarean (1st century). Descendent of David; husband to the Virgin Mary; foster father to Jesus Christ. Joseph had second thoughts about marrying Mary when he learned that she was pregnant until the angel Gabriel explained the Messiah's coming. After the birth of Christ, he was forewarned in a dream of Herod's exploits, so he took his young family to Egypt. After Herod's death, a dream directed them to return to Israel. Fearing Herod's replacement, Joseph chose to settle his family in Nazareth. Scholars believe he died before the crucifixion of Christ. Also patron of Belgium, Canada, carpenters, the church, the dying, fathers, Korea, social justice, and working men. Feast days, March 19 and May 1.

PHARMACISTS: 1) Gemma Galani, mystic. Italian (1878–1903). This nineteen-year-old orphan suffered from spinal tuberculosis, which kept her from becoming a Passionist nun. Praying to her intercessor, St. Gabriel Possenti, Gemma was miraculously cured. At twenty-one, she began to experience stigmata and other marks of the Lord's afflictions. The devil also paid her a visit, coaxing her to spit on a cross and break a rosary. Gemma died peacefully at the age of twenty-five. There was much opposition upon her canonization in 1940. Her patronage to pharmacists stems from her father's occupation. Also patron of tuberculosis sufferers. Feast day, April 11.

2) Cosmas and Damian, martyrs. Arabians (4th century). Known as "the holy moneyless ones." Twin physicians who took no payment from their patients, they were beheaded along with their three brothers for their Christian beliefs. Some critics feel that their legend derives from Greek mythology's Castor and Pollux. Also patrons of barbers, doctors, druggists, physicians, and surgeons. Feast day, September 26.

3) James the Greater, apostle. Galilee (1st century). His name James "the Greater" is to differentiate him from the other apostle, James "the Less." He and his brother John "dropped their fishing nets" at the Sea of Galilee and followed Jesus; they were witnesses to both the transfiguration and the agony of Jesus in the garden. James was beheaded in Jerusalem, the first apostle to be martyred. Also patron of Chile, furriers, Guatemala, Nicaragua, pilgrims, and Spain; he is invoked against arthritis and rheumatism. Feast day, July 25.

PHILIPPINES: Immaculate/Sacred Heart of Mary. In 1942, Pope Pius XII sanctified the holiness of Mary's heart, which has since been revered as the embodiment of purity and mercy. In order to achieve the Sacred Heart one must follow the code of the decent Christian: go to mass, recite the rosary, and receive communion, all of which must be done on a regular basis. Also patron of Angola, Ecuador, and Lesotho.

PHILOSOPHERS: 1) Catherine, martyr. Alexandrian (4th century). Religious legend. This woman of noble birth chose to study philosophy rather than relish her beauty. Her conversion to Christianity was prompted by a hermit's dream. She then converted Emperor Maxentius' wife, an officer, and two hundred soldiers. In retaliation, the emperor gathered fifty pagan scholars, then challenged her to a religious debate. After a long and heated exchange, Catherine's words swayed all of the fifty scholars to convert. Maxentius had Catherine tied to a wheel, which immediately broke into pieces. She was then beheaded. Also patron of eloquence, maidens, preachers, single women, spinners, and students. Feast day, November 25.

2) Justin, martyr. Palestinian (2nd century). After studying various philosophies, he embraced Christianity. He founded a school of philosophy in Rome. Justin was martyred along with five other men and a woman for refusing to worship pagan gods. Also patron of apologists. Feast day, June 1.

PHYSICAL ABUSE, INVOKED AGAINST: 1) Pharaildis, housewife. Flemish (8th century). When she was of marrying age, her parents betrothed her to a man of wealth. The vow of virginity to God that Pharaildis had taken as a youth angered her hot-tempered husband. He constantly abused her both physically and emotionally until his death. Pharaildis caused a well to spring at Braug. Its water is believed to cure children of disease. Also invoked against childhood diseases and marital problems. Feast day, January 4.

2) Louise de Marillac, founder. French (1591–1660). This wealthy widow chose to assist St. Vincent De Paul in establishing a number of institutions. She founded the Sisters of Charity, a group of nondenominational women brought together to aid the poor and abused. Also patron of social workers. Canonized 1934; feast day, March 15.

3) Fabiola, founder. Roman (3rd century). After divorcing her abusive husband, she remarried. This prevented her from receiving the Sacraments of the church. Fabiola performed public penance, then founded the first Christian hospital. Pope St. Siricus pardoned Fabiola her sins, after her second husband died. Also patron of divorce, infidelity, and widows. Feast day, December 27.

PHYSICALLY DISABLED: Giles, hermit. English (8th century). A forest hermit, he was wounded with an arrow while protecting a hind he had been suckling for a year. The king was so touched by the cripple's compassion, he appointed Giles as one of his advisors. Also patron of beggars, breast-feeding, hermits, horses, and the woods. Feast day, September 1.

PHYSICIANS: 1) Cosmas and Damian, martyrs. Arabians (4th century). Known as "the holy moneyless ones." Twin physicians who took no payment from their patients, they were beheaded along with their three brothers for their Christian beliefs. Some critics feel that their legend derives from Greek mythology's Castor and Pollux. Also patrons of barbers, doctors, druggists, pharmacists, and surgeons. Feast day, September 26.

2) Luke, evangelist. Greek (1st century). Physician and artist. Little is known of his early life. He was the author of the third Gospel and the Acts of the Apostles, which serve as a record of the progression of early Christianity. He died in Greece at the age of 84. Also patron

of artists, butchers, glassworkers, notaries, painters, and surgeons. Feast day, October 18.

3) Raphael, archangel. One of the seven archangels of God; one of the three archangels specified by name in the Bible. He has been venerated by both Jewish and Christian faiths. His name means "God heals." Also patron of the blind, lovers, nurses, and travelers. Feast day, September 29.

PILGRIMS: James the Greater, apostle. Galilean (1st century). His name James "the Greater" is to differentiate him from the other apostle, James "the Less." He and his brother John "dropped their fishing nets" at the Sea of Galilee and followed Jesus; they were witnesses to both the transfiguration and the agony of Jesus in the garden. James was beheaded in Jerusalem, the first apostle to be martyred. Also patron of Chile, furriers, Guatemala, Nicaragua, pharmacists, and Spain; he is invoked against arthritis and rheumatism. Feast day, July 25.

PILOTS: Joseph of Cupertino, ecstatic. Italian (1603–1663). Born in a shed to an impoverished family, this mentally challenged child was nicknamed "the gaper" by his peers. After failing twice, he was ordained a Franciscan in 1628. His miracles, raptures, and levitations became legendary. Flying over the altar was commonplace, as were his ecstasies. As his following grew, "the flying friar" was moved from one friary to another, eventually dying in obscure seclusion at Osimo. Also patron of astronauts and aviators. Canonized 1767; feast day, September 18.

PLAGUES, INVOKED AGAINST: 1) Agricola of Avignon, bishop. French (630–700). At the age of thirty, his father, Bishop (Saint) Magnus, appointed Agricola to co-bishop Avignon, thus creating a rare father and son team in the Roman Catholic church. He is best known for a prayer that ended an invasion of storks. Also patron of good weather and rain; he is invoked against misfortune. Feast day, September 2.

2) Genevieve, nun. French (420–500). After receiving the call of God at the age of seven, Genevieve predicted the invasion of Attila the Hun in 451. The sparing of Paris from the barbarian's invasion was attributed to her prayers. In 1129, Genevieve's relics were raised and an epidemic of ergot poisoning miraculously ceased. Also patron of the women's army corps; she is invoked against disasters. Feast day, January 3.

3) Roch (Rocco), hermit. French (1350–1380). Legend. He tended to plague sufferers in Italy, then became ill himself. Sick and alone, Roch was nourished back to health by a stray dog, who brought him food. He was then imprisoned as a spy by his unknowing uncle, the governor. After Roch's death in prison, a cross-shaped birthmark revealed his true identity. Also patron of the falsely accused and invalids; he is invoked against cholera. Feast day, March 28.

4) Walburga, abbess. English (8th century). Medicine woman. Shortly after following her uncle, St. Boniface, to Germany, she was named abbess to the monastery in Heidenheim. Stories of Walpurgis, as she was then named, can be found in Germany's folklore. On April 30, witches honor this holy healer on what is known as Walpurgisnacht. A slippery liquid with curing powers is said to flow from near her tomb. Walburga once suppressed the voracious appetite of a child by having her consume three ears of grain. Also patron of crops; she is invoked against famine. Feast day, February 25.

PLUMBERS: Vincent Ferrer, missionary. Spanish (1350–1419). Christ called upon this strikingly handsome man in a dream. Vincent successfully converted tens of thousands of people, including Rabbi Paul of Burgos, who became the bishop of Cartagena. He also converted St. Bernardine of Siena and St. Mary of Savoy. Vincent assisted in ending the great Western Schism by removing his support from Benedict XIII. Also patron of builders and pavement workers. Canonized 1455; feast day, April 5.

POETS: 1) Cecilia, martyr. Roman (unknown dates). Legend. On her wedding day Cecilia was unable to hear the music being performed; instead she only heard herself singing to God. Her husband, Valerian, agreed to live a life of chastity upon Cecilia's request. She, her husband, and his brother were caught burying the bodies of Christians. The others were beheaded first; her executioner botched her beheading and left her to endure a three-day death. Also patron of composers, musicians, organ builders, and singers. Feast day, November 22.

2) Columban, missionary. Irish (540–615). Europe acquired a most persuasive monk from Ireland; he founded monasteries in France, Germany, Switzerland, and Italy. In France, he refused to baptize the illegitimate children of King Thierry II; he and all of the other Irish monks were deported. On his way back to Ireland, Columban's ship was thrown off course by a storm, and he was taken in by King Theodebert II of Neustria. Again he founded monasteries. Thierry then defeated Theodebert's army, and once again Columban found himself forced to flee. This time he went to Italy, where he received a warm greeting from King Agilulf. Once again he founded monasteries. Columban left behind a number of sermons and poems. Also patron of Ireland. Feast day, November 23.

3) Caedmon, laybrother. English (7th century).

Known as "the father of English sacred poetry." Caedmon is accredited as the first English writer of religious poetry. One of the few hymns that has survived him is believed to have been composed while he was dreaming. Also patron of songwriters. Feast day, February 11.

POISON, INVOKED AGAINST: Benedict of Nursia, monk. Italian (480–547). Accredited as the father of Western monasticism. At fourteen, he left his noble family and sister, St. Scholastica, to further his studies in Rome; at twenty, he chose the life of a hermit and moved into a cave; at thirty, he had founded a dozen monasteries. Benedict's book of holy rules became the model for monastic life throughout Europe for centuries. After a poisoning attempt by a jealous monk named Florentius, who found his methods too fastidious, Benedict left the position of abbot. He systemized a dozen monasteries, establishing Western monasticism. Also patron of Europe, monks, and speleologists; he is invoked against witchcraft. Feast day, March 21.

POLAND: Casimir, Prince. Polish (1458–1484). Also known as the "Peace Maker." King Casimir ordered the young prince to seize Hungary. Casimir's refusal left the king with no choice but to imprison his thirteenth child. Prince Casimir never wavered, praying to the Blessed Virgin Mary for hours on end. He died after his release in Lithuania. Also patron of Lithuania and princes. Canonized 1522; feast day, March 4.

POLICE OFFICERS: Michael, archangel. One of the seven archangels of God; one of the three archangels mentioned by name in the Bible. He is cited twice in the Old Testament, appearing to Moses and Abraham. In the New Testament, he contends with Satan for the body of Moses and tosses Lucifer and his cohorts from heaven.

In art, he is often depicted with a scale (representing the weighing of souls) in one hand, while slaying a dragon (Satan) with the other. Also patron of battle, the dead, grocers, mariners, paratroopers, and radiologists. Feast day, September 29.

POLIO: Margaret Mary, visionary. French (1647–1690). As a youth, she was bedridden for two years with a form of rheumatism. Shortly before Margaret Mary was miraculously cured, her father died. She found herself a servant in her own home, by the order of her older sister. Margaret Mary then joined a convent at Paray-le-Monial, where her visions began. In one visit, Christ introduced the symbol of the Sacred Heart to Margaret Mary. In another, Christ invited her to join him at the last supper and gave her Peter's seat. The Feast of the Sacred Heart became universal in 1856. Feast day, October 16.

POLITICAL PRISONERS: Maximilian Kolbe, priest. Polish (1894–1941). Imprisoned in Auschwitz for his anti-Nazi publications. He traded places with a young married man, who was to be slaughtered in retribution for an escaped prisoner. Maximilian was killed by means of a carbonic acid injection. Also patron of drug addiction. Canonized 1982; feast day, August 14.

POOR: 1) Anthony of Padua, preacher. Portuguese (1195–1231). Born Ferdinand; known as "the Wonder Worker" for his preaching savvy; the first lector in theology; Doctor of the Church; colleague of St. Francis of Assisi. A disciple once took Anthony's psalter without asking. The terrorized novice promptly returned it, claiming that he was being haunted by apparitions for his act. Also the patron of barren women, lost articles, Portugal, shipwrecks, and travelers; he is invoked against starvation. Canonized 1232; feast day, June 13.

2) Lawrence, martyr. Spanish (3rd century). A prediction revealed that he had three days to live. The city prefect mandated the church's treasures be handed over to the emperor. Lawrence sold everything and donated the money to the poor. He returned on the third day with an array of societal misfits and said that they were the church's treasures. The prefect had him bound to a hot griddle. Lawrence asked to be flipped over at one point, claiming he was done on that side. Also patron of cooks, cutlers, glaziers, restaurateurs, and Sri Lanka. Feast day, July 29.

POPES: Gregory the Great, pope. Roman (540–604). Originator of the Gregorian chants; Doctor of the Church. His "height of embarrassment," as he put it, occurred when Gregory was named pope in 590. He converted England to Christianity, initiated medieval papacy, and authored fourteen books. Also patron of musicians, singers, and teachers. Canonized 604; feast day, September 3.

PORTERS: Christopher, martyr. Lycian (3rd century). Legend. There are a number of legends about the man martyred in Lycia. One goes like this: He was a hideous giant named Offero, who earned a living carrying travelers across the river. He carried a heavy lad one day, claiming to be weighted by the problems of the world. This child, of course, was the youthful Christ. The name Christopher itself means "carrier of Christ" in Greek. Also patron of bachelors, bus drivers, motorists, travelers, truck drivers; he is invoked against nightmares. Feast day, July 25.

PORTUGAL: 1) Immaculate Conception. In 1854, Pope Pius IX declared the Blessed Virgin Mary as born without original sin, having been immaculately conceived, and having lived a sin-free life. Also patron of Brazil, Corsica, Tanzania, and the United States.

2) Anthony of Padua, preacher. Portuguese (1195–1231). Born Ferdinand; known as "the Wonder Worker" for his preaching savvy; the first lector in theology; Doctor of the Church; colleague of St. Francis of Assisi. A disciple once took Anthony's psalter without asking. The terrorized novice promptly returned it, claiming that he was being haunted by apparitions for his act. Also the patron of barren women, lost articles, the poor, shipwrecks, and travelers; he is invoked against starvation. Canonized 1232; feast day, June 13.

POSTAL WORKERS: Gabriel, archangel. Messenger of God. One of the seven archangels of God; one of the three archangels referred to by name in the Bible. Announced the birth of Jesus to Mary (Luke 1:11–21). Also patron of broadcasters, clerics, diplomats, messengers, radio workers, stamp collectors, telecommunications workers, and television workers.

POTTERS: Justa and Rufina, martyrs. Roman (2nd century). These daughters of a potter were offered a considerable amount of money for their earthenware. When the siblings realized that the pottery was to be used in pagan rituals, they smashed the entire stock to pieces. After a short trial, the two were fed to the lions. Feast day, July 19.

POVERTY, INVOKED AGAINST: Regina, martyr. Burgundian (3rd century). After her mother's death during childbirth, Regina was sent to live with a poor shepherdess, who secretly raised her as a Christian. When Regina's pagan father learned of his daughter's faith, he attempted to marry her off to a fellow pagan named Olybrius. Regina was imprisoned, tortured, then beheaded. Also patron of shepherdesses and torture victims. Feast day, September 7.

PREACHERS: 1) Catherine, martyr. Alexandrian (4th century). Religious legend. This woman of noble birth chose to study philosophy rather than relish her beauty. Her conversion to Christianity was prompted by a hermit's dream. She then converted Emperor Maxentius' wife, an officer, and two hundred soldiers. In retaliation, the emperor gathered fifty pagan scholars, then challenged her to a religious debate. After a long and heated exchange, Catherine's words swayed all of the fifty scholars to convert. Maxentius had Catherine tied to a wheel, which immediately broke into pieces. She was then beheaded. Also patron of eloquence, maidens, philosophers, single women, spinners, and students. Feast day, November 25.

2) John Chrysostom, preacher. Antiochan (347–407). One of the four Greek Doctors of the Church. An eminent speaker, he was exiled for denouncing the Empress Eudoxia's plethoric lifestyle as well as her vanity. Chrysostom means "golden mouth." He authored ninety homilies on Matthew, eighty-eight on John, and thirty-two on Romans. Also patron to orators. Feast day, September 13.

PREGNANT WOMEN: 1) Margaret, martyr. Antiochan (4th century). Legend. She was disowned by her father, a pagan priest, for converting to Christianity. Margaret became a shepherdess, during which she was spotted by the governor. His failed attempts in seducing the young woman angered him to the point of incarcerating her. Margaret then revealed herself a Christian and was subjected to a number of gruesome tortures. One of these was being swallowed by a dragon whose belly was sliced open by the cross Margaret was wearing. Eventually she was beheaded. Also patron of birth and divine intervention. Feast day, July 20.

2) Raymond Nonnatus, cardinal. Spanish (1204–1240). He was taken from his dying mother by cesarian section. As a Mercedarian, he ransomed himself to the Moors in exchange for the freedom of slaves and Christian hostages. He converted within the prison walls, which angered the Muslims. His jailers realized that his ransom would exceed those of the other prisoners, so Raymond was continuously tortured for preaching. Negotiations for his release took eight months. Also patron of childbirth, the falsely accused, midwives, and obstetricians. Canonized 1657; feast day, August 31.

PRESS, THE: Edmund Campion, martyr. English (1540–1581). This son of a bookseller was a fellow at Oxford by the age of seventeen. During the persecution of Catholics in England, Edmund fled to France. He became a Jesuit and taught in Prague. Returning to England, Edmund began to distribute his underground papers, *Dememrationes* and *Brag*. One of England's largest manhunts in history was assembled to apprehend Edmund. The police were tipped off to his whereabouts, then locked him in the Tower of London. Edmund ignored the promises and threats of his captors, who then had him hanged, drawn, and quartered. Canonized 1970; feast day, December 1.

PRIESTS: John Baptist Vianney, priest. French (1786–1859). This military man deserted Napoleon's army, then was ordained in 1815. He was determined to rid the world of sin, partaking in confession for up to 16 hours a day. Also patron of parish priests. Canonized 1925. Feast day, August 4.

PRINCES: 1) Gotteschalc, Prince. German (11th century). This student of St. Michael broke with Christianity when he learned of his father Uto's death. While avenging his father, Gotteschalc was captured and imprisoned by Saxons. Upon his release, he returned to his native land and was confirmed once again to Christianity. Also patron of linguists. Feast day, June 7.

2) Casimir, Prince. Polish (1458–1484). Also known as the "Peace Maker." King Casimir ordered the young prince to seize Hungary. Casimir's refusal left the king with no choice but to imprison his thirteenth child. Prince Casimir never wavered, praying to the Blessed Virgin Mary for hours on end. He died after his release in Lithuania. Also patron of Lithuania and Poland. Canonized 1522; feast day, March 4.

PRINCESSES: Adelaide, Empress. Burgundian (931–991). A first marriage to Lothair, the king of Italy, was brief. Lothair died shortly after the birth of their daughter Emma. Adelaide was then kidnaped by Berengarius, who tried to force the young queen to marry his son. Adelaide refused and was thrown in the dungeon of a castle on Lake Garda. Otto the Great of Germany rescued Adelaide and defeated Berengarius' army. The two were wed on Christmas, which united the German and Italian empires. The couple raised their five children, along with Emma and Otto's son Rudolph. In 962, Otto became emperor of Rome. Empress Adelaide founded monasteries, convents, and donated generously to the needy. Also patron of empresses, parenthood, second marriages, and step-parents. Feast day, December 16.

PRINTERS: 1) Augustine of Hippo, bishop, doctor. North African (354–430). He was into parties, fun, and games. Augustine kept a mistress and sired a son out of wedlock. The conversion of Augustine is attributed to the prayers of his mother, Saint Monica, and a sermon by Saint Ambrose. As a convert, he authored numerous works, *Confessions* and *City of God*, to name two. He was one of the greatest intellectuals of the Catholic church and the first philosopher of Christianity, associating the term "original sin" with Adam and Eve. Also patron of brewers and theologians. Feast day, August 28.

2) Genesius, martyr. Roman (3rd century). Legend. This comedian converted to Christianity while performing a farce of Christian baptism on stage for the Emperor Diocletian in Rome. For refusing the emperor's order to recant, Genesius was tortured, then beheaded while still on stage. Also patron of actors, lawyers, secretaries, and stenographers. Feast day, August 25.

3) John of God, founder. Portuguese (1495–1550). He went from soldier, to shepherd, to drifter, to bookseller. At forty, he heard a sermon by John of Avila and went mad with guilt. John of Avila visited him in his cell, where John of God confessed his sins and converted to Christianity. Building a hospital, he devoted his life to the care of the sick and needy. John died trying to save a man from drowning. He was named founder of the Brothers Hospitallers after his death. Also patron of alcoholism sufferers, booksellers, heart patients, hospitals, nurses, and the sick. Canonized 1690; feast day, March 8.

PRISONERS: 1) Barbara, martyr. (4th century.) Religious fiction. A young woman whose pagan father locked her in a tower before leaving on a long journey. Within the walls, she converted to Christianity and had three windows built to signify the Trinity. When her father returned, he was so infuriated by his daughter's religious preference, he turned her over to the authorities. Barbara was subjected to heinous torture, yet refused to disavow her faith. The judge ordered the father to kill her himself. Atop a mountain he slew his daughter, then was immediately struck dead by a bolt of lightning. Also patron of architects, builders, dying, fire prevention, founders, miners, and stonemasons. Feast day, December 4.

2) Dismas, thief. (1st century.) All that is known of this "good thief" is that he was hanged on the cross next to Jesus. Also patron of death row inmates, funeral directors, thieves, and undertakers. Feast day, March 25.

3) Vincent de Paul, founder. French (1580–1660). The common myth of Vincent's life is that he was captured by pirates, who then sold him into slavery in North Africa, where he escaped to France. The truth is that upon listening to the final confession of a villager, Monsieur Vincent realized the plight of the peasants. He left his comfortable position as spiritual advisor to Madame de Gondi and began to work as a minister to galley slaves. Vincent then founded the Congregation of the Missions, the Sisters of Charity, orphanages, and hospitals. His savvy with wealthy women accounted for many of his accomplishments. A charity bearing his name was established in Paris in 1833. Also patron of charitable societies. Canonized 1737; feast day, September 27.

PRISONERS OF WAR: Leonard, founder. French (6th century). Legend. After he assisted his godfather's, King Clovis', wife in an arduous pregnancy, the king endowed to him the land that he could cover by riding on a donkey in a day. On his new property, Leonard founded Noblac monastery and the town of Saint-Leonard. The king also released any prisoner that Leonard went to visit. Most of the former inmates sought refuge in his abbey, and many stayed on to help run it. Also patron of women in labor; he is invoked against burglary. Feast day, November 6.

PRISONS: Joseph Cafasso, founder. Italian (1811–1860). This priest strove to improve the conditions of prisons in Turin and was the founder of various coalitions and religious fellowships. He once escorted sixty newly converted men to their hanging, then bestowed the title of the "hanged saints" upon them. Canonized 1947; feast day, June 23.

PROCRASTINATION, INVOKED AGAINST: Expiditus. (Unknown dates.) Absolutely no facts are known about this saint. An unreliable story claims the relics of an unknown saint were sent to a convent in France, with the word *spedito* across the lid. The nuns mistook this for the word *expedite*, which they thought must be the holy deceased's name. But, a Saint Expeditus is named in the eighteenth century, so one can only wonder. Also patron of emergencies and solutions. Feast day, April 19.

PROFESSORS: Alphonso Maria de'Liguori, theologian. Italian (1696–1787). At age sixteen, he had received his doctorate in canon and civil law. When not experiencing visions, ecstasies, or prophecies, he authored *Moral Theology* and *Glories of Mary*. Also patron of confessors, theologians, and vocations. Canonized 1839; feast day, August 1.

PRUSSIA: Dorothy of Montau, mystic. Prussian (14th century). In the twenty-five years of her marriage to Albert, Dorothy gave birth nine times. Only the youngest of her children survived to adulthood. When her disdainful husband died, Dorothy moved into a hermit's cell. There she healed and counseled visitors in the last year of her life. Also invoked against miscarriages. Feast day, October 30.

PSYCHICS: Agabus, prophet. Roman (1st century). After converting to Christianity, Agabus began to experience visions of the future. His predictions include the famine of 49, the incarceration of Saint Paul, and his own death. Also patron of clairvoyance. Feast day, February 13.

PUBLIC EDUCATION: Martin de Porres, laybrother. Peruvian (1579–1639). A barber-surgeon apprentice before joining the laybrothers. He attended to the African slaves brought into Peru, was founder of an orphanage and a foundling hospital, and experienced bilocation and aerial flights. Also patron of hairstylists (men), health workers, interracial justice, and race relations. Canonized 1962; feast day, November 3.

PUBLIC RELATIONS: 1) Bernardine of Siena, preacher. Italian (1380–1444). "The people's preacher." At the age of twenty, he took charge of a hospital in Siena during the plague of 1400. In 1417 he set out on foot preaching and converting thousands throughout Italy; he was the second founder of the Friars of the Strict Observance. In spite of his attributes, he believed that witchcraft was running rampant and appears to have been an anti-Semite. His sermons often denounced gambling. Also patron of advertising and communications personnel; he is invoked against uncontrolled gambling. Canonized 1450; feast day, May 20.

2) Paul, apostle. Tarsus (1st century). "The Great Apostle." A tentmaker by trade, Paul was a Jew named Saul who was one of the tormenters of the early Christians, until Christ's voice from heaven asked him why he was persecuting "His people." After converting, Paul traveled to Jerusalem, where he was welcomed by the apostles. From there, Paul ventured on three crucial missionary trips throughout Europe and Asia Minor. He converted thousands and authored fourteen New Testament letters. Paul and St. Peter were arrested in Rome. Paul was beheaded, and St. Peter was crucified upside

down, during Emperor Nero's persecutions of Christians. Also patron of Malta and tentmakers; he is invoked against snake bites. Feast day, June 29.

PUBLISHERS: John the Divine, apostle. Galilean (1st century). Brother of James. Christ called the siblings "sons of thunder." John was referred to as the "disciple whom Jesus loved" (John 21:20–24). Christ, on the cross, left his mother in John's care (John 19:25–27). He was eventually exiled to the island of Patmos. He was the author of the Fourth Gospel, three biblical epistles, and the book of the Revelation. Also patron of art dealers, Asia Minor, editors, and friendship. Feast day, December 27.

We should be simple in our affections, intentions, and words; we should do what we find to do without artifice or guile.

—St. Vincent de Paul

QUEENS: 1) Clotilde, Queen. French (6th century). She gave birth to the three sons and daughter of King Clovis, before the king's death in 511. The greedy children were at constant odds with one another over control of the kingdom. The rivalry led to the murder of Clodomir, her eldest son. Clotilde quickly adopted his three children, which angered Clotaire, her youngest son. He proceeded to murder two of the small children. Clotilde managed to sneak young Saint Cloud to safety away from his uncle's wrath. Clotilde then spent the rest of her life tending to the needy. Also patron of adopted children, the death of children, parenthood, and widows. Feast day, June 3.

2) Hedwig, Queen. Bavarian (1174–1243). She and her husband, Henry I, supported a number of charities. After Henry's death, Hedwig was beset by her six chil-

dren's tribulations. Hedwig found solace in a Cistercian abbey, an early endeavor of the royal couple, then committed herself to the care of the indigent. Also patron of Bavaria, children's death, duchesses, and Silesia; she is invoked against jealousy and marital problems. Feast day, October 16.

. . . Never assert anything without first being assured of it.

—St. Teresa of Avila

RABIES SUFFERERS (HYDROPHOBIA): Hubert, bishop. French (8th century). He put an end to idol worship in his diocese. The story of Hubert's conversion to Christianity is remarkably similar to Eustachius' conversion. He was on the trail of a stag, which turned to face him. Between the animal's antlers was the mark of a crucifix. His patronage came about when people suffering from rabies were cured at his grave. Also patron of dogs and hunters. Feast day, November 3.

RACE RELATIONS: Martin de Porres, laybrother. Peruvian (1579–1639). A barber-surgeon apprentice before joining the laybrothers. He attended to the African slaves brought into Peru, was founder of an orphanage and a foundling hospital, and experienced bilocation and aerial flights. Also patron of hairstylists (men), health workers, interracial justice, and public education. Canonized 1962; feast day, November 3.

RADIOLOGISTS: Michael, archangel. One of the seven archangels of God; one of the three archangels mentioned by name in the Bible. He is cited twice in the Old Testament, appearing to Moses and Abraham. In the New Testament, he contends with Satan for the body of Moses and tosses Lucifer and his cohorts from heaven. In art, he is often depicted with a scale (representing the weighing of souls) in one hand, while slaying a dragon (Satan) with the other. Also patron of battle, the dead, grocers, mariners, paratroopers, and police officers. Feast day, September 29.

RADIO WORKERS: Gabriel, archangel. Messenger of God. One of the seven archangels of God; one of the three archangels referred to by name in the Bible. Announced the birth of Jesus to Mary (Luke 1:11–21). Also patron of broadcasters, clerics, diplomats, messengers, postal workers, stamp collectors, telecommunications workers, and television workers.

RAIN: 1) Agricola of Avignon, bishop. French (630–700). At the age of thirty, his father, Bishop (Saint) Magnus, appointed Agricola to co-bishop Avignon, thus creating a rare father and son team in the Roman Catholic church. He is best known for a prayer that ended an invasion of storks. Also patron of good weather; he is invoked against bad luck, misfortune, and plague. Feast day, September 2.

2) Swithun (Swithin), bishop. English (9th century). On July 15th, 971, his relics were transferred to Winchester Cathedral. The heavy rain that followed initiated the English belief that if it rains on July 15, expect an-

other forty days of rain. Also invoked against drought. Feast day, July 15.

RAPE VICTIMS: 1) Agatha, martyr. Sicilian (3rd century). Legend. Governor Quintianis used the persecution of Christians as a way of possessing her. She refused his advances and was brutally tortured. Her captor starved her, sliced off her breasts, then rolled her in hot coals and broken pottery. She died in her cell. In early paintings of this saint, her breasts displayed on a platter have been mistaken for bread. Hence, the blessing of bread on her feast day. Also patron of nurses, and invoked against volcanic eruptions; she is also invoked against breast disease. Feast day, February 5.

2) Maria Goretti, child. Italian (1890–1902). After her mother's death, Maria's father moved the family to Ferriere di Conca, where he took on work as a farmhand. Though poor, the family found room to take in another farmhand by the name of Alexander Serenelli. Maria worked the fields, as well as helped in the running of the household. Her free time was devoted to prayer. Once when Maria was cooking the evening meal, Alexander made sexual advances to her. Maria was stabbed seventeen times and died that night. On her deathbed, she said, "I forgive Alexander. I forgive him with all my heart; and I want him to be with me in heaven." A penitent Alexander attended her canonization. Also patron of children. Feast day, July 6.

RATS, INVOKED AGAINST: Gertrude of Nivelles, abbess. Belgium (626–659). When Gertrude's father died, her mother, Itta, founded a monastery at Neville. The fourteen-year-old Gertrude was appointed as the abbess and proved herself deserving of the title. Gertrude's monastic center was known for its hospitality to pilgrims and monks. At the age of thirty, Gertrude lay on her deathbed, fearing that she was unworthy of heaven. St. Ultan assured her that St. Patrick was awaiting her. She died on St. Patrick's Day. The well at her monastery was said to have repellent properties against rodents. Also patron of accommodations, cats, and the recently dead. Feast day, March 17.

RECONCILIATION: Theodore, bishop. Galatian, Asia Minor (5th century). A vision of St. George converted Theodore's mother, who at the time was running a house of prostitution. The brothel was made into a family restaurant, and the young Theodore was sent to a monastery. Once ordained, he became known for his intuitive abilities. As bishop of Sykeon, Theodore used his capacities as a marriage counselor. Feast day, April 22.

REFUGEES: Alban, martyr. Roman (4th century). Legend. First martyr of Britain. He harbored a fugitive priest who had escaped Emperor Diocletian's persecution of Christians. While the father rested, Alban put on the priest's clothes and turned himself in as the renegade. He was tortured, then beheaded. Also patron of torture victims. Feast day, June 21.

RELIGIOUS ORDERS: Benedict Joseph Labre, transient. Boulognian (18th century). After being rejected from several religious orders, Benedict left his wealthy family to search for God. Traveling throughout Europe for three years, he visited every pilgrimage site in his holy quest. Ending up at the Colosseum, Benedict the beggar spent his last years in intense prayer. He died in church. Also patron of beggars, the homeless, and transients. Feast day, April 16.

REPENTANT PROSTITUTES: Mary Magdalen. Magdalene (1st century). She is known for washing Christ's feet with her tears, which she dried with her hair, then anointed with perfume. There is no reference that the repentant adulteress in the New Testament was actually Mary. Christ cast seven devils out of her (Mark 16:9; Luke 8:2), she was present at the crucifixion (Matthew 27:56; Mark 15:40; John 19:25), and was the first to see Christ after his resurrection (Matthew 28:9; Mark 16:9; John 20:1–18). Also patron of hairstylists for women and perfumers. Feast day, July 22.

RESTAURATEURS: Lawrence, martyr. Spanish (3rd century). A prediction revealed that he had three days to live. The city prefect mandated the church's treasures be handed over to the emperor. Lawrence sold everything and donated the money to the poor. He returned on the third day with an array of societal misfits and said that they were the church's treasures. The prefect had him bound to a hot griddle. Lawrence asked to be flipped over at one point, claiming he was done on that side. Also patron of cooks, cutlers, glaziers, the poor, and Sri Lanka. Feast day, July 29.

RETREATS: Ignatius Loyola, founder. Basque Spanish (1491–1556). A war injury he received in Pamplona left this brave soldier bedridden long enough to read the biographies of Christ and the saints. He hung up his sword and went on a retreat to Manresa, where he authored *Spiritual Exercises* in 1522. Ignatius founded the Society of Jesus (Jesuits) in 1534. He devoted the rest of his life to the founding and running of schools and seminaries. Also patron of soldiers. Canonized 1622; feast day, July 31.

RHEUMATISM, INVOKED AGAINST: James the Greater, apostle. Galilean (1st century). His name James "the Greater" is to differentiate him from the other apostle, James "the Less." He and his brother John "dropped their fishing nets" at the Sea of Galilee and followed Jesus; they were witnesses to both the transfiguration and the agony of Jesus in the garden. James was beheaded in Jerusalem, the first apostle to be martyred. Also patron of Chile, furriers, Guatemala, Nicaragua, pharmacists, pilgrims, and Spain; he is invoked against arthritis. Feast day, July 25.

ROME: Philip Neri, priest. Italian (1515–1595). Arriving in Rome during its religious low point of 1527, Philip roomed in the attic of an officer's home. He earned his keep by tutoring the officer's son and spent the rest of his time devouring books on philosophy and religion. After a couple of years, Philip began to preach on the streets of post-Renaissance Rome. The response of the citizens was so favorable that Philip was ordained and reformed the failing churches of Rome. On May 25, 1595, Philip heard confessions all day. When he was through, he announced to his parish that "Last of all, we must die." He passed away around midnight. Also patron of orators. Canonized 1622; feast day, May 26.

RULERS: Ferdinand III, King. Castilian (1198–1252). Married Princess Beatrice; fathered ten children. He and King Alfonso, his father, teamed up to drive the Moors out of Spain. He was the founder of the University of Salamanca and the cathedral of Burgos, and reformer of the canon code of laws. Also patron of engineers, governors, magistrates, and parenthood. Canonized 1671; feast day, May 30.

RUNAWAYS: 1) Alodia, martyr. Spanish (9th century). She, and her sister, St. Nunilo, were frequently beaten by their Muslim stepfather. The two ran away when their vows of virginity were threatened by the stepfather's attempt to marry them off to his peers. Alodia and Nunilo were reported to the authorities as Christians, apprehended, then beheaded. Also patrons of child abuse victims. Feast day, October 22.

2) Dymphna, martyr. Irish (7th century). Folktale. She and her confessor ran away from her incestuous father, a pagan chieftain. In Belgium, the two lived as hermits in an oratory they had built, until her father and his men hunted them down. The confessor was murdered and Dymphna was beheaded for refusing to return home. Many have been cured at Dymphna's tomb. Also patron of epileptics; she is invoked against diabolic possession, mental disorders, and sleepwalking. Feast day, May 15.

RUSSIA: 1) Vladimir, King. Russian (975–1015). He murdered his half brother, Yarapolk, ruler of Russia, then crowned himself king of Russia. He led a reign of terror until his conversion to Catholicism in 989. Giving up his five wives and dozen concubines, Vladimir demanded that all his subjects in Kiev become baptized. This marked the beginning of Catholicism in Russia. Also patron of converts, kings, and murderers. Feast day, July 15.

2) Andrew, apostle. Bethsaidan (1st century). Son of Jonah. This fisherman was the first called by Jesus Christ, who then recruited his brother Peter; he was a witness to the Feeding of the Five Thousand (John 6:8–9). After the resurrection of Christ, Andrew made his way to Greece and was crucified in Achaia. Also patron of fishermen, Greece, and Scotland. Feast day, November 30.

Sorrow can be alleviated by good sleep, a bath, and a glass of wine.

—St. Thomas Aquinas

SADDLERS: Crispin and Crispinian, martyrs. Roman (3rd century). Legend. These brothers were Christian converters by day and shoemakers by night. Their torturer, Maximian, took his own life in frustration when his attempts to execute the siblings failed. The two were then beheaded. Also patrons of cobblers, leatherworkers, shoemakers, and tanners. Feast day, October 25.

SAILORS: 1) Brendan the Navigator, founder/explorer. Irish (1303–1373). The Clonfert monastery, which he founded, was the core of missionary endeavors for centuries. Some scholars believe that his book *Navigato Sancti Brenardani Abbatis* was based on his accounts of an expedition to North America. Also patron of whales. Feast day, May 16.

2) Elmo (Erasmus), martyr. Italian (4th century). Legend. One legend has him surviving unharmed Emperor Diocletian's order of execution by bonfire during

the Christian persecutions. Another has him tortured to death by having his intestines pulled from him by a windlass. The electrical discharge on a ship's masthead, which sometimes occurs before or after a storm, is believed to be a sign that St. Elmo is protecting the vessel. Also invoked against appendicitis, intestinal disease, and seasickness. Feast day, June 2.

SCANDINAVIA: Ansgar, monk. French (801–865). The "Apostle of the North." He devoted his life to Christianizing Scandinavia, which then slipped back to its pagan ways, upon his death. Scandinavia began to have a more prominent Christian presence two hundred years later. Also patron of Denmark. Feast day, February 3.

SCHOLARS: 1) Bede the Venerable, monk. Northumbrian (673–735). Doctor of the Church. Although the "father" of English history never ventured farther than a few miles from his monastery in Wearmouth-Jarrow, Bede goes down in the canon as one of the most learned men in Catholic history. Author of *The History of the English Church and People*, and a number of hymns and homilies; first author of English prose. Bede's last breath was spent translating the last words of St. John's Gospel. Feast day, May 25.

2) Bridget (Brigid), nun. Irish (450–525). St. Patrick baptized her parents. Brigid became a nun; she founded the first convent in Ireland, a monastery, and a school of art in Kildare. Also patron of dairyworkers, Ireland, and nuns. Feast day, February 1.

SCHOOLGIRLS: Ursula, martyr. German (unknown dates). Myth. According to the chiseled words on a stone in Cologne, a group of Christian maidens were martyred in the fourth century. Four hundred years later, the tales of the women flowered into this legend. Ursula was the

Christian daughter of a British king, whose wedding date to a pagan prince had been set. In an attempt to postpone the nuptials, she boarded a ship with her ladies-in-waiting. They set out for a pilgrimage to Rome. In Cologne, Ursula and her young maidens (numbering anywhere from a dozen to a thousand) were attacked by the Huns. Ursula rejected the chieftain's marriage proposal and all of the women were murdered. Also patron of drapers and young women. Feast day, October 21.

SCHOOLS: Joseph Calasanz, founder. Aragonian (1557–1648). In 1597 this priest with degrees in both divinity and law opened a school in the squalid part of Tiber. Thus began the Clerks Regular of the Religious Schools, an order focused on educating elementary school children. His Piarist schools can be found throughout Europe. Canonized 1767; feast day, August 25.

2) Thomas Aquinas, theologian. Neapolitan (1225–1274). His aristocratic family was so against his religious pursuits, they locked him away for fifteen months. The attempt to change his mind proved futile. The greatest thinker of the Middle Ages; author of volumes of theological works, including *Summa contra Gentiles* and *Summa theologica*. Declared a Doctor of the Church in 1567. Also patron of academics, chastity, colleges, and pencil makers. Canonized 1323: feast day, January 28.

SCIENTISTS: Albert the Great, theologian. German (1206–1280). "The Universal Doctor." A great intellectual of the medieval church; mentor to St. Thomas Aquinas; believed the earth to be round; a pioneer of natural sciences. Also patron of medical technicians. Canonized 1931; feast day, November 15.

SCOTLAND: Andrew, apostle. Bethsaidan (1st century). Son of Jonah. This fisherman was the first called by

Jesus Christ, who then recruited his brother Peter; he was a witness to the Feeding of the Five Thousand (John 6:8–9). After the resurrection of Christ, Andrew made his way to Greece and was crucified in Achaia. Also patron of fishermen, Greece, and Russia. Feast day, November 30.

SCULPTORS: Four Crowned Martyrs, martyrs. Yugoslavians (3rd century). Castorius, Claudius, Nicostratus, and Simpronian were skilled carvers who declined to sculpt a pagan statue for the Roman Emperor Diocletian. They were weighted with lead, then drowned in the river. Also patrons of freemasons. Feast day, November 8.

SEAMEN: Francis of Paola, founder. Italian (1416–1507). At the age of fifteen, Francis chose the life of a hermit; at the age of twenty, he founded his own order, the Minims. He founded a monastery in Plessis, France. Francis' nautical patronages emanate from a tale in which Francis once placed his shawl on the water of an Italian channel and navigated the cloth home. Also patron of naval officers. Canonized 1519; feast day, April 2.

SEAFOOD: Corentin, bishop. English (6th century). Religious fiction. Every day this bishop would pluck the same fish from the waters of a holy stream, chop off enough for his meals, then set it back in the water. The next day the fish would be complete again. Upon learning of this daily miracle, a curious neighbor gave the fish a whack. Corentin healed the dying creature, then freed it. Feast day, December 12.

SEASICKNESS, INVOKED AGAINST: Elmo (Erasmus), martyr. Italian (4th century). Legend. One legend has him surviving unharmed Emperor Diocletian's order of execution by bonfire during the Christian persecutions.

Another has him tortured to death by having his intestines pulled from him by a windlass. The electrical discharge on a ship's masthead, which sometimes occurs before or after a storm, is believed to be a sign that St. Elmo is protecting the vessel. Also patron of sailors; he is invoked against appendicitis and intestinal disease. Feast day, June 2.

SECOND MARRIAGES: 1) Adelaide, Empress. Burgundian (931–991). A first marriage to Lothair, the king of Italy, was brief. Lothair died shortly after the birth of their daughter Emma. Adelaide was then kidnaped by Berengarius, who tried to force the young queen to marry his son. Adelaide refused and was thrown in the dungeon of a castle on Lake Garda. Otto the Great of Germany rescued Adelaide and defeated Berengarius' army. The two were wed on Christmas, which united the German and Italian empires. The couple raised their five children, along with Emma and Otto's son Rudolph. In 962, Otto became emperor of Rome. Empress Adelaide founded monasteries, convents, and donated generously to the needy. Also patron of empresses, parenthood, princesses, and step-parents. Feast day, December 16.

SECRETARIES: Genesius, martyr. Roman (3rd century). Legend. This comedian converted to Christianity while performing a farce of Christian baptism on stage for the Emperor Diocletian in Rome. For refusing the emperor's order to recant, Genesius was tortured, then beheaded while still on stage. Also patron of actors, lawyers, printers, and stenographers. Feast day, August 25.

SECURITY GUARDS: Matthew, apostle. Galilean (1st century). His name means "Gift of God." Also known as Levi; no records of his early life. Tax collector turned apostle; he wrote the first Gospel between 60 and 90, which contains quotes from the Old Testament. He was martyred either in Ethiopia or Persia. Also patron of accountants, bankers, bookkeepers, customs agents, and tax collectors. Feast day, September 21.

SEMINARIANS: Charles Borromeo, bishop/cardinal. Italian (1538–1584). A speech impediment did nothing to stop him from preaching. His uncle, Pope Pius IV, appointed this twenty-two-year-old as cardinal before he was even a priest. He was one of the predominant figures among Roman Catholic reformers in clerical education, which constantly put him at odds with the clergy and aristocracy of the time. He was the originator of Sunday schools for children. Also patron of apple orchards and catechists. Canonized 1610; feast day, November 4.

SEPARATION, SPOUSAL: 1) Gummarus, courtier. Flemish (8th century). Also known as Gomer. As a servant to the court of Pepin, Gummarus married the nefarious Guinimaria. After a number of years of persecution from this brutal woman, Gummarus paid off the money kept from the servants' wages by his wife and joined a hermitage. He founded the abbey at Lierre. Also patron of cowherds and unhappily married men; he is invoked against impotence. Feast day, October 11.

2) Nicholas von Flue, layman. Swiss (1417–1487). After fighting in two wars, raising ten children, and holding the offices of magistrate and councilor, Nicholas received the calling from God. He left his family and lived the remainder of his life as a hermit. It is said that from that day forth, he was solely nourished by the Holy Eucharist. Also patron of councilmen. Feast day, March 21.

3) Gengulphus, knight. Burgundian (8th century). Also known as Gengulf; one of King Pepin the Short's compatriots. Upon learning of his wife's infidelity, Gen-

gulphus left her, moving to a castle in Avalon. He devoted his time to prayer and aiding the less fortunate. He was murdered while he slept, by his wife's lover. Also patron of infidelity and knights. Feast day, May 11.

SERVANTS: 1) Martha, homemaker. Bethanian (1st century). A friend of Jesus; older sister of Mary and Lazarus. During one of Jesus' many visits to their home, Martha fussed away in the kitchen, while Mary listened attentively to Christ. Jesus then said to her, "Martha, Martha, thou art careful and troubled about many things; but one thing is needful; and Mary hath chosen that good part, which shall not be taken away from her" (Luke 10: 41–42). Also patron of cooks, dietitians, and waitpersons. Feast day, July 29.

2) Zita, servant. Italian (1218–1278). Legend has it that this servant of the Fatinelli family would take bits of food from her rich employers to give to the poor. One day she was caught by the mistress while leaving the house with her apron stuffed with leftovers. When forced to disclose the contents, roses spilled out onto the floor. Also patron of domestic help, housekeepers, and maids. Canonized 1696; feast day, April 27.

SHEPHERDESSES: 1) Bernadette, nun. French (1844–1879). In 1858, the Blessed Virgin Mary first appeared to a young girl named Bernadette Soubirous. The illumination was dressed in white and referred to herself as the "Immaculate Conception." On the site of her eighteen visits, a spring of curing water emerged. A church has since been built. Bernadette joined the Sisters of Notre Dame in 1866. Lourdes is one of the most popular pilgrimage sites for Catholics in the world, drawing over four million visitors a year. Canonized 1933; feast day, April 16.

2) Regina, martyr. Burgundian (3rd century). After

her mother's death during childbirth, Regina was sent to live with a poor shepherdess, who secretly raised her as a Christian. When Regina's pagan father learned of his daughter's faith, he attempted to marry her off to a fellow pagan named Olybrius. Regina was imprisoned, then beheaded. Also patron of poverty and torture victims. Feast day, September 7.

SHEPHERDS: 1) Drogo, shepherd. Flemish (1105–1189). As a child, Drogo learned that his father died before he was born, and his mother had given her life for his. This made a great impact on the ten-year-old youth of noble lineage. While tending to sheep in his mid-forties, Drogo suffered a ruptured hernia, which disfigured him. He drilled a hole through a wall of the church to be able to attend mass without attracting attention away from the sermon. He lived his remaining forty years in prayer and penitence. Also patron of coffeehouse keepers, hernia sufferers, and homely people. Feast day, April 16.

SHIPWRECKS: Anthony of Padua, preacher. Portuguese (1195–1231). Born Ferdinand; known as "the Wonder Worker" for his preaching savvy; the first lector in theology; Doctor of the Church; colleague of St. Francis of Assisi. A disciple once took Anthony's psalter without asking. The terrorized novice promptly returned it, claiming that he was being haunted by apparitions for his act. Also the patron of barren women, lost articles, the poor, Portugal, and travelers; he is invoked against starvation. Canonized 1232; feast day, June 13.

SHOEMAKERS: Crispin and Crispinian, martyrs. Roman (3rd century). Legend. These brothers were Christian converters by day and shoemakers by night. Their torturer, Maximian, took his own life in frustration when his attempts to execute the siblings failed. The two were then beheaded. Also patrons of cobblers, leatherworkers, saddlers, and tanners. Feast day, October 25.

SICK: 1) John of God, founder. Portuguese (1495–1550). He went from soldier, to shepherd, to drifter, to bookseller. At forty, he heard a sermon by John of Avila and went mad with guilt. John of Avila visited him in his cell, where John of God confessed his sins and converted to Christianity. Building a hospital, he devoted his life to the care of the sick and needy. John died trying to save a man from drowning. He was named founder of the Brothers Hospitallers after his death. Also patron of alcoholism sufferers, booksellers, heart patients, hospitals, nurses, and printers. Canonized 1690; feast day, March 8.

2) Camillus de Lellis, founder. Italian (1550–1614). A festering inflammation on his foot kept him from joining the Capuchin order. He became a hospital director and was ordained. Camillus then founded the Servants of the Sick, a lay order of male nurses, which organized the first military ambulance task force. Also patron of hospitals, infirmarians, and nurses. Feast day, July 14.

3) Michael, archangel. One of the seven archangels of God; one of the three archangels mentioned by name in the Bible. He is cited twice in the Old Testament, appearing to Moses and Abraham. In the New Testament, he contends with Satan for the body of Moses and tosses Lucifer and his cohorts from heaven. In art, he is often depicted with a scale (representing the weighing of souls) in one hand, while slaying a dragon (Satan) with the other. Also patron of battle, grocers, mariners, paratroopers, police officers, and radiologists. Feast day, September 29.

SILENCE: John of Nepomucene, bishop and martyr. Czechoslovakian (1345–1393). Until 1961, John was believed to have been thrown from a bridge for refusing to crack the seal of the confessional, when the jealous King Wenceslaus IV demanded to know what disclosures his wife, Queen Sophia, had made to the bishop. A more logical reason for his drowning is religious and political differences. Also patron of bridges, Czechoslovakia, and discretion; he is invoked against slander. Canonized 1729; feast day, May 16.

SILESIA: Hedwig, Queen. Bavarian (1174–1243). She and her husband, Henry I, supported a number of charities. After Henry's death, Hedwig was beset by her six children's tribulations. Hedwig found solace in a Cistercian abbey, an early endeavor of the royal couple, then committed herself to the care of the indigent. Also patron of Bavaria, children's death, duchesses, and queens; she is invoked against jealousy, marital problems. Feast day, October 16.

SILVERSMITH: 1) Andronicus, silversmith. Alexandrian (5th century). When their children died on the same day, his wife put on men's clothing and the two joined a monastery, where St. Daniel assigned each to a different task. Twelve years later, Andronicus accompanied a monk to Alexandria. It was only after the monk's death that a note was found, disclosing the true identity of his wife. He died within the week. The two were buried together. Feast day, October 9.

2) Dunstan, bishop. English (910–988). One of the great reformers of church life in England during the tenth century. He rectified Bath and Westminster Abbey. He was advisor to King Edwy, until his accusation of the king's sexual exploits caused Dunstan's exile. A skillful metalworker and harpist. Also patron of armorers, black-

smiths, goldsmiths, locksmiths, and musicians. Feast day, May 19.

SINGERS: 1) Cecilia, martyr. Roman (unknown dates). Legend. On her wedding day Cecilia was unable to hear the music being performed; instead she only heard herself singing to God. Her husband, Valerian, agreed to live a life of chastity upon Cecilia's request. She, her husband, and his brother were caught burying the bodies of Christians. The others were beheaded first; her executioner botched her beheading and left her to endure a three-day death. Also patron of composers, poets, organ builders, and musicians. Feast day, November 22.

2) Gregory the Great, pope. Roman (540–604). Originator of the Gregorian chants; Doctor of the Church. His "height of embarrassment," as he put it, occurred when Gregory was named pope in 590. He converted England to Christianity, initiated medieval papacy, and authored fourteen books. Also patron of musicians, popes, and teachers. Canonized 604; feast day, September 3.

SINGLE MOTHERS: Margaret of Cortona, mystic. Italian (1247–1297). At the age of seven, Margaret's mother suddenly died. Her father remarried a woman who was cruel to the girl. When old enough, Margaret left the farm and moved in with a knight. She was the mistress of the castle for nine years, and she bore a son before her lover's murder. She publicly confessed, then served her penance. Margaret's father turned the two away from his home. It was at this time that Margaret joined the Franciscan tertiaries and began to experience visions and healing powers. She devoted the rest of her life to the neglected. Also patron of the homeless, midwives, and tertiaries. Canonized 1728; feast day, February 22.

SINGLE WOMEN: Catherine, martyr. Alexandrian (4th century). Religious legend. This woman of noble birth chose to study philosophy rather than relish her beauty. Her conversion to Christianity was prompted by a hermit's dream. She then converted Emperor Maxentius' wife, an officer, and two hundred soldiers. In retaliation, the emperor gathered fifty pagan scholars, then challenged her to a religious debate. After a long and heated exchange, Catherine's words swayed all of the fifty scholars to convert. Maxentius had Catherine tied to a wheel, which immediately broke into pieces. She was then beheaded. Also patron of eloquence, maidens, philosophers, preachers, spinners, and students. Feast day, November 25.

SKATERS: Lidwina. Dutch (1380–1433). Her visions of heaven and hell began after an ice-skating accident, which left her an invalid. Canonized 1890; feast day, April 14.

SKIERS: Bernard of Montijoix, priest. Italian (996–1081). He devoted his forty years as a priest to the residence of the Alps. Builder of schools and churches; best known for Great and Little Bernard, two shelters on mountain passes created for travelers of all religions and origins. Also patron of alpinists and mountaineers. Feast day, May 28.

SKIN DISEASES, INVOKED AGAINST: Peregrine Laziosi. Italian (14th century). As a political activist for the antipapal party, Peregrine was once cuffed by the leader of the opposition. Peregrine responded by turning the other cheek. Realizing what he had done, the assailant repented on the spot. Within the Servite order, Peregrine's self-mortification of choice was to stand. For the later thirty years of his life, Peregrine never sat down. A cancerous growth developed on his foot, which disappeared on the morning of the scheduled amputation. He died a very old man, with both feet firmly planted on the ground. Canonized 1726; feast day, May 1.

SLANDER, INVOKED AGAINST: John of Nepomucene, bishop and martyr. Czechoslovakian (1345–1393). Until 1961, John was believed to have been thrown from a bridge for refusing to crack the seal of the confessional, when the jealous King Wenceslaus IV demanded to know what disclosures his wife, Queen Sophia, had made to the bishop. A more logical reason for his drowning is religious and political differences. Also patron of Czechoslovakia, detraction, discretion, and silence. Canonized 1729; feast day, May 16.

SLAVERY VICTIMS: Peter Claver, missionary. Catalonian (1580–1654). As a missionary in New Granada (Colombia), he ministered to the 300,000 African slaves brought to Cartagena to work the mines and plantations. Also patron of African Americans and Colombia. Canonized 1888; feast day, September 9.

SLEEP DISORDERS, INVOKED AGAINST: The Seven Sleepers. Ephesian (unknown dates). Religious folklore. During the persecutions by Decian, these seven Christians sealed themselves into a cave. The year was 250. When they awoke, two hundred years had passed, and Christianity was the official religion in Ephesus. This tale can be found in *The Golden Legend*. Feast day, July 27.

SLEEPWALKING, INVOKED AGAINST: Dymphna, martyr. Irish (7th century). Folktale. She and her confessor ran away from her incestuous father, a pagan chieftain. In Belgium, the two lived as hermits in an oratory they had built, until her father and his men hunted them down. The confessor was murdered and Dymphna was beheaded for refusing to return home. Many have been cured at Dymphna's tomb. Also patron of epileptics and runaways; she is invoked against diabolic possession and mental disorders. Feast day, May 15.

SLOVAKIA: Our Lady of Sorrows. The Blessed Virgin Mary's seven sorrows are as follows: 1) The arrest of Christ, 2) Christ being taken to Pontius Pilate for conviction, 3) Christ found guilty before Pilate and the Jewish people, 4) The crucifixion of Christ, 5) The death of Christ on the cross, 6) Christ being brought down from the cross, and 7) The burial of Christ.

SMELTERS: Stephen the Younger, martyr. Constantinopolitan (8th century). To prove the point of how important it is to respect religious artifacts, this monk once tossed a coin with the likeness of Emperor Constantine V on the floor. He then proceeded to stomp on it, in the presence of the emperor. Stephen was sent to jail for eleven months. After his release, Stephen stood before a bewildered Constantine and chose to prove yet other points. The aggravated emperor gave up and ordered the execution of Stephen. Also patron of coin collectors. Feast day, November 28.

SNAKE BITES, INVOKED AGAINST: Paul, apostle. Tarsus (1st century). "The Great Apostle." A tentmaker by trade, Paul was a Jew named Saul who was one of the tormenters of the early Christians, until Christ's voice from heaven asked him why he was persecuting "His people." After converting, Paul traveled to Jerusalem, where he was welcomed by the apostles. From there, Paul ventured on three crucial missionary trips throughout Europe and Asia Minor. He converted thousands and authored fourteen New Testament letters. Paul and St. Peter were arrested in Rome. Paul was beheaded, and

St. Peter was crucified upside down, during Emperor Nero's persecutions of Christians. While on a mission, Paul was bitten by a poisonous snake. Its fatal venom had no effect on him. Also patron of Malta, public relations, and tentmakers. Feast day, June 29.

SNAKES: Patrick, bishop. Romano-Briton (389–461). It's difficult to separate the myth from the man. At the age of sixteen, he was abducted from his hometown of Kilpatrick and enslaved in Ireland. After six years of working as a herdsman, he escaped to Gaul, where he was ordained. Returning to Ireland, Patrick carried on the work of St. Pallidius in the successful conversion of much of Ireland. Though the snake is one of his emblems (the other being a shamrock), scholars have ruled out that the creatures were ever native to Irish soil. Also patron of Ireland. Feast day, March 17.

SOCIAL JUSTICE: Joseph, carpenter. Nazarean (1st century). Descendent of David; husband to the Virgin Mary; foster father to Jesus Christ. Joseph had second thoughts about marrying Mary when he learned that she was pregnant until the angel Gabriel explained the Messiah's coming. After the birth of Christ, he was forewarned in a dream of Herod's exploits, so he took his young family to Egypt. After Herod's death, a dream directed them to return to Israel. Fearing Herod's replacement, Joseph chose to settle his family in Nazareth. Scholars believe he died before the crucifixion of Christ. Joseph was declared patron of social justice by Pope Pius IX in 1870. Also patron of Belgium, Canada, carpenters, the church, the dying, fathers, Korea, Peru, and working men. Feast days, March 19 and May 1.

SOCIAL WORKERS: Louise de Marillac, founder. French (1591–1660). This wealthy widow chose to assist St.

Vincent De Paul in establishing a number of institutions. She founded the Sisters of Charity, a group of nondenominational women brought together to aid the poor and abused. Also invoked against physical abuse. Canonized 1934; feast day, March 15.

SOLDIERS: 1) Joan of Arc, soldier. French (1412–1431). Known in France as Jean La Pucelle. At the age of fourteen, this daughter of a peasant farmer began hearing voices directing her to her destiny of saving France from English rule. After a panel of theologians found Joan to be sane, King Charles VII provided her with an army which defeated the English, who had been invaders to their native soil. She was captured and sold to the British. King Charles did not lift a finger to save her. Since the English could not openly admit that she had defeated them, they drummed up the charge of heresy and witchcraft, then burned her at the stake. Joan was nineteen years old when she died. Also patron of France. Canonized 1920; feast day, May 30.

2) George, martyr. English (3rd century). Aside from being martyred in Palestine, this Christian knight's life is pure fiction. He is best known for a dragonslaying incident, in which he saved a princess from being sacrificed, then married her. An account of his life is found in the thirteenth-century *The Golden Legend*. Also patron of Boy Scouts, England, and farmers. Feast day, February 21.

3) Hadrian (Adrian) martyr. Roman (3rd–4th century). As a pagan military officer, he was amazed by the Christians' refusal to recant their faith. When the prefect learned that Hadrian had been baptized, he had him broken limb from limb. Also patron of butchers. Feast day, September 8.

4) Ignatius Loyola, founder. Basque Spanish (1491–

1556). A war injury he received in Pamplona left this brave soldier bedridden long enough to read the biographies of Christ and the saints. He hung up his sword and went on a retreat to Manresa, where he authored *Spiritual Exercises* in 1522. Ignatius founded the Society of Jesus (Jesuits) in 1534. He devoted the rest of his life to the founding and running of schools and seminaries. Also patron of retreats. Canonized 1622; feast day, July 31.

5) Sebastian, martyr. Gaul (3rd century). A favorite among Renaissance painters. According to legend, he was an officer of the imperial guard. When Sebastian admitted his Christian faith, he was shot with arrows by his former coworkers. Surviving the execution, Sebastian was nurtured back to health by the widow of St. Castulus. When Emperor Diocletian received word of Sebastian's recovery, he sent his guards to club him to death. Also patron to archers and athletes. Feast day, January 20.

6) Demetrius, martyr. Salonikan (unknown dates). Legend. This "soldier of God" was imprisoned for preaching the gospel. He was then lanced with a spear before his trial got underway, by the order of Emperor Maximian. Also patron of chivalry. Feast day, October 8.

SOLUTIONS: Expeditus. (Unknown dates.) Absolutely no facts are known about this saint. An unreliable story claims the relics of an unknown saint were sent to a convent in France, with the word *spedito* across the lid. The nuns mistook this for the word *expedite*, which they thought must be the holy deceased's name. But, a Saint Expeditus is named in the eighteenth century, so one can only wonder. Also patron of emergencies; he is invoked against procrastination. Feast day, April 19.

SONGWRITERS: Caedmon, laybrother. English (7th century). Known as "the father of English sacred poetry." Caedmon is accredited as the first English writer of religious poetry. One of the few hymns that has survived him is believed to have been composed while dreaming. Also patron of poets. Feast day, February 11.

SOUTH AFRICA: Our Lady of the Assumption. In 1950, Pope Pius XII surmised that since the Blessed Virgin Mary was born without original sin (Pope Pius IX, 1854), she was elevated (body and soul) to heaven upon her death. Also patron of France, India, Malta, and Paraguay.

SPAIN: James the Greater, apostle. Galilee (1st century). His name James "the Greater" is to differentiate him from the other apostle, James "the Less." He and his brother John "dropped their fishing nets" at the Sea of Galilee and followed Jesus; they were witnesses to both the transfiguration and the agony of Jesus in the garden. James was beheaded in Jerusalem, the first apostle to be martyred. Also patron of Chile, furriers, Guatemala, Nicaragua, pharmacists, and pilgrims; he is invoked against arthritis and rheumatism. Feast day, July 25.

SPASMS, INVOKED AGAINST: John the Baptist, martyr. Israelite (1st century). Cousin to Jesus Christ; his birth was announced by an angel to his father, Zachary. John baptized several of the apostles, including Jesus himself. He was imprisoned for condemning the incestuous relationship Herod was carrying on with his niece, Herodias, who happened to be the wife of Phillip, his half-brother. Herod offered Herodias' daughter, Salome, anything she wanted. Salome requested John's head on a platter, upon her mother's prodding. Also patron of baptism and farriers. Feast day, June 24.

SPELEOLOGISTS: Benedict of Nursia, monk. Italian (480–547). Accredited as the father of Western monasticism. At fourteen, he left his noble family and sister, St. Scholastica, to further his studies in Rome; at twenty, he chose the life of a hermit and moved into a cave; at thirty, he had founded a dozen monasteries. Benedict's book of holy rules became the model for monastic life throughout Europe for centuries. After a poisoning attempt by a jealous monk named Florentius, who found his methods too fastidious, Benedict left the position of abbot. He systemized a dozen monasteries, establishing Western monasticism. Also patron of Europe and monks; he is invoked against poison and witchcraft. Feast day, March 21.

SPINNERS: Catherine, martyr. Alexandrian (4th century). Religious legend. This woman of noble birth chose to study philosophy rather than relish her beauty. Her conversion to Christianity was prompted by a hermit's dream. She then converted Emperor Maxentius' wife, an officer, and two hundred soldiers. In retaliation, the emperor gathered fifty pagan scholars, then challenged her to a religious debate. After a long and heated exchange, Catherine's words swayed all of the fifty scholars to convert. Maxentius had Catherine tied to a wheel, which immediately broke into pieces. She was then beheaded. Also patron of eloquence, maidens, philosophers, preachers, single women, and students. Feast day, November 25.

SPINSTERS: 1) Nicholas of Myra, bishop. Lycian (4th century). Better known as Saint Nick. The facts are few. He ran a monastery, was a prisoner during the time of Christian persecutions, and was present at the Council of Nicaea. The rest is myth. One tale tells of a father who was so poor he couldn't afford his three daughters' dowries. Nick tossed three bags of gold through the kitchen window, and the three daughters married soon after. Also patron of boys, brides, children, dockworkers, Greece, merchants, pawnbrokers, and travelers. Feast day, December 6.

2) Catherine of Siena, mystic. Italian (1347–1380). The twenty-fourth of twenty-five children; one of the great Christian mystics; suffered the pain of stigmata without the visible marks; worked tirelessly with leprosy patients; Doctor of the Church. She convinced Pope Gregory XI to leave Avignon, which returned the papacy to Rome after 68 years. Dictated *Dialogue*, since she was illiterate. Also patron of fire prevention, Italy, and nursing homes. Canonized 1461; feast day, April 29.

SRI LANKA: Lawrence, martyr. Spanish (3rd century). A prediction revealed that he had three days to live. The city prefect mandated the church's treasures be handed over to the emperor. Lawrence sold everything and donated the money to the poor. He returned on the third day with an array of societal misfits and said that they were the church's treasures. The prefect had him bound to a hot griddle. Lawrence asked to be flipped over at one point, claiming he was done on that side. Also patron of cooks, cutlers, glaziers, the poor, and restaurateurs. Feast day, July 29.

STAMP COLLECTORS: Gabriel, archangel. Messenger of God. One of the seven archangels of God; one of the three archangels referred to by name in the Bible. Announced the birth of Jesus to Mary (Luke 1:11–21). Also patron of clerics, diplomats, messengers, postal workers, radio workers, telecommunications workers, and television workers.

Starvation, invoked against: Anthony of Padua, preacher. Portuguese (1195–1231). Born Ferdinand; known as "the Wonder Worker" for his preaching savvy; the first lector in theology; Doctor of the Church; colleague of St. Francis of Assisi. A disciple once took Anthony's psalter without asking. The terrorized novice promptly returned it, claiming that he was being haunted by apparitions for his act. Also the patron of barren women, lost articles, the poor, Portugal, shipwrecks, and travelers. Canonized 1232; feast day, June 13.

Steel workers: Eligius (Eloi), bishop. French (588–660). As a metalsmith, he crafted two thrones for King Choltar II with the portions of gold and jewels provided to him for one. He was then appointed as the master of the mint and used his influence to help the sick and homeless. Also patron of farriers, garage workers, and jewelers. Feast day, December 1.

Stenographers: 1) Cassian, stenographer. Tangarine (3rd century). He became a Christian after being the official recorder at the unjust trial of St. Marcellus. He threw his tablet and writing implement on the floor when the sentence was announced and was immediately put to death. Also patron of court clerks. Feast day, December 3.

  2) Genesius, martyr. Roman (3rd century). Legend. This comedian converted to Christianity while performing a farce of Christian baptism on stage for the Emperor Diocletian in Rome. For refusing the emperor's order to recant, Genesius was tortured, then beheaded while still on stage. Also patron of actors, lawyers, printers, and secretaries. Feast day, August 25.

Step-parents: Adelaide, Empress. Burgundian (931–991). A first marriage to Lothair, the king of Italy, was brief. Lothair died shortly after the birth of their daughter Emma. Adelaide was then kidnaped by Berengarius, who tried to force the young queen to marry his son. Adelaide refused and was thrown in the dungeon of a castle on Lake Garda. Otto the Great of Germany rescued Adelaide and defeated Berengarius' army. The two were wed on Christmas, which united the German and Italian empires. The couple raised their five children, along with Emma and Otto's son Rudolph. In 962, Otto became emperor of Rome. Empress Adelaide founded monasteries, convents, and donated generously to the needy. Also patron of empresses, parenthood, princesses, and second marriages. Feast day, December 16.

STERILITY, INVOKED AGAINST: Henry II, emperor. Bavarian (11th century). Good King Henry and his wife, St. Cunegund, were childless. Unwarranted rumors after the couple's death claim the two had taken a vow of celibacy. They were cofounders of schools and reformers of the church. Henry died with the title of emperor of the Holy Roman Empire. Also patron of dukes. Feast day, July 15.

STOMACHACHES, INVOKED AGAINST: Wolfgang, bishop. Swabian (924–994). The tomb site of this educator of both clergymen and his future king (Henry II) is believed to cure sufferers of stomach ailments. Also patron of woodsmen. Canonized 1052; feast day, October 31.

STOMACH DISEASE, INVOKED AGAINST: Brice, bishop. French (5th century). Also known as Britus and Brictio. As the precocious student of St. Martin, Brice thought his teacher to be a fool. St. Martin was patient with the lad, knowing the cleric would someday succeed him as bishop. When that day arrived, Brice was unable to assume the bishop's mitre. He was accused of lewd behavior by a woman from his own parish, then banished for seven years. Brice returned to his see a new man. He even performed a miracle to prove his innocence. Years later, when Brice died, he was almost immediately venerated. Feast day, November 13.

STONECUTTERS: Clement I, martyr. Roman (1st–2nd century). The third pope (Peter was the first, Cletus was the second). When Emperor Trajan banished Clement from Rome, he was forced to work the quarries in Russia. It is said that during a water shortage in the mines, a spring suddenly flowed from the earth, quenching the prisoners' thirst. Clement founded seventy-five churches in his absence from Rome. He was martyred when thrown into the Black Sea with an anchor tied to him. Also patron of marble workers. Feast day, November 23.

STONEMASONS: 1) Barbara, martyr. (4th century.) Religious fiction. A young woman whose pagan father locked her in a tower before leaving on a long journey. Within the walls, she converted to Christianity and had three windows built to signify the Trinity. When her father returned, he was so infuriated by his daughter's religious preference, he turned her over to the authorities. Barbara was subjected to heinous torture, yet refused to disavow her faith. The judge ordered the father to kill her himself. Atop a mountain he slew his daughter, then was immediately struck dead by a bolt of lightning. Also patron of architects, builders, dying, fire prevention, founders, and prisoners. Feast day, December 4.

2) Reinhold, monk. French (10th century). Jealous stonemasons murdered this overseer for laboring more diligently than they were willing to work. Feast day, January 7.

3) Stephen, martyr. Hellenist (of the Dispersion) (1st century). The first martyr for Christ. The Jewish council

stoned Stephen to death after he denounced them. Also patron of bricklayers and deacons. Feast day, December 26.

STORMS, INVOKED AGAINST: Scholastica, abbess. Norcian (480–543). She was the sister of St. Benedict; some historians believe they were fraternal twins. Founder of a convent near Monte Cassino, she was the first Benedictine nun. Her brother paid a visit at her convent one day. When it grew late, Benedict prepared to leave. Scholastica prayed for a storm, keeping her brother a few extra days, until she died. Also patron of convulsive children. Feast day, February 10.

STRESS: Walter of Pontnoise, abbot. French (17th century). This professor of philosophy was recruited by King Philip I, who persuaded him to become the abbot of a local monastery. Walter agreed on the condition that he would not be subordinate to the crown. Feeling overwhelmed by his responsibilities soon after taking office, Walter began his search for prayer in solitude. But as abbot he was in such high demand that every time he found a place of retreat, zealots would search him out. The situation only worsened when Pope Gregory XV refused his resignation. Walter spent the rest of his life aiding others and searching for quiet corners for self-mortification. Also patron of job-related stress and wine merchants. Feast day, April 8.

STUDENTS: Catherine, martyr. Alexandrian (4th century). Religious legend. This woman of noble birth chose to study philosophy rather than relish her beauty. Her conversion to Christianity was prompted by a hermit's dream. She then converted Emperor Maxentius' wife, an officer, and two hundred soldiers. In retaliation, the emperor gathered fifty pagan scholars, then challenged her to a religious debate. After a long and heated exchange, Catherine's words swayed all of the fifty scholars to convert. Maxentius had Catherine tied to a wheel, which immediately broke into pieces. She was then beheaded. Also patron of eloquence, maidens, philosophers, preachers, single women, and spinners. Feast day, November 25.

SUCCESSFUL ENTERPRISES: Servatius, bishop. Armenian (4th century). This native Armenian gave refuge to St. Athanasius while he was in exile. Servatius foresaw the invasion of the Huns seventy years before Attila devastated Gaul, then died shortly after he returned from a penitential trip to Rome. His staff, cup, and a key, presented to him by St. Peter's apparition, are kept in Maestricht. Also invoked against leg disorders and vermin. Feast day, May 13.

SURGEONS: 1) Cosmas and Damian, martyrs. Arabians (4th century). Known as "the holy moneyless ones." Twin physicians who took no payment from their patients, they were beheaded along with their three brothers for their Christian beliefs. Some critics feel that their legend derives from Greek mythology's Castor and Pollux. Also patrons of barbers, doctors, druggists, pharmacists, and physicians. Feast day, September 26.

2) Luke, evangelist. Greek (1st century). Physician and artist. Little is known of his early life. He was the author of the third Gospel and the Acts of the Apostles, which serve as a record of the progression of early Christianity. He died in Greece at the age of 84. Also patron of artists, butchers, glassworkers, notaries, painters, and physicians. Feast day, October 18.

SWEDEN: Bridget of Sweden, Princess. Swedish (1303–1373). Mystic, prophet; wife of Ulf Gudmarrson;

mother of eight, including St. Catherine. She reformed much of the lapsed attitude in the convents, cared for the sick, and was the founder of a monastery in Vadstena. For some reason, Bridget was canonized three times. Also patron of healers; she is invoked against miscarriages. Canonized 1391; feast day, July 23.

SWIMMERS: Adjutor, monk. French (12th century). Knight and the Lord of Vernon-sur-Seine. While sailing to his first crusade in 1095, he was captured by Muslims but managed to escape. Back in France, he became a monk. Adjutor's final years were devoted to prayer and meditation; he died at Tiron. Also patron of yachtsmen; he is invoked against drowning. Feast day, April 30.

SWORDSMITHS: Maurice, officer. Egyptian (3rd century). Legend. As officer in the Theban Legion, Maurice encouraged his Christian platoon to refuse Maximian Herculius' request to worship pagan gods. Maximian ordered the execution of every tenth man, which proved to be an ineffective deterrent. A second, then third decimation began. Eventually, the entire unit was put to death. Also patron of dyers, infantrymen, knife sharpeners, and weavers; he is invoked against gout. Feast day, September 22.

SYPHILIS, INVOKED AGAINST: Fiacre, hermit. Irish (7th century). Healer; built a refuge for the sick and poor. He was once endowed by St. Faro with all the land he could clear in a single day. When the saint returned at dusk, a large field was clear and ready for planting. The first cabstand in Paris was near the Hotel Saint Fiacre. As a result, the French word for taxi is *fiacre*. Also patron of cab drivers and gardeners; he is invoked against hemorrhoids. Feast day, September 1.

Drunkenness is the ruin of reason. It is premature old age. It is temporary death.

—St. Basil

TAILORS: 1) Homobonus, cloth worker. Italian (12th century). A wealthy merchant who went into the family's tailoring business, he donated most of his money to the needy. Homobonus died during mass. Also patron of businessmen and cloth workers. Feast day, November 13.

2) Martin of Tours, bishop. Hungarian (316–397). One night, this soldier came upon a peasant shivering in the doorway. He tore his cape in half and covered the old man with it. Through a dream, Martin saw Christ wearing the half-cloak and awoke a converted man. After his baptism, Martin advanced to the battlefield as a conscientious objector. Martin then left the military to begin his work as one of the forefathers of monasticism, where he and his followers practiced mortification and penance. The people of Tours elected an uneager Martin as their bishop. Leaving his monastery in the countryside, Bishop

Martin took his place at the see wearing his animal skins. The oldest church in England is named after him. Also patron of horsemen and the impoverished. Feast day, November 8.

TANNERS: Crispin and Crispinian, martyrs. Roman (3rd century). Legend. These brothers were Christian converters by day and shoemakers by night. Their torturer, Maximian, took his own life in frustration when his attempts to execute the siblings failed. The two were then beheaded. Also patrons of cobblers, leatherworkers, saddlers, and shoemakers. Feast day, October 25.

TANZANIA: Immaculate Conception. In 1854, Pope Pius IX declared the Blessed Virgin Mary as born without original sin, having been immaculately conceived, and having lived a sin-free life. Also patron of Brazil, Corsica, Portugal, and the United States.

TAX COLLECTORS: Matthew, apostle. Galilee (1st century). His name means "Gift of God." Also known as Levi; no records of his early life. Tax collector turned apostle; he wrote the first Gospel between 60 and 90, which contains quotes from the Old Testament. He was martyred either in Ethiopia or Persia. Also patron of accountants, bankers, customs agents, and security guards. Feast day, September 21.

TEACHERS: 1) Gregory the Great, pope. Roman (540–604). Originator of the Gregorian chants; Doctor of the Church. His "height of embarrassment," as he put it, occurred when Gregory was named pope in 590. He converted England to Christianity, initiated medieval papacy, and authored fourteen books. Also patron of musicians, popes, and singers. Canonized 604; feast day, September 3.

2) John Baptist de la Salle, educator. French (1651–

1719). Gave his fortune to the poor, then dedicated his life to education. He created the classroom method of teaching, as opposed to one-on-one instruction, then founded numerous schools. Also patron of schoolteachers. Canonized 1900; feast day, April 7.

TEENAGERS: Aloysius Gonzaga, priest. Spanish (1568–1591). At seventeen, Aloysius announced to his prestigious family that he planned to join a new order known as the Jesuits. They preferred that he become a soldier, until a bad kidney quashed the family's hopes of grandeur. As a seminary student, Aloysius taught catechism to poor youths. He died while tending to plague victims. Canonized 1727; feast day, June 21.

TELECOMMUNICATIONS WORKERS: Gabriel, archangel. Messenger of God. One of the seven archangels of God; one of the three archangels referred to by name in the Bible. Announced the birth of Jesus to Mary (Luke 1:11–21). Also patron of broadcasters, clerics, diplomats, messengers, postal workers, radio workers, stamp collectors, and television workers.

TELEVISION: Clare of Assisi, nun. Italian (1194–1253). At the age of eighteen, Clare ran away from home to follow the examples of St. Francis. Clare was appointed the superior of a church in San Damiano. She founded the Poor Clares, an order of barefoot nuns who took a vow of poverty. St. Francis aside, she is most responsible for the furtherance of the Franciscans. Pope Pius XII declared her as patron of television in 1958. Apparently, Clare was able to watch midnight mass from her deathbed, though many walls should have made this impossible. Canonized 1255; feast day, August 11.

TELEVISION WORKERS: Gabriel, archangel. Messenger of God. One of the seven archangels of God; one of the three archangels referred to by name in the Bible. Announced the birth of Jesus to Mary (Luke 1:11–21). Also patron of broadcasters, clerics, diplomats, messengers, postal workers, radio workers, stamp collectors, and telecommunications workers.

TENTMAKERS: Paul, apostle. Tarsus (1st century). "The Great Apostle." A tentmaker by trade, Paul was a Jew named Saul who was one of the tormenters of the early Christians, until Christ's voice from heaven asked him why he was persecuting "His people." After converting, Paul traveled to Jerusalem, where he was welcomed by the apostles. From there, Paul ventured on three crucial missionary trips throughout Europe and Asia Minor. He converted thousands and authored fourteen New Testament letters. Paul and St. Peter were arrested in Rome. Paul was beheaded, and St. Peter was crucified upside down, during Emperor Nero's persecutions of Christians. Also patron of Malta, public relations; he is invoked against snake bites. Feast day, June 29.

TERTIARIES (LAY PEOPLE IN RELIGIOUS ORDERS):
1) Elizabeth, Queen. Hungarian (1207–1231). Although her marriage to Ludwig IV was arranged, the two were in love and had three children. In 1227 Ludwig died while on crusade. Elizabeth and her children were kicked out of the Wartburg castle by the in-laws. She made arrangements for her children, then relinquished herself of her title. Joining the Franciscan order, she devoted herself to the care of those in need. She was counseled by a tyrant named Conrad of Marburg. He was insistent that she suffer extreme deprivation and humility for the rest of her short life, which ended at the tender age of twenty-three. Also patron of bakers and nursing homes. Canonized 1235; feast day, November 17.

2) Elizabeth of Portugal, Queen. Aragonian (1271–1336). Niece of Elizabeth of Hungary. King Peter III of Aragon offered his twelve-year-old daughter's hand to King Denis of Portugal. She was constantly interceding as peacemaker between her son, Alfonso, and his father. King Denis once believed her to be endorsing her son for the throne; he then banished Elizabeth from Portugal. After the king's death, Elizabeth joined the Secular Franciscan order and moved to a convent of the Sisters of St. Claire, which she had founded in Coimbra. Also patron of brides and war; she is invoked against jealousy and marital problems. Canonized 1626; feast day, July 4.

3) Margaret of Cortona, mystic. Italian (1247–1297). At the age of seven, Margaret's mother suddenly died. Her father remarried a woman who was cruel to the girl. When old enough, Margaret left the farm and moved in with a knight. She was the mistress of the castle for nine years, and she bore a son before her lover's murder. She publicly confessed, then served her penance. Margaret's father turned the two away from his home. It was at this time that Margaret joined the Franciscan tertiaries and began to experience visions and healing powers. She devoted the rest of her life to the neglected. Also patron of the homeless, midwives, and single mothers. Canonized 1728; feast day, February 22.

THEOLOGIANS: 1) Alphonso Maria de'Liguori, theologian. Italian (1696–1787). At age sixteen, he had received his doctorate in canon and civil law. When not experiencing visions, ecstasies, or prophecies, he authored *Moral Theology* and *Glories of Mary*. Also patron of confessors, professors, and vocations. Canonized 1839; feast day, August 1.

2) Augustine of Hippo, bishop, doctor. North Afri-

can (354–430). He was into parties, fun, and games. Augustine kept a mistress and sired a son out of wedlock. The conversion of Augustine is attributed to the prayers of his mother, Saint Monica, and a sermon by Saint Ambrose. As a convert, he authored numerous works, *Confessions* and *City of God*, to name two. He was one of the greatest intellectuals of the Catholic church and the first philosopher of Christianity, associating the term "original sin" with Adam and Eve. Also patron of brewers and printers. Feast day, August 28.

THERAPISTS: Christina the Astonishing, laywoman. Flemish (1150–1224). At the age of twenty-one, Christina had a seizure which appeared to kill her. During her funeral mass, Christina opened her eyes, then flew to the rafters of the cathedral. She landed on the altar and spoke of her journey through heaven, hell, purgatory, and back. Christina believed she was released from the afterlife to pray for the souls in purgatory. It is said that Christina was never the same, being repulsed by the scent of people. She would hide in small spaces, such as cupboards or ovens. Christina died in St. Catherine's convent some years later. Also patron of lunatics. Feast day, July 24.

THIEVES: Dismas, thief. (1st century.) All that is known of this "good thief" is that he was hanged on the cross next to Jesus. Also patron of death row inmates, funeral directors, prisoners, and undertakers. Feast day, March 25.

THROAT DISEASE, INVOKED AGAINST: Blaise, bishop. Armenian (4th century). Legend. The particulars of this bishop are a union of tales. During the persecution of Christians, Blaise hid in a cave. He tended there to wounded animals, who had been harmed by the traps and arrows of hunters. Blaise was martyred during Lininius' persecutions. His patronage comes from once saving a boy from choking on a fish bone. Also patron of veterinarians and wild animals. Feast day, February 3.

THUNDERSTORMS, INVOKED AGAINST: Agrippina, martyr. Roman (3rd century). During the persecution of Christians, Agrippina was tortured then executed when she refused to renounce her faith to Emperors Valerian or Diocletian. Her body was taken to Sicily by three women, where the afflicted have been cured at her tomb for centuries. She is invoked against bacterial diseases and evil spirits. Feast day, June 23.

TODDLERS: Vaast, bishop. French (6th century). King Clovis I was en route to Rheims when he stopped at Toul long enough to find a priest to escort him to his baptism. Vaast reluctantly complied with the king's wishes. On the way, Vaast cured a number of lame people, which prompted the king's men to convert. Upon reaching Rheims, Vaast found that Christianity was all but a memory there. He built a church, then resuscitated the faith in Rheims. Feast day, February 6.

TOOTHACHE SUFFERERS: Apollonia, martyr. Alexandrian (3rd century). An elderly deaconess who refused to denounce her faith during a riot against Christians. Her beating was so severe, her teeth were smashed. Saying a prayer, she flung herself into her captors' bonfire. Also patron of dentists. Feast day, February 9.

TORTURE VICTIMS: 1) Alban, martyr. Roman (4th century). Legend. First martyr of Britain. He harbored a fugitive priest who had escaped Emperor Diocletian's persecution of Christians. While the father rested, Alban put on the priest's clothes and turned himself in as the renegade. He was tortured, then beheaded. Also patron of refugees. Feast day, June 21.

2) Eustachius (Eustace), martyr. Roman (1st century). Pious legend. One of the fourteen "Holy Helpers." He was a general with Emperor Trajan's army. Eustachius converted to Christianity while hunting a stag with the shape of a crucifix between its antlers. He and his family were burnt to death for refusing to denounce their Christian faith. Also patron of hunters. Feast day, September 20.

3) Regina, martyr. Burgundian (3rd century). After her mother's death during childbirth, Regina was sent to live with a poor shepherdess, who secretly raised her as a Christian. When Regina's pagan father learned of his daughter's faith, he attempted to marry her off to a fellow pagan named Olybrius. Regina was imprisoned, tortured, then beheaded. Also patron of poverty and shepherdesses. Feast day, September 7.

4) Vincent, martyr. Saragossan (4th century). Emperors Diocletian and Maximian had teamed up in their efforts to punish those practicing Christianity. Vincent was caught, tried, then sent to prison. He seemed to thrive under prison conditions, which caused the emperors to suspect their guards of going easy on the prisoner. Vincent was thrown back into his cell; this time the orders were to have the prisoner tortured by the cruelest means devised by man. When brought before the emperors this time, Vincent called his torturers "faint-hearted." The baffled executioners were severely reprimanded before getting another crack at Vincent. After a successful execution, Vincent's body was tossed into a nearby field. A raven protected the holy corpse from predators until nightfall, when his fellow Christians were able to retrieve his body. Also patron of wineries. Feast day, January 22.

5) Victor of Marseilles, martyr. Gaulish (3rd century). Pious legend. When Emperor Maximian discovered that his favorite Roman guard was a Christian, Victor was subjected to a number of tortures. As he was being stretched on a rack for refusing to worship pagan deities, Jesus Christ appeared to Victor. That night, God sent his angels to his cell, causing the conversion of three prison guards. The next day, Emperor Maximian had the new converts beheaded. Victor was brought before the emperor again. Maximian ordered the battered man to offer incense to Jupiter. Victor kicked the statue, which enraged Maximian. The Christian's foot was ordered to be hacked off before he was crushed in a mill. The grindstone broke about halfway through the execution, yet a partially pulverized Victor still lived on. One of his executioners drew a sword and beheaded him. Also patron of millers; he is invoked against foot trouble. Feast day, July 21.

TOYMAKERS: Claud, bishop. French (7th century). Instead of joining the military, this son from a congressional family joined the priesthood. Under the rule of the Benedictine order, he reformed a monastery in the Jura Mountains. Claud was then elected bishop of Besançon. In art, he is depicted as bringing a child back to life. Also patron of tuners. Feast day, June 6.

TRANSIENTS: Benedict Joseph Labre, transient. Boulognian (18th century). After being rejected from several religious orders, Benedict left his wealthy family to search for God. Traveling throughout Europe for three years, he visited every pilgrimage site in his holy quest. Ending up at the Colosseum, Benedict the beggar spent his last years in intense prayer. He died in church. Also patron of beggars, the homeless, and religious orders. Feast day, April 16.

TRAPPERS: Bartholomew, apostle. Israelite (1st century). Also known as Nathaniel. The authorship of the extrabiblical gospel attributed to Bartholomew is questionable. Little else is known about the son of Tolomai. He is believed to have traveled to Ethiopia, India, and Persia; he was martyred in Armenia. In art, he is often depicted flayed. Also patron of Armenia. Feast day, August 24.

TRAVELERS: 1) Anthony of Padua, preacher. Portuguese (1195–1231). Born Ferdinand; known as "the Wonder Worker" for his preaching savvy; the first lector in theology; Doctor of the Church; colleague of St. Francis of Assisi. A disciple once took Anthony's psalter without asking. The terrorized novice promptly returned it, claiming that he was being haunted by apparitions for his act. Also the patron of barren women, lost articles, the poor, Portugal, shipwrecks; he is invoked against starvation. Canonized 1232; feast day, June 13.

2) Christopher, martyr. Lycian (3rd century). Legend. There are a number of legends about the man martyred in Lycia. One goes like this: He was a hideous giant named Offero, who earned a living carrying travelers across the river. He carried a heavy lad one day, claiming to be weighted by the problems of the world. This child, of course, was a youthful Christ. The name Christopher itself means "carrier of Christ" in Greek. Also patron of bachelors, bus drivers, motorists, porters, and truck drivers; he is invoked against nightmares. Feast day, July 25.

3) Nicholas of Myra, bishop. Lycian (4th century). Better known as Saint Nick. The facts are few. He ran a monastery, was a prisoner during the time of Christian persecutions, and was present at the Council of Nicaea. The rest is myth. One tale tells of a father who was so poor he couldn't afford his three daughters' dowries.

Nick tossed three bags of gold through the kitchen window, and the three daughters married soon after. Also patron of boys, brides, children, dockworkers, Greece, merchants, pawnbrokers, and spinsters. Feast day, December 6.

4) Raphael, archangel. One of the seven archangels of God; one of the three archangels specified by name in the Bible. He has been venerated by both Jewish and Christian faiths. His name means "God heals." Also patron of the blind, lovers, nurses, and physicians. Feast day, September 29.

5) Three Magi—Caspar, Melchior, and Balthasar (1st century). Better known as the three wisemen who visited the newborn Jesus. It is believed that they were astrologers from Babylonia or Arabia. Feast day, July 23.

TRUCK DRIVERS: Christopher, martyr. Lycian (3rd century). Legend. There are a number of legends about the man martyred in Lycia. One goes like this: He was a hideous giant named Offero, who earned a living carrying travelers across the river. He carried a heavy lad one day, claiming to be weighted by the problems of the world. This child, of course, was a youthful Christ. The name Christopher itself means "carrier of Christ" in Greek. Also patron of bachelors, bus drivers, motorists, porters, and travelers; he is invoked against nightmares. Feast day, July 25.

TUBERCULOSIS SUFFERERS: 1) Pantaleon, martyr. Bithynian (4th century). Pious legend. This respected man of medicine lived a privileged life as the personal physician to Emperor Galerius. When the emperor learned that Pantaleon had converted to Christianity, he had him sentenced to death. The six attempts to execute the convert (burning, molten lead, being thrown to the lions, drowning, the wheel, and stabbing) all failed. Once Pantaleon was confident that he had proved his theological point, he bowed his head and allowed the haggard executioner to behead him. Also patron of doctors and endurance. Feast day, July 27.

2) Gemma Galani, mystic. Italian (1878–1903). This nineteen-year-old orphan suffered from spinal tuberculosis, which kept her from becoming a Passionist nun. Praying to her intercessor, St. Gabriel Possenti, Gemma was miraculously cured. At twenty-one, she began to experience stigmata and other marks of the Lord's afflictions. The devil also paid her a visit, coaxing her to spit on a cross and break a rosary. Gemma died peacefully at the age of twenty-five. There was much opposition upon her canonization in 1940. Also patron of pharmacists. Feast day, April 11.

TUNERS: Claud, bishop. French (7th century). Instead of joining the military, this son from a congressional family joined the priesthood. Under the rule of the Benedictine order, he reformed a monastery in the Jura Mountains. Claud was then elected bishop of Besançon. In art, he is depicted as bringing a child back to life. Also patron of toymakers. Feast day, June 6.

. . . The gifts of grace increase as the struggles increase.

—St. Rose of Lima

UKRAINE: Josaphat, martyr. Polish (1580–1623). The Byzantine archbishop accused Josaphat of being a Roman Catholic, which divided the people of Poletsk. A priest named Elias was arrested for an assassination attempt on the bishop's life. This caused an angry mob to storm Josaphat's chambers, where they beat and shot him. Josaphat has the distinction of being the first Eastern saint to be canonized in Rome, in 1876. Feast day, November 12.

UNDERTAKERS: 1) Joseph of Arimathea, disciple. Arimathean (1st century). He witnessed Christ's crucifixion, then laid Christ's body in a tomb. His name is cited in the four gospels. Legend has it that he obtained the holy grail from the last supper. Also patron of funeral directors. Feast day, March 17.

   2) Dismas, thief. (1st century.) All that is known of this "good thief" is that he was hanged on the cross next

to Jesus. Also patron of death row inmates, funeral directors, prisoners, and thieves. Feast day, March 25.

UNHAPPILY MARRIED MEN: Gummarus, courtier. Flemish (8th century). Also known as Gomer. As a servant to the court of Pepin, Gummarus married the nefarious Guinimaria. After a number of years of persecution from this brutal woman, Gummarus paid off the money kept from the servants' wages by his wife and joined a hermitage. He founded the abbey at Lierre. Also patron of cowherds and spousal separation; he is invoked against impotence. Feast day, October 11.

UNHAPPILY MARRIED WOMEN: Wilgefortis, martyr. Portuguese (unknown dates). Legend. Her father, the king of Portugal, had betrothed her to the king of Sicily against her will. She prayed so intensely, she sprouted facial hair. The king of Sicily backed out of the arrangement. Her outraged father then crucified her. Feast day, July 20.

UNITED STATES OF AMERICA: Immaculate Conception. In 1854, Pope Pius IX declared the Blessed Virgin Mary as born without original sin, having been immaculately conceived, and having lived a sin-free life. Also patron of Brazil, Corsica, Portugal, and Tanzania.

UNIVERSITIES: Contardo Ferrini, professor. Italian (1859–1902). This professor of Roman law co-founded the St. Severinus Boethius Society for university students. He was fluent in a dozen languages. Feast day, October 20.

URUGUAY: Our Lady of Lujan. Over three hundred years ago, a two-foot-tall statue of the Immaculate Conception disappeared from Buenos Aires, then miraculously turned up in Lujan. In 1904, a church was erected around the fragile figurine. Also patron of Argentina.

Belligerents are not reluctant to have peace, but they want it of their own liking.

—St. Augustine of Hippo

VERMIN, INVOKED AGAINST: Servatius, bishop. Armenian (4th century). This native Armenian gave refuge to St. Athanasius while he was in exile. Servatius foresaw the invasion of the Huns seventy years before Attila devastated Gaul, then died shortly after he returned from a penitential trip to Rome. His staff, cup, and a key, presented to him by St. Peter's apparition, are kept in Maestricht. Also patron to successful enterprises; he is invoked against leg disorders. Feast day, May 13.

VETERINARIANS: Blaise, bishop. Armenian (4th century). Legend. The particulars of this bishop are a union of tales. During the persecution of Christians, Blaise hid in a cave. He tended there to wounded animals, who had been harmed by the traps and arrows of hunters. Blaise was martyred during Lininius' persecutions. Also patron of wild animals; he is invoked against throat disease. Feast day, February 3.

VINEGROWERS: Tychon, bishop. Cyprene (5th century). According to tradition, Bishop Tychon was granted a small, barren vineyard. He planted a dead vine branch, then said a prayer for an early harvest. The next autumn, Tychon's vines had not only multiplied but the sweet grapes had matured before those in any other vineyard. Critics believe that the tale of Tychon evolved from those of the pagan god Priapus. Feast day, June 16.

VINTAGES: Medard, bishop. French (470–560). Medard was appointed to the dioceses of Tournai and Noyan after the attack by the Huns. According to local belief, if it rains on Medard's feast day, expect forty more days of wet weather. If it's sunny on his feast day, the next forty will be as well. This legend is remarkably similar to St. Swithun's. Also patron of corn harvests. Feast day, June 8.

VIRGINS: Blessed Virgin Mary. (1st century.) Mother of God. The second holiest person (Christ, her son, is first); daughter of Anne and Joachim; born free of original sin; wife of Joseph; impregnated by the Holy Spirit; mother of Jesus; witness to Christ's first miracle in Cana, where he turned water into wine (John 2:1–11); was present when Christ was nailed to the cross (John 19:25–27); prayed for her son after his death (Acts 1:12–14). Her body was raised to heaven upon her death, where it was reunited with her soul. Mary is the most sought-after saint in heaven. She has appeared with messages and prophesies and is venerated throughout the world. Also patron of Korea and mothers. Feast day, August 15.

VIRTUE: Hallvard, martyr. Norwegian. (11th century.) Religious folktale. One day this son of a landowner was about to take his boat out for a leisurely day of fishing. A frantic woman burst from the wilderness and told a startled Hallvard that she had wrongly been accused of stealing, then asked for his aid. As the two rowed away, the mob reached the shore. They insisted that the woman be returned; Hallvard continued rowing. Both were then shot with arrows by her pursuers. Also patron of innocence. Feast day, May 15.

VOCATIONS: Alphonso Maria de'Liguori, theologian. Italian (1696–1787). At age sixteen, he had received his doctorate in canon and civil law. When not experiencing visions, ecstasies, or prophecies, he authored *Moral Theology* and *Glories of Mary*. His patronage to confessors is attributed to the large crowds he attracted to the confessionals. Also patron of confessors, professors, and theologians. Canonized 1839; feast day, August 1.

VOLCANIC ERUPTIONS, INVOKED AGAINST: Agatha, martyr. Sicilian (unknown dates). Legend. The governor Quintianis used the persecution of Christians as a way of possessing her. She refused his advances and was brutally tortured. Her captor starved her, sliced off her breasts, then rolled her in hot coals and broken pottery. She died in her cell. In early paintings of this saint, her breasts displayed on a platter have been mistaken for bread. Hence, the blessing of bread on her feast day. Also patron of nurses and rape victims; she is invoked against breast disease. Feast day, February 5.

. . . Of two imperfect things, holy rusticity is better than sinful eloquence.

—St. Jerome

WAITPERSONS: Martha, homemaker. Bethanian (1st century). A friend of Jesus; older sister of Mary and Lazarus. During one of Jesus' many visits to their home, Martha fussed away in the kitchen, while Mary listened attentively to Christ. Jesus then said to her, "Martha, Martha, thou art careful and troubled about many things; but one thing is needful; and Mary hath chosen that good part, which shall not be taken away from her" (Luke 10:41–42). Also patron of cooks, dietitians, and servants. Feast day, July 29.

WALES: David (Dewi), bishop. Welsh (6th century). This third son of King Sant and St. Non was ordained, then founded twelve monasteries. According to the legend, David was about to give a sermon in Brefi. The ground beneath him swelled enough for him to be visible from the back of the crowd. Just then a dove landed on David's shoulder. Also patron of doves. Feast day, March 1.

WAR: Elizabeth of Portugal, Queen. Aragonian (1271–1336). Niece of Elizabeth of Hungary. King Peter III of Aragon offered his twelve-year-old daughter's hand to King Denis of Portugal. She was constantly interceding as peacemaker between her son, Alfonso, and his father. King Denis once believed her to be endorsing her son for the throne; he then banished Elizabeth from Portugal. After the king's death, Elizabeth joined the Secular Franciscan order and moved to a convent of the Sisters of St. Claire, which she had founded in Coimbra. Also patron of brides, tertiaries, and war; she is invoked against jealousy and marital problems. Canonized 1626; feast day, July 4.

WATCHMEN: Peter of Alcantara, monk. Spanish (1499–1562). He instilled more atonement and rigidity to the order of friars. He even prayed throughout the night on his knees. When he grew sleepy, Peter would lean his head against the wall and doze. Hence, his patronage to watchmen. Canonized 1669; feast day, October 22.

WEAVERS: 1) Paul the Hermit, hermit. Roman (4th century). The protohermit. Fleeing from the persecutions of Christians, Paul sought temporary refuge in a cave. He remained there for the next seventy-five years or so. Upon his death, St. Anthony and his two lions (gifts from St. Athanasius) buried Paul. Feast day, January 15.

2) Maurice, officer. Egyptian (3rd century). Legend. As officer in the Theban Legion, Maurice encouraged his Christian platoon to refuse Maximian Herculius' request to worship pagan gods. Maximian ordered the execution of every tenth man, which proved to be an ineffective deterrent. A second, then third decimation

began. Eventually, the entire unit was put to death. Also patron of dyers, infantrymen, knife sharpeners, and swordsmiths; he is invoked against gout. Feast day, September 22.

WEST INDIES: Gertrude, mystic. Saxon (1256–1302). This orphan ended up on the doorstep of the Benedictine nuns, who took her in and raised her. Gertrude's visions of Christ are reflected in her writings, such as the *Revelation of St. Gertrude*. Feast day, November 16.

WHALES: Brendan the Navigator, founder/explorer. Irish (1303–1373). The Clonfert monastery, which he founded, was the core of missionary endeavors for centuries. Some scholars believe that his book *Navigato Sancti Brenardani Abbatis* was based on his accounts of an expedition to North America. Also patron of sailors. Feast day, May 16.

WIDOWS: 1) Paula, founder. Roman (347–404). After her husband died, she devoted her life to assisting St Jerome's many projects. They built churches, hospices, monasteries, and convents. Feast day, January 26.

2) Clotilde, Queen. French (6th century). She gave birth to the three sons and daughter of King Clovis, before the king's death in 511. The greedy children were at constant odds with one another over control of the kingdom. The rivalry led to the murder of Clodomir, her eldest son. Clotilde quickly adopted his three children, which angered Clotaire, her youngest son. He proceeded to murder two of the small children. Clotilde managed to sneak young Saint Cloud to safety away from his uncle's wrath. Clotilde then spent the rest of her life tending to the needy. Also patron of adopted children, the death of children, parenthood, and queens. Feast day, June 3.

3) Fabiola, founder. Roman (3rd century). After divorcing her abusive husband, she remarried. This prevented her from receiving the Sacraments of the church. Fabiola performed public penance, then founded the first Christian hospital. Pope St. Siricus pardoned Fabiola her sins, after her second husband died. Also patron of divorce and infidelity; she is invoked against physical abuse. Feast day, December 27.

WIDOWERS: Edgar, King. English (944–975). After the death of his first wife, Ethelfreda, Edgar married Ethelfrida. A young St. Wilfreda was raped by Prince Edgar, from which event St. Edith was born. St. Dunstan's penance on the penitent prince delayed his coronation for seven years. The king's reign was brief. In the two years before his death, he reformed the secular clergy. Though the church has declared Edgar a saint, his feast day has yet to be selected.

WILD ANIMALS: Blaise, bishop. Armenian (4th century). Legend. The particulars of this bishop are a union of tales. During the persecution of Christians, Blaise hid in a cave. He tended there to wounded animals, who had been harmed by the traps and arrows of hunters. Blaise was martyred during Lininius' persecutions. Also patron of veterinarians; he is invoked against throat disease. Feast day, February 3.

WINERIES: 1) Morand, monk. German (12th century). This Benedictine monk was an advisor to Count Frederick Pferez of Alsace. His patronage derives from eating only grapes during Lent. Feast day, June 3.

2) Vincent, martyr. Saragossan (4th century). Emperors Diocletian and Maximian had teamed up in their efforts to punish those practicing Christianity. Vincent was caught, tried, then sent to prison. He seemed to

thrive under prison conditions, which caused the emperors to suspect their guards of going easy on the prisoner. Vincent was thrown back into his cell; this time the orders were to have the prisoner tortured by the cruelest means devised by man. When brought before the emperors this time, Vincent called his torturers "faint-hearted." The baffled executioners were severely reprimanded before getting another crack at Vincent. After a successful execution, Vincent's body was tossed into a nearby field. A raven protected the holy corpse from predators until nightfall, when his fellow Christians were able to retrieve his body. Also patron of torture victims. Feast day, January 22.

WINE MERCHANTS: 1) Amand, missionary. French (584–679). After leaving the hermitage, he founded monasteries in Belgium; made converts in Flanders, Carinthia, and Germany. Feast day, February 6.

2) Walter of Pontnoise, abbot. French (17th century). This professor of philosophy was recruited by King Philip I, who persuaded him to become the abbot of a local monastery. Walter agreed on the condition that he would not be subordinate to the crown. Feeling overwhelmed by his responsibilities soon after taking office, Walter began his search for prayer in solitude. But as abbot he was in such high demand that every time he found a place of retreat, zealots would search him out. The situation only worsened when Pope Gregory XV refused his resignation. Walter spent the rest of his life aiding others and searching for quiet corners for self-mortification. Also patron of job-related stress. Feast day, April 8.

WITCHCRAFT, INVOKED AGAINST: Benedict of Nursia, monk. Italian (480–547). Accredited as the father of Western monasticism. At fourteen, he left his noble family and sister, St. Scholastica, to further his studies in Rome; at twenty, he chose the life of a hermit and moved into a cave; at thirty, he had founded a dozen monasteries. Benedict's book of holy rules became the model for monastic life throughout Europe for centuries. After a poisoning attempt by a jealous monk named Florentius, who found his methods too fastidious, Benedict left the position of abbot. He systemized a dozen monasteries, establishing Western monasticism. Also patron of Europe, monks, and speleologists; he is invoked against poison. Feast day, March 21.

WOLVES, INVOKED AGAINST: Herve (Harvey), abbot. English (6th century). Pious myth. This musician was born blind and is said to have wandered the countryside converting people with song. One of his most popular miracles occurred one day while plowing. A wolf killed and ate his beast of burden. No sooner had Harvey said "Amen," when the wolf strapped on the harness and finished plowing the field. Another story tells of a fox that stole a chicken from his coop and returned the bird alive. Also invoked against eye trouble and foxes. Feast day, June 17.

WOMEN IN LABOR: 1) Anne, housewife. Nazarean (1st century B.C.). Grandmother of Jesus; wife of Joachim. Aside from giving birth to the Blessed Mary at the age of forty, little is known of her. Also patron of cabinetmakers, grandmothers, and housewives. Feast day, July 26.

2) Leonard, founder. French (6th century). Legend. After he assisted his godfather's, King Clovis', wife in an arduous pregnancy, the king endowed to him the land that he could cover by riding on a donkey in a day. On his new property, Leonard founded Noblac monastery and the town of Saint-Leonard. The king also released

any prisoner that Leonard went to visit. Most of the former inmates sought refuge in his abbey, and many stayed on to help run it. Also patron of prisoners of war; he is invoked against burglary. Feast day, November 6.

WOMEN'S ARMY CORPS: Genevieve, nun. French (420–500). After receiving the call of God at the age of seven, Genevieve predicted the invasion of Attila the Hun in 451. The sparing of Paris from the barbarian's invasion was attributed to her prayers. In 1129, Genevieve's relics were raised and an epidemic of ergot poisoning miraculously ceased. Also invoked against disasters and plagues. Feast day, January 3.

WOODS: Giles, hermit. English (8th century). A forest hermit, he was wounded with an arrow while protecting a hind he had been suckling for a year. The king was so touched by the cripple's compassion, he appointed Giles as one of his advisors. Also patron of beggars, breastfeeding, hermits, horses, and the physically disabled. Feast day, September 1.

WOODSMEN: Wolfgang, bishop. Swabian (924–994). The tomb site of this educator of both clergymen and his future king (Henry II) is believed to cure sufferers of stomach ailments, which he is invoked against. Canonized 1052; feast day, October 31.

WORKING MEN: Joseph, carpenter. Israelite (1st century). Descendent of David; husband to the Virgin Mary; foster father to Jesus Christ. Joseph had second thoughts about marrying Mary when he learned that she was pregnant until the angel Gabriel explained the Messiah's coming. After the birth of Christ, he was forewarned in a dream of Herod's exploits, so he took his young family to Egypt. After Herod's death, a dream directed them to return to Israel. Fearing Herod's replacement, Joseph chose to settle his family in Nazareth. Scholars believe he died before the crucifixion of Christ. Also patron of Belgium, Canada, carpenters, the church, the dying, fathers, Korea, Peru, and social justice. Feast days, March 19 and May 1.

WORKING WOMEN: Flora, martyr. Spanish (9th century). Though Flora's mother was a Christian, the household was run with the strict Muslim beliefs of her father. Flora's rejection of the Islamic faith caused severe beatings by her brother and father, which worsened when she converted to Christianity. She and her best friend, Mary, chose to leave home when Flora's parents announced her engagement to a Muhammedan. The two hid in Flora's sister's home for a brief time. The fear of being associated with Christians led Flora's sister to throw them back out on the street. Flora and Mary confessed themselves to the Islamic council as Christians, and they were tortured before being beheaded. Also patron of victims of betrayal and converts. Feast day, November 24.

WRITERS: 1) Francis de Sales, bishop, writer. French (1567–1622). He earned a doctorate in law at the age of twenty-four. Within five years, surviving numerous assassination attempts, he managed to convert thousands of Calvinists back to Catholicism. Francis' writings include *Introduction to the Devout Life* (1609) and *Treatise on the Love of God* (1616). He was the first to receive beatification at St. Peter's. Also patron of authors, the Catholic press, the deaf, and journalists. Canonized 1877; feast day, January 24.

2) Lucy, martyr. Italian (4th century). Pious myth. It is said that she was once told how pretty her eyes were by an arranged suitor. Lucy gouged them from their sockets and handed them to her horrified future hus-

band, who promptly had her condemned for her Christian beliefs. Proving to be flame-proof when flung in the fire, Lucy was eventually stabbed in the throat. Her name translates to "light." Also patron of cutlers; she is invoked against eye trouble and hemorrhaging. Feast December 13.

Patience is not good if when you may be free you allow yourself to become a slave.

—St. Bernard

YACHTSMEN: Adjutor, monk. French (12th century). Knight and the Lord of Vernon-sur-Seine. While sailing to his first crusade in 1095, he was captured by Muslims but managed to escape. Back in France, he became a monk. Adjutor's final years were devoted to prayer and meditation; he died at Tiron. Also patron of swimmers; he is invoked against drowning. Feast day, April 30.

YOUNG WOMEN: Ursula, martyr. German (unknown dates). Myth. According to the chiseled words on a stone in Cologne, a group of Christian maidens were martyred in the fourth century. Four hundred years later, the tales of the women flowered into this legend. Ursula was the Christian daughter of a British king, whose wedding date to a pagan prince had been set. In an attempt to postpone the nuptials, she boarded a ship with her ladies-in-waiting. They set out for a pilgrimage to Rome. In Cologne, Ursula and her maidens (numbering anywhere from a dozen to a thousand) were attacked by the Huns. Ursula rejected the chieftain's marriage proposal and all of the women were murdered. Also patron of drapers and schoolgirls. Feast day, October 21.

YOUTHS: John Berchmans. Brabanterian (1599–1621). Somehow this Jesuit novice managed hosts of miracles after his death. Also patron of altar boys. Canonized 1888; feast day, November 26.

The gate of heaven is very low; only the humble can enter it.

—St. Elizabeth of Seton

Zoos: Francis of Assisi, founder. (1181–1226.) Although never a priest, he is one of the dominant figures of the Christian religion. Born the son of a wealthy cloth merchant, Francis lived a lavish and irresponsible life. At 20, he went to war against Perugia, where he was captured and imprisoned. After his release, Francis experienced several visions of Christ. He then renounced his inheritance and founded the Friars Minor. The first person ever to receive stigmata (five wounds, concurring with the five wounds of Christ) while praying, which never healed. He created the first Nativity scene in 1223. Also patron of animals, Catholic action, ecologists, Italy, and merchants. Canonized 1228; feast day, October 4.

PART TWO

PRAYERS FROM THE SAINTS

CALENDAR OF ROMAN CATHOLIC FEAST DAYS

BAPTISMAL NAMES FOR CHILDREN

EMBLEMS AND SYMBOLS

PATRONS OF COUNTRIES AND PLACES

Prayers from the Saints

✛

Give me chastity and continence,
but not yet.

> St. Augustine of Hippo (354–430)
> Author, theologian

. . . O divine Master, grant that I may not so much seek
to be consoled, as to console; to be understood, as to under-
stand; to be loved, as to love. For it is in giving that we
receive; it is in pardoning that we are pardoned; and it is
in dying that we are born to eternal life.

> St. Francis of Assisi (1181–1286)
> Founder

Teach us, good Lord, to serve you as you deserve:
To give and not to count the cost;
To fight and not to heed the wounds;
To toil and not to seek for rest;
To labor and not to ask for any reward
Save that of knowing that we do your will.

> St. Ignatius of Loyola (1491–1556)
> Founder, author

O abyss, O eternal Godhead, O sea profound,
what more could you give me than yourself? . . .

> St. Catherine of Siena (1347–1380)
> Dominican nun

I did not know you, my Lord, because I still
desired to know and delight in things.
Well and good of all things change, Lord God,
provided we are rooted in you.
If I go everywhere with you, my God, everywhere
things will happen as I desire for your sake.

> St. John of the Cross (1542–1591)
> Mystic, poet

From silly devotions
and from sour-faced saints,
good Lord, deliver us.

> St. Teresa of Avila (1515–1582)
> Nun, founder, author

Those things, good Lord, that we pray for,
Give us thy grace to labor for.

> Sir Thomas More (1478–1535)
> Martyr

Give me, O Lord,
A steadfast heart, which no unworthy affection may drag
downwards;
Give me an unconquered heart, which no tribulation can
wear out;

give me an upright heart, which no unworthy purpose may tempt aside.

> St. Thomas Aquinas (1225–1274)
> Theologian

My God, I love you.

> The final words of St. Therese of Lisieux
> (1873–1897)
> Nun

Calendar of Roman Catholic Feast Days

✛

The Catholic calendar is organized according to the progression of seasons, revolving around Easter. The tradition of Easter appearing on different dates goes back to the Council of Nicaea in 325. It was then decided that Jesus Christ's resurrection would be celebrated the first Sunday following the first full moon after the vernal equinox of March 21.

The seasons are Advent, Christmas, Lent, Easter Triduum, and the Ordinary Time. The cycles include the life, death, and resurrection of Jesus Christ; homage to the Blessed Virgin Mary; and the veneration of saints. These days of remembrance are celebrated through prayers, festivals and penances. The revised calendar went into effect in 1972.

Floating Feast Days

Year:	1996	1997	1998	1999	2000
Ash Wednesday:	Feb. 21	Feb. 12	Feb. 25	Feb. 17	March 8
Easter Sunday:	April 7	March 30	April 12	April 4	April 23
Ascension:	May 16	May 8	May 21	May 13	June 1
Pentecost:	May 26	May 18	May 31	May 23	June 11
Advent:	Dec. 1	Nov. 30	Nov. 29	Nov. 28	Dec. 3

(The patron saints are listed in bold type below.)

January 1 **Clarus**
January 2 **Basil the Great**
January 3 **Genevieve**
January 4 **Pharaildis**
January 5 **John Nepomucene**
January 6 John de Ribera
January 7 **Bonaventure of Potenza, Raymond of Peñafort, Reinhold**
January 8 **Amalburga**
January 9 Adrian of Canterbury
January 10 Peter Orseolo
January 11 Theodosius the Cenobiarch
January 12 **Benedict Biscop**
January 13 **Hilary of Poitiers**
January 14 **Felix of Nola, Sabas**
January 15 **Maurus, Paul the Hermit**
January 16 Honoratus
January 17 **Anthony the Great**
January 18 Deicolus
January 19 **Fillan, Gervase and Protase, Henry of Uppsala**
January 20 **Sebastian**
January 21 **Agnes**
January 22 **Vincent of Saragossa**
January 23 John the Almsgiver
January 24 **Francis de Sales**
January 25 **Paul**
January 26 **Paula**
January 27 **Devota**
January 28 **Thomas Aquinas**
January 29 Gildas the Wise
January 30 **Adelelm, Aldegonda**
January 31 **John Bosco**

February 1 **Bridget of Ireland**
February 2 **Blaise, Walburga**
February 3 **Ansgar, Blaise**
February 4 **Andrew Corsini**
February 5 **Agatha**
February 6 **Amand, Dorothy, Peter Baptist, Vaast**
February 7 Luke the Younger
February 8 **Jerome Emiliani**
February 9 **Apollonia**
February 10 **Scholastica**
February 11 **Caedmon, Margaret of Cortona**
February 12 **Julian the Hospitaler**
February 13 **Agabus**
February 14 **Cyril and Methodius, Valentine**
February 15 Sigfrid of Vaxjo
February 16 Gilbert of Sempringham
February 17 The Seven Holy Founders
February 18 Theotonius
February 19 **Conrad**
February 20 Wulfric
February 21 Peter Damian
February 22 **Margaret of Cortona**
February 23 **Polycarp**
February 24 Praetexatus
February 25 **Tarasius**
February 26 Alexander of Alexandria
February 27 **Gabriel of the Sorrowful Mother**
February 28 **Romanus**
March 1 **David, Swithbert**
March 2 Chad
March 3 **Winwaloe**
March 4 **Casimir of Poland**
March 5 **John of the Cross**
March 6 Colette
March 7 **Drausius, Perpetua**

March 8 **John of God**
March 9 **Catherine of Bologna, Dominic Savio, Frances of Rome, Gregory of Neocaesarea**
March 10 **Drogo**
March 11 Oengus
March 12 Theophanes
March 13 **Ansovinus**
March 14 Leobinus
March 15 **Louise de Marillac, Matrona**
March 16 Abraham Kidunaia
March 17 **Gertrude, Joseph of Arimathea, Patrick**
March 18 Cyril of Jerusalem
March 19 **Joseph**
March 20 **Cuthbert**
March 21 Enda
March 22 **Nicholas von Flue**
March 23 Turibius
March 24 Irenaeus
March 25 **Dismas, Margaret Clitherow**
March 26 Braulio
March 27 John of Egypt
March 28 Tutilo
March 29 Rupert
March 30 Zosimus
March 31 Guy of Pamposa
April 1 Hugh
April 2 **Francis of Paola**
April 3 **Irene**
April 4 **Benedict the Black**
April 5 **Vincent Ferrer**
April 6 **Notkar Balbulus**
April 7 **John Baptist de La Salle**
April 8 **Walter of Pontnoise**

April 9 Waldertrudis
April 10 Fulbert
April 11 **Gemma Galgani, Godberta**
April 12 **Zeno**
April 13 Hermenegild
April 14 **Lidwina**
April 15 **Hunna**
April 16 **Benedict Joseph Labre, Bernadette, Magnus**
April 17 Stephen Harding
April 18 Galdinus
April 19 **Expiditus**
April 20 Agnes of Montepulciano
April 21 **Beuno**
April 22 **Theodore of Sykeon**
April 23 **George**
April 24 **Bona**
April 25 **Mark**
April 26 **Stephen**
April 27 **Zita**
April 28 **Pollio**
April 29 **Catherine of Siena**
April 30 Pius V
May 1 **Peregrine Laziosi**
May 2 Athanasius
May 3 **James the Less**
May 4 **Florian**
May 5 Hilary of Arles
May 6 Petronax
May 7 **Domitian**
May 8 Peter of Tarentaise
May 9 Pachomius
May 10 **Antoninus of Florence**
May 11 **Genulphus**
May 12 **Pancras**

May 13 **Servatius**
May 14 Michael Garicoits
May 15 **Dymphna, Hallvard, Isidore the Farmer**
May 16 **Brendan, Honortus**
May 17 **Madron, Paschal Baylon**
May 18 Eric of Sweden
May 19 **Dunstan, Ivo of Kermartin, Peter Celestine V**
May 20 **Bernardine of Sienna**
May 21 Andrew Bobola
May 22 **Rita of Cascia**
May 23 John Baptist Rossi
May 24 Vincent of Lerins
May 25 **Bede**
May 26 **Philip Neri**
May 27 Augustine of Canterbury
May 28 **Bernard of Montijoux**
May 29 Stephen
May 30 **Ferdinand III, Joan of Arc**
June 1 **Justin, Wite**
June 2 **Elmo**
June 3 **Clotilde, Morand**
June 4 **Quirnus**
June 5 **Boniface of Germany**
June 6 **Claud**
June 7 **Gotteschale**
June 8 **Medard**
June 9 **Columba**
June 10 Ithamar
June 11 Barnabas
June 12 John of Sahagun
June 13 **Anthony of Padua**
June 14 Methodius I
June 15 **Vitus**

June 16 **John Francis Regis, Tychon**
June 17 **Avertinius, Herve**
June 18 Elizabeth of Schonau
June 19 Juliana Falconieri
June 20 Silverius
June 21 **Alban, Aloysius**
June 22 **Thomas More**
June 23 **Agrippina, Joseph Cafasso**
June 24 **John the Baptist**
June 25 **Eurosia**
June 26 Anthelm
June 27 Cyril of Alexandria
June 28 Irenaeus of Lyons
June 29 **Peter**
June 30 **Theobald**
July 1 Oliver Plunket
July 2 Otto
July 3 **Thomas**
July 4 **Elizabeth of Portugal, Ulric**
July 5 Athanasius
July 6 **Maria Goretti**
July 7 Palladius
July 8 Withburga
July 9 Nicholas Pieck
July 10 **Felicity**
July 11 **Benedict of Nursia**
July 12 **John Gualbert, Veronica**
July 13 **Henry II**
July 14 **Camillus de Lellis**
July 15 **Alexis, Swithun, Vladmir**
July 16 Fulrad
July 17 **Alexis**
July 18 **Arnulph, Bruno**
July 19 **Justa and Rufina**
July 20 **Margaret of Antioch, Wilgefortis**

July 21 **Victor of Marseilles**
July 22 **Mary Magdalen**
July 23 **Bridget of Sweden, The Three Magi**
July 24 **Christina the Astonishing**
July 25 **Christopher, James the Greater**
July 26 **Anne**
July 27 **Pantaleon, The Seven Sleepers**
July 28 Samson of Dole
July 29 **Martha, Olaf of Norway**
July 30 **Abdon and Senen**
July 31 **Ignatius Loyola**
August 1 **Alphonsus Liguori**
August 2 Eusebius
August 3 **Lydia Purpuria**
August 4 **John Baptist Vianney**
August 5 Addai and Mari
August 6 Hormisdas
August 7 **Albert of Trapani**
August 8 **Dominic Guzman**
August 9 **Emydius**
August 10 **Lawrence**
August 11 **Clare of Assisi**
August 12 Porcarius
August 13 **Concordia, Hippolytus**
August 14 **Maximillian Kolbe**
August 15 **Arnulf, The Blessed Virgin Mary**
August 16 **Stephen of Hungary**
August 17 **Mamas, Roch**
August 18 **Agapitus, Helena**
August 19 **Sebald**
August 20 **Bernard of Clairvaux**
August 21 Pius X
August 22 Sigfrid
August 23 **Rose of Lima**
August 24 **Bartholomew**

August 25 **Genesius, Louis IX**
August 26 Elizabeth Birchier
August 27 **Monica**
August 28 **Augustine of Hippo, Moses the Black**
August 29 Medericus
August 30 Pammachius
August 31 **Raymond Nonnatus**
September 1 **Adjutor, Agia, Fiacre, Giles**
September 2 **Agricola of Avignon**
September 3 **Gregory the Great**
September 4 Rose of Viterbo
September 5 Laurence of Guistiniani
September 6 Bega
September 7 **Cloud, Regina**
September 8 **Hadrian**
September 9 **Peter Claver**
September 10 **Nicholas of Tolentino**
September 11 Paphnutius
September 12 Guy of Anderlecht
September 13 **John Chrysostom, Venerius**
September 14 **Notburga**
September 15 Catherine of Genoa
September 16 Cyprian
September 17 Hildegard
September 18 **Joseph of Cupertino**
September 19 **Januarius**
September 20 **Eustachius**
September 21 **Matthew**
September 22 **Maurice, Phocas**
September 23 **Cadoc**
September 24 Gerard
September 25 **Joseph Calasanz**
September 26 **Cosmas and Damian**
September 27 **Vincent de Paul**
September 28 **Wenceslaus of Bohemia**

September 29 **Gabriel, Michael, Raphael**
September 30 **Gregory the Illuminator, Jerome**
October 1 **Therese of Lisieux**
October 2 The Guardian Angels
October 3 Thomas Cantelupe
October 4 **Francis of Assisi**
October 5 **Placid**
October 6 **Bruno**
October 7 Osith
October 8 **Demetrius, Pelagia**
October 9 **Andronicus, Denis**
October 10 **Gereon**
October 11 **Gummarus, James Grissinger**
October 12 Wilfrid
October 13 **Colman**
October 14 Callistus
October 15 **Teresa of Avila**
October 16 **Gall, Gerard of Majella, Hedwig, Margaret-Mary**
October 17 **Contardo Ferrini**
October 18 **Luke**
October 19 **Peter Alcantara, Rene Groupil**
October 20 Bertilla Boscardin
October 21 **Ursula**
October 22 **Alodia**
October 23 **John of Capistrano**
October 24 **Antony Claret**
October 25 **Crispin and Crispinian**
October 26 **Bonaventure**
October 27 Frumentius
October 28 **Jude**
October 29 **Baldus**
October 30 **Dorothy of Montau**
October 31 **Quentin, Wolfgang**
November 1 All Saints

November 2 Marcian
November 3 **Hubert, Martin de Porres**
November 4 **Charles Borromeo**
November 5 Bertilla
November 6 **Leonard of Noblac**
November 7 **Willibroad**
November 8 **The Four Crowned Martyrs**
November 9 **Theodore Tiro**
November 10 **Andrew Avellino**
November 11 **Martin of Tours**
November 12 **Josaphat**
November 13 **Brice, Francis Xavier Cabrini, Homobonus, Stanislaus Kostka**
November 14 Laurence O'Toole
November 15 **Albert the Great**
November 16 Margaret of Scotland
November 17 **Elizabeth of Hungary**
November 18 **Odo of Cluny**
November 19 Nerses I
November 20 Edmund the Martyr
November 21 Albert of Louvain
November 22 **Cecilia**
November 23 **Clement I, Columban**
November 24 **Flora**
November 25 **Catherine of Alexandria**
November 26 **John Berchmans, Leonard of Port Maurice**
November 27 Virgil
November 28 **Stephen the Younger**
November 29 Radbod
November 30 **Andrew**
December 1 **Edmund Campion, Eligius**
December 2 **Bibliana**
December 3 **Cassian, Francis Xavier**
December 4 **Barbara**

December 5 **Sabas**
December 6 **Nicholas of Myra**
December 7 **Ambrose**
December 8 **Immaculate Conception**
December 9 Peter Fourier
December 10 Gregory III
December 11 **Damasus**
December 12 **Corentin**
December 13 **Odilia, Lucy**
December 14 **John of the Cross**
December 15 **Valerian**
December 16 **Adelaide**
December 17 Sturmi
December 18 Flannan
December 19 Anastasius I
December 20 Dominic Silos
December 21 Peter Canisius
December 22 Ischyrion and companions
December 23 **Thorac Thorhallsson**
December 24 Irmina and Adela
December 25 **Anastasia**
December 26 **Stephen**
December 27 **Fabiola, John the Divine**
December 28 **Holy Innocents**
December 29 **Thomas Becket**
December 30 Egwin
December 31 Sylvester I

Baptismal Names for Children

The tradition of selecting a saint's name during baptism serves not only as a protector for the infant, but as a role model for the new Catholic. Celebrating one's name-day on their feast day acts as a second birthday in Catholic homes around the world.

Female

Abigail (Abby, Gail): Our father is happy
Adele (Adelaide, Dell): Noble
Adria (Adriana, Adrienne): Dark
Agatha (Agathe): Good
Agnes (Inez, Neysa, Nina, Rachel): Pure
Albina (Bianca, Blanch): White
Alexandria (Alessandra, Aleth, Alexis, Cassandra) *Feminine*, Alexander: Helper of men
Alice (Alison, Elissa): Noble cheer
Alma ( ): Loving
Amanda ( ) *Feminine*, Amandus: Worthy of love
Amy (Amata): Beloved, a friend

Anastasia (Stacey, Statia): The one who will rise again

Andrea ( ) *Feminine*, Andrew: Manly

Angela (Angie, Angelica): Angel

Ann (Anita, Annabel, Annette, Hannah, Nancy): Grace

Barbara (Beatrix, Beatriz): Happiness

Bernadette (Bernardine, Nadine) *Feminine*, Bernard: Bold as a bear

Bertha ( ): The strong one

Brenda ( ) *Feminine*, Bernard: Sword

Bridget (Brigit, Brigid): Strength

Camille (Camelia) *Feminine*, Camillus: The servant of the temple

Carol (Arlene, Carey, Carla, Caroline, Charlene, Cheryl) *Feminine*, Charles: Strong

Catherine (Karen, Kate, Kathleen): Pure

Cecilia (Sheila): Dim sighted

Christina (Kirsten, Nina) *Feminine*, Christ: Anointed

Clare (Clarissa): Illustrious

Claudia (Claudette) *Feminine*, Claude: The lame one

Constance (Connie) *Feminine*, Constantine: Standing firm

Crystal (Chrysa): Clarity

Cynthia ( ) *Feminine*, Synesius: Understanding

Daniela (Danielle, Danette) *Feminine*, Daniel: The Lord is judge

Deborah (Debra): Bee

Denise ( ) *Feminine*, Denis: God of Nyssa

Desiree ( ): Longed for

Diana (Cynthia, Dinah): Divine

Dolores (Lola, Lolita): Sorrows

Dominica (Dominique) *Feminine*, Dominic: I belong to the Lord

Doris (Dorothy) *Feminine*, Theodore: God's gift

Edith (Eda): Happiness

Edwina (Edna) *Feminine*, Edwin: Fire

Elizabeth (Alise, Bess, Beth, Elisa, Elise, Isabella, Lee, Lisa, Lison): God has sworn

Emily (Amelia, Emma): Excelling

Enrica (Henrietta) *Feminine*, Henry: The ruler of the house

Erica ( ) *Feminine*, Eric: Ever ruler

Erin ( ): From Ireland

Esther (Edissa, Vanessa): Star

Etheldra (Audrey, Ethel): Noble maiden

Eve (Evelyn): Life

Frances (Cecca, Fran, Frankie): Free one

Freda (Alfreda, Althryda) *Feminine*, Alfred: Good counsellor

Frederica ( ) *Feminine*, Fred: Peace ruler

Gabriela (Briel, Ella) *Feminine*, Gabriel: God's strength

Gemma ( ): Jewel

Genevieve (Violane, Yolanda): White wave

Georgia (Georgianna, Georgette) *Feminine*, George: Farmer

Germaine ( ) *Feminine*, Germain: Kin

Gloria ( ): Glory

Grace (Engracia, Giorsal, Grazia): Graceful

Helen (Aileen, Celine, Elaine, Eleanore, Ilona, Lena, Selina): Light

Hilary ( ): Hundred rolls

Hilda ( ): Battle maiden

Hope ( ): Hope, expectation, desire

Irene (Renata, Rene): Peace

Irma (Irmina): Strong

Jacqueline ( ) *Feminine*, James: Supplanter

Jane (Janet, Jeanine, Jessica, Joan, June, Nita): God has mercy

Jean (Joan, Jodie): God is gracious

Jennifer ( ) *Feminine*, Wilfred: Firm peace

Judith (Judy) *Feminine*, Jude: Praised
Julia (Jill, Juliet): Downy
Justina (Tina): Just
Laura (Lauren, Lorraine) *Feminine*, Lawrence: Laurel
Lilian (Lila): Lily
Linda (Lindy, Lynn): Beautiful one
Louise (Alison, Eloise) *Feminine*, Louis: Famous warrior
Lucy (Lucilla, Luz) *Feminine*, Luke: Light
Margaret (Greta, Maggie, Marina, Peggy, Rita): Pearl
Marian (Mary Ann, Mariana): Bitter, graceful
Martha (Marta): Lady
Mary (Mae, Mara, Marilyn, Mariann, Maureen, Miriam):
   Rebellion
Melanie (Melinda): Dark
Monica (Mona, Monique): Counselor
Natalie (Natasha, Nathalie): Birth
Nicole (Nicolette) *Feminine*, Nicholas: People's victory
Olivia (Oliva): Olive
Patricia ( ) *Feminine*, Patrick: Nobly born
Paula (Paulette, Pauline) *Feminine*, Paul: Little
Phoebe (Phebe) *Feminine*, Phobas: Brilliant one
Rachael (Rachel, Rae, Raquel, Rahal): A lamb
Regina (Reine, Rene): Queen
Rose (Rosalyn, Roseann): Rose
Ruth ( ): Friend
Sandra ( ) *Feminine*, Alexander: Helper of men
Sarah (Sally, Shari): Princess
Sharon ( ): Plain
Silvia (Sylvette, Sylvie): Lady of the forest
Sophia (Nadia, Sonia): Wisdom
Stephanie (Esta, Estancia) *Feminine*, Stephen: Crowned
Susan (Suki, Susette, Shoshana, Zsa Zsa): Lily
Theresa (Terry, Tracy): Reaper
Ursula ( ): Little bear
Valerie (Valery): Brave

Veronica (Bernice, Vera): Victory Bringer
Victoria ( ): Victory
Vivian (Bibliana): Lively
Winifred (Genevieve): White wave
Yvette (Yvonne): Praised
Zita ( ): Little hope
Zoe ( ): Life

Male

Aaron ( ): Lofty mountain
Abraham (Abram): Father of many
Adam (Adan): First of earth
Adrian (Adrien, Hadrian): Brave
Alan (Allen): Harmony
Albert (Bert, Delbert): Illustrious
Alexander (Alistair, Alec, Sacha, Sandor): Helper of men
Alphonse (Alonzo, Lon): Eager for battle
Ambrose ( ): Immortal
Andrew (Andreas, Drew): Manly
Angelo ( ): Angel
Anthony (Anton): Priceless
Arnold (Arnaud): Strong as an eagle
Augustine (Agostino, Austin): Majestic
Bartholomew (Bart, Barry): Son of Talmai
Basil (Vasily, Vassily): Royal
Benedict (Bennett, Benito): Blessing
Benjamin (Benson): Son of the right hand
Bernard (Nardo): Bold as a bear
Blase (Blaise): Babbler
Bonaventure ( ): Good attempt
Brendan (Brandon, Brennan): Sword
Brian (Bryant): Strong
Brice (Bruce): Breach

Camillus (Camillo): Temple servant
Casimir (Cass, Casper): Peaceful
Charles (Carl, Carlos, Cary, Karl): Strong
Christian ( ): Belonging to Christ
Christopher (Cristobal): Carrier of Christ
Claude (Claudius): Lame
Clement ( ): Merciful
Constantine: Firm
Daniel (Neil): The Lord is judge
David ( ): Beloved
Denis (Dion, Sidney): God of Nyssa
Dominic (Domingo): I belong to the Lord
Donald (Don): Dark stranger
Edmund (Eamon, Ned): Happy protection
Edward (Edoardo, Ned): Rich guardian
Edwin ( ): Rich friend
Eric (Erich): Ever-ruler
Ernest (Ernst, Ernestus): Earnest one
Ferdinand (Ferde, Hernando): Adventurous
Francis (Franco, Franz): Free
Frederick (Fred, Fritz, Frederigo): Peaceful ruler
Gabriel ( ): God's strength
George (Igor, Jurgen): Farmer
Gerald (Garcia, Gary, Jerold): Spear ruler
Godfrey (Geoffrey, Jeff): God's peace
Gregory (Gregor, Gregorio): Watchman
Harold ( ): Strong warrior
Henry (Emeric, Harry, Rico): Home ruler
Hilarion (Hilaire, Hillary): Merry
Ignatius (Ignacio, Nacho): Fiery
Isaac ( ): He laughs
Isidore (Dorian): Strong gift
James (Diego, Jacob, Jacques, Santiago, Shamus, Yakov): Supplanter
Jason (Iason): Healer

Jerome (Hieronymus): Holy name

Joel ( ): The coming of dawn

John (Evan, Giovanni, Hans, Ian, Ivan, Johann, Joua, Sean, Shane): God has mercy

Joseph (Giuseppe, Jose): Increase

Joshua (Josh) God is salvation

Justin ( ): Just

Kenneth (Canice, Kent): Handsome

Kevin ( ): Handsome

Lawrence (Lars, Lauren, Lorenzo): Laurel

Leonard (Leon, Leonardo): Lionhearted

Lepold ( ): People's prince

Louis (Aloysius, Lewis, Ludwig): Famous warrior

Luke (Luca, Luciano): Light

Mark (Marcel, Marco): Mars

Martin (Martino): Warlike

Matthew (Matthias): The Lord's gift

Maximilian (Massimiliano, Maxim): Greatest

Mel ( ): Honey

Michael (Miguel, Mikhail, Mitchell): Who is like God

Nathaniel ( ): Gift of God

Nicholas (Colin, Klaus, Niles): People's victory

Oliver ( ): Peace

Owen ( ): To possess

Patrick (Patricio, Patriatus): Nobly born

Paul (Pablo, Pawel): Little

Peter (Perrin, Pierce, Piers, Piotr): Rock

Philip (Felipe, Phelps): Lover of horses

Quentin (Quin, Quintus): Fifth

Ralph (Rafe, Raul, Rodolfo, Rudolph): Good omen

Raphael (Raffaello): God's healer

Raymond (Raimondo, Ramon): Wise protection

Rene (Renato, Renatus): Reborn

Richard (Ricardo): Firm ruler

Robert (Robin, Rupert): Bright flame

Roderic (Rodrigo, Rory): Noble ruler
Roger (Hodge, Rory, Ruggero): Famous spear
Samuel ( ): Asked of the Lord
Sebastian ( ): Venerable
Simon (Simeon, Simone): Obedient
Stephen (Esteban, Sven): Crowned
Terence (Terry): Smooth
Theodore (Tad, Theo): God's gift
Thomas (Tomas, Tommaso): Twin
Timothy (Timoteo): God fearing
Valerius (Valentine, Valerio): Valiant
Victor ( ): Winner
Vincent (Vincenzo): Conquering
Walter (Gualtieri, Wenceslas): Great glory
William (Guiliermo, Wilhelm, Willis): Strong helmet
Xavier (Javier): Bright
Zachary (Zaccaria, Zechariah): Remembered by God

The Emblems and Symbols of Saints

✤

Emblems are a representation of saints through symbolic devices. By combining selected devices, a pictoral depiction of the saint emerges.

Anchor: Clement, Felix, Nicholas
Angels: Cecilia, Frances of Rome, Genevieve, Matthew, Catherine, The Blessed Virgin Mary
Anvil: Adrian, Baldomerus, Eligius
Apples: Dorothy, Nicholas
Armour: Eligius, George, Joan of Arc, Martin, Michael, Olaf II, Quentin, Quirinus, Sebastian, Theodore
Arrows, in hand: Augustine of Hippo, Edmund, Gereon, Sebastian, Ursula
Arrows, shot with: Edmund, Giles, Sebastian, Teresa
Ax: Boniface, John Fisher, Magnus, Olav, Thomas More, Winifred
Axhead: Thomas Becket
Baker's peel: Authbert, Honorius
Balls: Nicholas
Barrel: Antonis, John the Divine, Willibrord
Basket: Dorothy
Bears: Columban, Gall

Beehive: Ambrose, Bernard, Isidore, John Chrysostom

Bell: Anthony, Benedict, Winwaloe

Birds: Benedict, Blaise, Colette, David, Francis of Assisi

Boat: John Roche, Jude, Julian, Mary Magdalene, Simon

Book: Anne, Boniface, Bridget of Sweden, Elizabeth of Hungary, Stephen, Walburga

Bowl: Oswald

Branch: Brendan, Bridget, Kentigern

Bread: Anthony of Padua, Cuthbert, Nicholas, Zita

Breast: Agatha, Justina, Ursula

Broom: Petronilla, Zita

Bull: Blandina, Thecla

Burning bush: The Blessed Virgin Mary

Candle: Genevieve

Cannon: Barbara

Candle: Bridget of Ireland

Cardinal's hat: Bonaventure, Jerome, John Fisher, Vincent Ferrer

Carpenter's square: Joseph, Jude, Thomas

Cave: Anthony, Benedict, Gall, Sabbas, Seven Sleepers

Chalice: Benedict, Eloi, John the Divine

Chain: Bridget of Sweden, Germanus, Leonard of Noblac, Radegund

Child: Anthony of Padua, Blessed Virgin Mary, Christopher, Elizabeth, Rose, Vincent de Paul

Church: Amandus, Winwaloe, Withburga

Club: Boniface, Christopher, Jude, Magnus

Coals: Brice, Lambert

Cock: Peter, Vitus

Cold: Medard

Communion: Charles Borromeo

Cow: Bridget, Perpetua

Cross: Augustine of Hippo, Bridget of Ireland, Francis of Assisi

Cross and rosary: Dominic Guzman

Crowns: Henry, Elizabeth of Hungary
Crown of thorns: Francis of Assisi, Louis, Teresa
Crucifix: Aloysius, Charles, Scholastica, Vincent Ferrer
Cup, broken: Benedict
Dagger: Edward
Digger: Fiacre, Phocas
Doe: Withburga
Dog: Bernard, Dominic Guzman, Roch
Door: Anne, Margaret Clitherow
Dove: David, Gregory, Scholastica
Dragon: George, Juliana, Margaret, Silvester
Eagle: John the Divine
Eyes: Lucy, Alban
Feather: Barbara
Fire: Agnes, Anthony
Fish: Raphael, Simon, Zeno
Flame: Brigid of Ireland
Flask: Raphael, Walburga
Flowers: Dorothy, Zita
Forceps with tooth: Apollonia
Fuller's club: James the Less, Simon
Geese: Martin
Gridiron: Lawrence, Vincent
Hair: Mary Magdalene, Sabas
Hammer: Apollonia, Eligius
Harp: Cecilia, David
Head: Alban, Cuthbert, Dionysius, John the Baptist, Oswald, Sidwell, Winefred
Heart: Augustine of Hippo, Catherine of Siena, Gertrude, Teresa
Hinds: Fiacre, Giles, Withburga
Hog: Anthony
Hooks: Agatha, Vincent
Horse: Eloi, George, Paul, Theodore
Horseshoe: Eligius

Intestines: Vincent, Claudius, Elmo
Keys: Martha, Peter, Petronilla, Zita
Knife: Agatha, Bartholomew
Lamb: Agnes, John
Lance: Barnabas
Lantern: Lucy
Lily: Casimir, Dominic Guzman, Joseph
Lion: Daniel, Jerome, Mark, Paul the Hermit
Lock: Leonard of Noblac
Millstone: Crispin and Crispinian, Vincent
Money pouch: Martin, Matthew, Nicholas
Monstrance: Clare, Norbert
Mortar and pestle: Cosmas and Damian
Mouse: Gertrude
Nails: Andrew, Helena, Louis
Necklace: Etheldreda
Noose: Mark
Oar: John Roche, Julian, Jude, Simon
Ointment: Joseph of Arimathaea, Mary Magdalene
Organ: Cecilia
Otter: Cuthbert
Ox: Ambrose, Luke
Palm: Agnes, Barbara
Pen: Ambrose
Phial: Cosmas and Damian
Pig: Anthony
Pincers: Agatha, Apollonia, Dunstan, Lucy
Raven: Benedict, Oswald, Vincent
Ring: Catherine of Siena, Edward the Confessor, Oswald
River: Christopher
Rosary: Dominic
Rose: Cecilia, Dorothy, Elizabeth of Hungary, Rose, Therese of Lisieux
Salmon: Kentigern
Saw: James, Joseph, Simon

Scales: Michael
Scourge: Ambrose, Gervase and Protase, Lawrence
Shears: Agatha
Shell: Augustine of Hippo, James the Greater
Shepherd: David
Shepherdess: Genevieve, Joan of Arc
Ship: Anselm, Jude, Nicholas, Ursula
Shoes: Crispin and Crispinian
Sieve: Benedict
Skin, animal: John the Baptist
Skin, human: Bartholomew
Skull: Jerome, Mary of Egypt
Snake: John the Divine, Patrick, Paul
Spade: Fiacre, Phocas
Spear: George, Louis, Margaret, Thomas
Spit: Quentin
Spring: Paul, Winefred
Staff: Etheldreda, Bridget of Sweden, Joseph of Arimathaea
Stag: Aidan, Eustace, Hubert
Star: Dominic, Thomas Aquinas
Stars: The Blessed Virgin Mary
Stigmata: Catherine of Siena, Francis of Assisi
Stones: Barnabas, Jerome, Stephen
Surgical implements: Cosmas and Damian, Luke
Swan: Cuthbert
Sword: Dionysius, Justina, Lucy, Matthew, Mathias, Michael, Paul, Thomas Becket
Tablet or Sun with the inscription IHS: Bernardine of Siena
Taper: Blaise
Tears: Monica
Tiara: Gregory the Great
Tongs: Agatha
Tooth: Apollonia

Torch: Anthony, Barbara
Tower: Barbara
Transverse cross: Andrew
Tree: Boniface
Tub: Nicholas
Veil: Agatha
Well: Vitalis
Wheel: Catherine, Willigis
Windlass: Elmo
Windmill: Victor
Wolf: Francis

Patrons of Countries
and Places

✦

Africa: St. Moses the Black, Our Lady Queen of Africa
Albania: Our Lady of Good Counsel
Alps: St. Bernard
Alsace: St. Odile
Angola: Immaculate Heart of Mary
Argentina: Our Lady of Lujan
Armenia: Sts. Bartholomew, Gregory the Illuminator
Asia Minor: St. John the Divine
Australia: Our Lady Help of Christians
Austria: Our Lady of Mariazell
Bavaria: St. Hedwig
Belgium: St. Joseph
Bohemia: Sts. Wenceslaus, Ludmilla
Bolivia: Our Lady of Copacabana
Borneo: St. Francis Xavier
Brazil: Nossa Senhora de Aparecida, Immaculate Conception
Bulgaria: St. Demetrius
Canada: Sts. Joseph, Anne
Central America: St. Rose of Lima
Ceylon (Sri Lanka): St. Lawrence
Chile: St. James the Greater, Our Lady of Mt. Carmel

China: St. Joseph
Colombia: Sts. Peter Claver, Louis Bertran
Corsica: St. Devota, Immaculate Conception
Cuba: Our Lady of Charity
Cyprus: St. Barnabas
Czechoslovakia: Sts. Wenceslaus, John Nepomucene
Denmark: St. Ansgar
Dominican Republic: St. Dominic, Our Lady of Grace
East Indies: St. Thomas
Ecuador: Sacred Heart of Mary
Egypt: St. Mark
El Salvador: Our Lady of Peace
England: St. George
Ethiopia: St. Frumentius
Europe: Sts. Benedict of Nursia, Cyril and Methodius
Finland: St. Henry of Uppsala
France: Sts. Denis, Joan of Arc, Therese, Our Lady of
    the Assumption
Germany: Sts. Boniface, Michael
Gibraltar: Our Lady of Europe
Greece: Sts. Andrew, Nicholas
Guatemala: St. James the Greater
Holland: St. Willibrord
Hungary: St. Stephen, The Blessed Virgin Mary
Iceland: Sts. Anskar, Thorlac Thorhallsson
India: St. Thomas, Our Lady of the Assumption
Iran: Sts. Addai and Mari
Ireland: Sts. Bridget, Patrick, and Columban
Italy: Sts. Francis of Assisi, Catherine of Siena
Japan: Sts. Peter Baptist, Francis Xavier
Korea: St. Joseph, The Blessed Virgin Mary
Lesotho: Immaculate Heart of Mary
Lithuania: St. Casimir
Luxembourg: St. Willibrord
Madagascar: St. Vincent de Paul

Malta: Sts. Devota, Paul, Our Lady of the Assumption
Mexico: Our Lady of Guadalupe
Moravia: Sts. Cyril and Methodius
New Zealand: Our Lady Help of Christians
Nicaragua: St. James the Greater
North Africa: St. Cyprian
North America: Our Lady of Guadalupe
Norway: St. Olaf
Pakistan: St. Thomas
Papua New Guinea: St. Michael
Paraguay: Our Lady of the Assumption
Persia: St. Maruthas
Peru: St. Joseph
Philippines: Sacred Heart of Mary
Poland: Sts. Casimir, Stanislaus of Cracow
Portugal: St. Francis Borgia, Immaculate Conception
Prussia: Dorothy of Mantau
Rome: St. Philip Neri
Romania: St. Nicetas
Russia: Sts. Andrew, Nicholas of Myra, Vladimir
Scandinavia: St. Ansgar
Scotland: Sts. Andrew, Columba
Silesia: St. Hedwig
Slovakia: Our Lady of Sorrows
South Africa: Our Lady of the Assumption
South America: St. Rose of Lima
Spain: St. James the Greater
Sri Lanka: Lawrence
Sweden: Sts. Bridget, Eric
Syria: Sts. Addai, Mari
Tanzania: Immaculate Conception
Turkey: St. John the Divine
Ukraine: St. Josaphat
United States of America: Immaculate Conception, Our
    Lady of Guadalupe

Uruguay: Our Lady of Lujan (*La Virgen de los Treinte y Tres*)
Venezuela: Our Lady of Comotomo
Wales: St. David
West Indies: St. Gertrude

Bibliography Listing

✤

Aldrich, Donald Bradshaw. *The Golden Book of Prayer: An Anthology of Prayer.* New York: Dodd, Mead, & Company, 1941.

Attwater, Donald. *A Catholic Dictionary.* New York: The Macmillan Company, 1941.

Attwater, Donald. *The Penguin Dictionary of Saints.* New York: Penguin, 1985.

Ayscough, John. *Saints and Places.* New York: Cincinnati Benziger brothers, 1912.

Baring-Gould, Sabine. *Lives of the Saints* (14 volumes). Edinburgh: John Grant, 1914.

Broderick, Robert C. *Catholic Encyclopedia.* New York: Nelson, 1967.

Catholic Almanac 1995. Huntington, Indiana: Our Sunday Visitor, Inc., 1994.

The Communion of Saints, Prayers of the Famous. Wm. B. Eerdmans Publishing Co., 1990.

Coulson, John. *The Saints: A Concise Biographical Dictionary.* New York: Hawthorn, 1958.

Delaney, John J. *Dictionary of Saints.* New York: Doubleday, 1979.

De Sola Chervin, Ronda. *Quotable Saints.* Michigan: Servant Publications, 1992.

Drake, Maurice. *Saints and Their Emblems.* London: T. W. Laurie, 1916.

Eerdman's Book of Famous Prayers. Wm. B. Eerdmans Publishing Co., 1983.

Estavan, Lawrence. *How Quaint the Saint.* Redwood City, Calif.: Creekside Press, 1979.

Familiar Quotations: A Collection of Passages, Phrases, and Proverbs Traced to Their Sources in Ancient and Modern Literature. Boston: Little, Brown, and Company, 1992.

Farmer, David Hugh. *The Oxford Dictionary of Saints.* New York: Oxford University Press, 1987.

Foy, Felician A., O.F.M., and Rose M. Avato. *A Concise Guide to the Catholic Church II.* Huntington, Indiana: Our Sunday Visitor, Inc., 1986.

Freze, Michael, S.F.O. *Patron Saints.* Huntington, Indiana: Our Sunday Visitor Inc., 1992.

Hallam, Elizabeth. *Saints: Who They Are and How They Help You.* New York: Simon & Schuster, 1994.

Kelly, Sean, and Rosemary Rogers. *Saints Preserve Us!: Everything You Need to Know About Every Saint You'll Ever Need.* New York: Random House, 1993.

Leckie, Robert. *These Are My Heroes: A Study of the Saints.* New York: Random House, 1964.

McCollister, John C. *The Christian Book of Why*. New York: Jonathan David Publishers, Inc., 1983.

Nevins, Albert J. *A Saint for Your Name: Saints for Boys*. Huntington, Indiana: Our Sunday Visitor Inc., 1980.

Nevins, Albert J. *A Saint for Your Name: Saints for Girls*. Huntington, Indiana: Our Sunday Visitor Inc., 1980.

New Catholic Encyclopedia (volumes 1–15). New York: McGraw-Hill, 1967.

Quadflieg, Joseph. *The Saints and Your Name*. New York: Pantheon, 1958.

Sharkey, Don, and Sister Loretta. *Popular Patron Saints*. Milwaukee: Bruce Publishing Company, 1960.

Thurston, H., and D. Attwater. *Butler's Lives of the Saints* (4 volumes). New York: P. J. Kennedy and Sons, 1956.

Walsh, Michael (ed.). *Butler's Lives of the Saints: Concise Edition*. San Francisco: Harper & Row, 1985.

Woodward, Kenneth. *Making Saints*. New York: Simon & Schuster, from 1985 to 1990.

Index of Patron Saints and Intercessors

✛